JAPAN'S POSTWAR PARTY POLITICS

JAPAN'S POSTWAR PARTY POLITICS

Masaru Kohno

PRINCETON UNIVERSITY PRESS

PRINCETON, NEW JERSEY

PUBLISHED BY PRINCETON UNIVERSITY PRESS, 41 WILLIAM STREET,
PRINCETON, NEW JERSEY 08540
IN THE UNITED KINGDOM: PRINCETON UNIVERSITY PRESS, CHICHESTER, WEST SUSSEX

LIBRARY OF CONGRESS CATALOGING-IN-PUBLICATION DATA

KOHNO, MASARU, 1962–
JAPAN'S POSTWAR PARTY POLITICS / MASARU KOHNO.
P. CM.
INCLUDES BIBLIOGRAPHICAL REFERENCES AND INDEX.
ISBN 0-691-02629-7 (CLOTH : ALK. PAPER)—ISBN 0-691-01596-1 (PBK. : ALK. PAPER)
1. POLITICAL PARTIES—JAPAN—HISTORY—20TH CENTURY. 2. JAPAN—POLITICS AND GOVERNMENT—1945– I. TITLE.
JQ1698.A1K64 1997 96-26393 324.252—DC20 CIP

THIS BOOK HAS BEEN COMPOSED IN TIMES ROMAN

PRINCETON UNIVERSITY PRESS BOOKS ARE PRINTED
ON ACID-FREE PAPER AND MEET THE GUIDELINES FOR
PERMANENCE AND DURABILITY OF THE COMMITTEE ON
PRODUCTION GUIDELINES FOR BOOK LONGEVITY
OF THE COUNCIL ON LIBRARY RESOURCES

PRINTED IN THE UNITED STATES OF AMERICA BY PRINCETON ACADEMIC PRESS

2 4 6 8 10 9 7 5 3 1

2 4 6 8 10 9 7 5 3 1
(PBK)

For my mother, Miyuki Kohno

CONTENTS

FIGURES

TABLES

ACKNOWLEDGMENTS

THIS BOOK, which is based on my Ph.D. dissertation submitted to Stanford University, could not have been completed without the support of numerous individuals and organizations. I would like to express my sincere appreciation to Professor Daniel Okimoto for his intellectual and moral support throughout my Ph.D. program. I am grateful to Stephen Krasner and Barry Weingast, each of whom provided many helpful criticisms on various earlier drafts. Special thanks go to Geoffrey Garrett who introduced me to innovative applications of contemporary political science theories and who assisted the completion of this study in every way possible.

Other faculty members and fellow students also gave me invaluable inspiration and encouragement during my stay at Stanford. I thank Sun-Ki Chai, Michael Caldwell, Christophe Crombez, Brian Gaines, Judith Goldstein, Lloyd Gruber, Terry Moe, Gabriella Montinola, Douglas Rivers, Amy Searight, Scott Wilson, and Belinda Yeomans, all of whom had to put up with my countless office visits and telephone calls. I am indebted to scholars outside Stanford as well, including Gary Cox, Bernie Grofman, Takashi Inoguchi, Yoshitaka Nishizawa, Hideo Otake, Mark Ramseyer, and Frances Rosenbluth, who shared their views and made helpful comments. I thank especially Steven Reed who reviewed my manuscript for publication and helped me to tighten many of the loose ends in my arguments.

Some chapters of this book have already been published in academic journals. I am grateful to the editors of *World Politics* (which published an early version of chapter 6) and of the *British Journal of Political Science* (which published parts of chapter 4) for their editorial assistance, and I thank both The Johns Hopkins University Press and Cambridge University Press for granting permission to reprint my articles.

While revising the manuscript I was provided with institutional support from the Institute of Asian Research, the Faculty of Law, and the Department of Political Science at the University of British Columbia. I thank Director Mark Fruin, Dean Lynn Smith, and departmental head Don Blake for their generosity. I am grateful to the Suntory Foundation for financial assistance that made the completion of this book possible.

Finally, I wish to extend my deep appreciation to my wife, Isabel Grant, without whose patience and editing skills this project could not have been completed, and to my mother Miyuki Kohno, for her unending support over the years.

JAPAN'S POSTWAR PARTY POLITICS

1

INTRODUCTION

SINCE THE END of World War II Japan has developed a democratic polity under its newly adopted Constitution and a set of rules and procedures that govern the interactions of political actors. While the national Parliament, "the Diet," has become formally "the highest organ of state power,"[1] the expansion of popular suffrage and the emergence of new political parties have given substance to the Japanese parliamentary democracy, which existed only nominally before the war. In contemporary Japan, as in any other modern democracy, elections take place, politicians and societal forces organize political parties, and those parties compete for power and influence in public policy.

These fundamental attributes of competitive democracy have rarely occupied a central place in the literature of Japanese political studies. For decades there has been a strong view that the whole Japanese political system is dominated or led by the state bureaucracy, whose entrenched policy-making power survived the war and was reinforced during the subsequent American occupation period. Since the early 1980s an increasing number of studies have challenged the bureaucracy-dominant view, but even in these recent studies, political parties (and other political actors) are recognized as relevant mostly in the context of the shifting "balance of power" between them and the bureaucrats in the policy-making process.[2]

A related and perhaps more direct reason for the limited scholarly emphasis on party competition in Japan is the unarguable fact that, for a large part of the postwar era, a single conservative party, the Liberal Democratic Party (LDP), dominated both houses of Parliament and continuously formed a majority government. The political success of the LDP was indeed remarkable given that, over the period the party was in power, Japan underwent a radical change in its social and economic conditions. The LDP's record was also extraordinary from a comparative perspective: although it was often compared with other dominant parties, such as the Social Democrats in Sweden and the Christian Democrats in Italy, the LDP was an exceptional case in terms of both its longevity and the degree of its dominance.[3] One consequence of the LDP's one-

[1] *The Constitution of Japan*, Article 41.

[2] For a survey of the development of the bureaucracy-dominant view and its recent critics, see chapter 2.

[3] The Swedish Social Democratic Party formed the government from 1932 to 1976 and returned to power in 1982, but throughout these years it obtained a parliamentary majority only

party dominance is that, within the already relatively scant literature, the analysis of Japanese party politics has been equated with the analysis of how the LDP maintained its rule so successfully; few studies on other political parties have been included in this literature, which has failed to address systematically the key analytical issues of competitive partisan interactions.[4]

The preeminent focus on the LDP, and on the period of its one-party dominance, has also had theoretical and normative ramifications; that is, in surveying the nature of postwar Japanese party politics, many of the perspectives that have been developed in the literature highlight features such as continuity, stability, and lack of meaningful competition in Japanese parliamentary democracy. Accordingly, what have been discussed as the determinants of Japanese party politics are, as detailed below, macroscopic, structural factors, such as Japanese political culture, the legacy from previous historical periods, and the underlying ideological cleavages of Japanese society. Furthermore, these determinants are often emphasized as unique or distinctive to the Japanese context. Thus, as the LDP's conservative hegemony continued, Japanologists perpetuated the image that Japan is somehow different from other advanced democracies, describing the LDP's one-party rule as an "uncommon democracy" and suggesting that there is a distinctive "Japanese way" in which politics operates in Japan.[5]

This study offers a different perspective on Japanese politics and advances a set of alternative interpretations for the evolution of Japanese parliamentary democracy. As I argue throughout the subsequent chapters, the central problem with the above conventional perspectives is that they cannot adequately explain some of the most important *changes* that have taken place in Japanese party politics over the postwar years. These changes include both big, sudden changes and more gradual and evolutionary ones. The former include events such as the formation of the Socialist-led coalition government formed in 1947, the creation of the LDP itself in 1955, and, most recently, the demise of the LDP's one-party regime in 1993. The latter includes the fragmentation of the opposition camp during the 1960s and changes in the nature of intraparty politics within the LDP during the 1970s and 1980s. In order to explain these changes, this study highlights the incentives of individual political actors, their relative bargaining power, and their strategic behavior under the given institutional constraints. I demonstrate that this alternative perspective, an-

twice, in 1940 and 1968. In Italy, until recently, the Christian Democratic Party had been the largest party throughout the post-World War II period, but its government had always been based on a coalition with other parties. The LDP in Japan maintained its majority in the House of Representatives from 1955 to 1993 and in the upper house (the House of Councillors) until 1989.

[4] For the LDP's rule, see Thayer, *How the Conservatives Rule Japan*; Fukui, *Party in Power*; Sato and Matsuzaki, *Jiminto Seiken* [The LDP's Rule]; Calder, *Crisis and Compensation*; and Ramseyer and Rosenbluth, *Japan's Political Marketplace*.

[5] Pempel, ed., *Uncommon Democracies*; and Curtis, *Japanese Way of Politics*.

chored in the microanalytic paradigm, provides a coherent account of the development of party politics in postwar Japan. Hence, by shifting the explanatory emphasis away from unique macrostructural factors, this study aims to explain Japan's parliamentary democracy in a manner that facilitates comparative analysis with political parties and competitive party systems in other advanced countries.[6]

The Evolution of Postwar Japanese Party Politics

It has become common practice among observers of modern Japan to document the development of Japanese parliamentary democracy by focusing on important events and phenomena in certain watershed years. With regard to the post-World War II development, many analysts would agree that the two most critical years were 1955 and 1993. Accordingly, postwar Japanese party politics has been seen as having gone through three different historical stages: 1945 to 1955, 1955 to 1993, and 1993 to the present.

For the first decade of the postwar period, Japan's parliamentary democracy represented a typical multiparty system. During this period, several major parties, from both conservative and progressive camps, competed for legislative seats and took turns forming coalition and minority governments.[7] This early period also witnessed constant party switching by individual politicians and a series of mergers and breakups of political parties, and thus was characterized by a fluid partisan alignment.

Second, the multiparty framework was replaced by a new party system in 1955, when the LDP was established, following the amalgamation of the conservative forces. For the next thirty-eight years, the LDP continuously formed a majority government; the Japan Socialist Party (JSP), also created in 1955, never became a viable alternative to the LDP.[8] The LDP did suffer a long-term decline in its popular support during the 1960s, with two centrist parties entering the electoral race—the Democratic Socialist Party (DSP) and the Clean Government Party (CGP). During the period between 1983 and 1986 the LDP entered a coalition with the New Liberal Club (NLC), a small conservative group that had broken away from the LDP in 1976. But for this exception, however, the LDP consistently formed a single-party government

[6] Similar explorations of the microfoundations of Japan's political development are currently under way in other subfields within Japanese political studies, especially in public policy analyses (see chapter 9).

[7] Only one of nine governments formed during this period was based on a single-party legislative majority (see chapter 4).

[8] In 1991 the party changed its official English name to the Social Democratic Party of Japan. In order to avoid confusion with the Democratic Socialist Party, however, I use the name Japan Socialist Party (and JSP) throughout this study.

throughout these years, maintaining its majority in the House of Representatives, the more important lower house.[9]

The third and current phase began in the early 1990s, when the LDP's conservative regime finally started to crumble owing to sweeping political distrust born out of a series of scandals involving high-profile politicians. In 1993 the largest faction within the LDP broke into two groups, one of which eventually joined the opposition in passing a nonconfidence bill against the LDP government and went on to create a new political party. In the subsequent general election the LDP failed to obtain a majority and was thus forced to hand over its power to a non-LDP coalition government, under the leadership of another newly established party, the Japan New Party (JNP).[10]

The above periodization certainly serves as a useful device for describing the development of postwar Japanese party politics. However, it should not lead one to overlook the continuity of the development and its basic evolutionary nature. For example, with the benefit of hindsight, it is easy to regard 1955 as the beginning of the LDP's long-lasting one-party rule, but a closer analysis reveals that the momentum for the conservative merger had actually evolved out of the interactions and bargaining under the previous multiparty framework. Many witnesses of the merger have confirmed that, at the time of its creation, the LDP was seen as a fragile federation of conservative and centrist parties and the merger itself was viewed as exemplifying simply one more development in the ongoing partisan alignment.[11] A closer examination of the post-1955 development also reveals that a number of salient changes have taken place in and outside the LDP over the long period of its governance. Most notably, by the end of the 1960s the framework within which the LDP competed with the opposition changed from a quasi two-party system to a multiparty system. With regard to the internal structure of the LDP, there have been significant organizational developments, especially in the factionalization and processes of promotion and appointment. Furthermore, although the

[9] The coalition with the NLC barely interrupted the dominant rule of the LDP, since the two parties were so different in size. A large part of the NLC was absorbed by the LDP after the 1986 election.

[10] The non-LDP coalition government turned out to be short-lived. In 1994, by offering the socialist leader the position of prime minister, the LDP was able to form an alternative majority coalition with the JSP and another small new party (*Sakigake*), both of which by then had departed from the non-LDP coalition government because of disagreements over policy issues and coalition management procedures. The power transition from the LDP to the non-LDP government resulted in the introduction of a new electoral system, which is bound to have pervasive consequences for party realignment. A systematic assessment of the post-1993 development must thus await one or two future general elections; for this reason the present study will not address the fluid and ongoing development of Japanese party politics in the aftermath of the 1993 political change.

[11] See, for example, a discussion by veteran Japanese journalists Motoo Goto, Kenzo Uchida, and Masumi Ishikawa, *Sengo Hoshu Seiji no Kiseki* [The course of postwar conservative politics].

exogenous forces of political scandals and public distrust were certainly significant, what finally triggered the demise of the LDP's regime was the breakup of the LDP itself, which introduced tremendous fluidity into the pattern of partisan alignment. Historical periodization, although a convenient device, may obscure all these facts.

To understand the development of contemporary Japanese party politics, then, one must account not only for the changes that occurred in a given stage but also for the transitions from one stage to another. Explanations applicable only to a specific event or a certain time period are inadequate. Interpretations must be *systematic* and *consistent* for the postwar Japanese parliamentary democracy in its entirety. Furthermore, in order to highlight the evolutionary nature of the development, explanations that rely on hindsight must be avoided. Rather, interpretations must be *forward-looking* in reconstructing events and decision-making processes. These are but some of the basic analytical requirements to which this study seeks to adhere.

Conventional Views

Much of the prevailing literature on Japanese party politics is descriptive in nature, and many Japanologists do not make explicit efforts to associate themselves with a particular theoretical approach. It is possible nevertheless to extrapolate at least three different schools of thought that underlie much of the existing work. They are the political-culture approach, the historical approach, and the socio-ideological approach. The intellectual origins of each school are reviewed critically and more thoroughly in chapter 2, and their specific claims about particular aspects of postwar party politics are challenged throughout the subsequent chapters. For now, a brief description may help to contrast these conventional approaches with the perspective developed in this study.

The political-culture approach emphasizes the cultural underpinnings of Japanese political systems and processes. Based on the work of Japanese anthropologists and social psychologists, this approach influences a wide range of contemporary research on Japanese politics. Scholars engaged in the study of Japanese voting behavior and political participation are particularly captivated by the notion that cultural attributes determine outcomes in Japanese politics. They typically focus on the conservative and passive nature of Japanese attitudes and behavior in explaining the long-lasting electoral fortunes of the LDP.

The historical approach emphasizes the enduring legacy and particular "lessons" learned from past experience in explaining the development of Japan's parliamentary democracy. Scholars affiliated with this school of thought observe the continuity of Japanese political history, linking the Taisho democracy era, the wartime experience, and the early postwar American occupation period with the postwar evolution of Japanese party politics. In accounting for the post-1955 conservative hegemony, these scholars focus on the underdevelopment of Japanese labor movements during the prewar period and the historical lessons the Japanese learned from the devastating consequences of the Socialist-led coalition government during 1947–48.

The socio-ideological approach emphasizes the societal and ideological foundations of Japanese politics. This approach is represented by those scholars who adhere to the concept of the "1955 system," a party system entrenched in the socio-ideological cleavage that resulted from a series of salient events during the late 1940s and early 1950s. These scholars argue that the socio-ideological cleavage in Japan has been extremely clear-cut because it originally formed at a time when the Japanese public was harshly divided into two opposing camps over the highly ideological issues of postwar settlement and the U.S.-Japan security arrangement. Thus the socio-ideological view attributes much of the LDP's extraordinary success to the rigid and polarized nature of the Japanese cleavage that prevented the leading opposition party, the Japan Socialist Party, from becoming a viable alternative to the ruling conservative party.

What are the problems with these conventional approaches? There are three major shortcomings. First, empirically, each approach is limited in its predictive power, leaving unexplained many important facts about postwar Japanese party politics. In particular, to the extent that they highlight cultural, historical, and socio-ideological foundations as the determinants, these approaches often overlook the important changes that have taken place in the pattern of party competition over the last fifty years.

Second, methodologically, the political-culture, historical, and socio-ideological approaches all face the difficulty of formulating causal arguments in a positive and falsifiable way. The basic problem is the operationalizability of the key explanatory variables. If one wants to argue, for example, that the configuration of political parties is determined by the underlying socio-ideological cleavage, then the specification of this cleavage must be done prior to and independent of observing the party system itself in order to avoid a circular argument. The exact nature of such a cleavage, however, is almost impossible to identify and its influence difficult to measure. Similarly, it is extremely difficult to define *ex ante* the impact of traditional Japanese culture and the historical legacy without referring to the behavioral outcomes associated with such an impact.[12]

Third, theoretically, the existing three approaches are too macroscopic to

[12] Arguably one could escape from this problem by employing large-scale survey data and thus identifying the impact of these macrostructural factors independently. In the case of Japan, however, no meaningful panel survey has been conducted at the national level, and the lack of such data is critical in interpreting any intertemporal change. For more on this problem, see chapter 7.

constitute an analytical framework for Japanese politics. According to these conventional views, individual political actors, their power, incentives, and strategies, do not play an independent and significant role in determining political outcomes. Instead, Japanese voters, politicians, and political parties are described as prisoners of the underlying culture, historical background, and socio-ideological structure. As a result, these perspectives are often too deterministic to advance a forward-looking account of the evolutionary changes in Japanese politics: no matter what incentives, power, and strategies each relevant political actor has, the Japanese political systems and processes would have evolved the way they actually did.

This study aims to overcome these shortcomings. As noted earlier, this study emphasizes important changes in Japanese party politics, which have not been adequately explained in the conventional literature. This study is also committed to the tradition of positive research, and the set of explanations offered below is therefore built on concepts and assumptions widely accepted in various strands of contemporary political theories. Finally, the present study seeks to "bring politics back" into the analysis of Japanese politics, highlighting the role of individual political actors and thus exploring the microfoundations for the development of postwar Japanese parliamentary democracy.

A Microanalytic Approach to Japanese Party Politics

The alternative microanalytic perspective developed in this study draws on several strands of contemporary positive theories. Such a perspective has already been applied to a wide range of subject areas in political science—from voting behavior to legislative politics in industrial democracies, from bureaucratic institutions to peasant revolutions in developing countries, from international wars to bi- and multilateral cooperation among nation states—and it is beyond the scope of this section to survey all the relevant literature. The purpose here is limited to outlining the basic tenets of the approach adopted in this study and to offering some general and preliminary justifications for applying it to the Japanese case.

Generally those who adhere to the microanalytic approach regard observed political phenomena as products of conscious choices made by individual, rational actors. The concept of rationality, in its purest form, is reflected in the axiomatic assumption that actors maximize, albeit under the given constraints, their own utilities that are defined exogenously based on their beliefs, values, and perceived strategic opportunities.[13] Starting with this assumption, and

[13] As John Ferejohn has articulated nicely, this assumption enables explanations to be systematic. Suppose, for example, the actor is making a choice from a set of alternative actions, {a1, a2,

often borrowing the analytical tools of game theory, theorists try to explain policy, institutional, and other behavioral outcomes by showing that those outcomes correspond to equilibrium behavior. In other words, based on deductive reasoning independent of empirical observations, they try to reconstruct the process through which such behavior is chosen and to demonstrate that the actual outcomes match their predictions.[14]

In applying this approach to the field of comparative politics per se, analysts often make more specific assumptions about relevant actors' utility functions. Typically, for example, it is assumed that politicians try to increase their chances of (re)election. Voters are assumed to seek to establish a government that will implement their preferred policies. Political parties are assumed to try to maximize their representation in public office and policy influence. These latter assumptions are sometimes called "auxiliary" or "thick rationality" assumptions, and they are presented as general, if not universal, characterizations of the actors' incentives. It is the presentation of these assumptions prior to their empirical investigation that permits analysts to posit specific predictions about the political outcomes in question.[15]

Over the last decade or so, the microanalytic approach, focusing as it does on individual political actors and their strategic behavior, has contributed innovative theoretical insights and methodological rigor to various subfields of political science. Nevertheless, with few recent exceptions, students of Japanese politics have neither fully embraced this approach nor incorporated its merits into their analyses.[16] Why have Japanologists thus far chosen to ignore the scholarly excitement that this approach has brought to their colleagues?

One reason may lie in the mistake of equating the uniqueness of Japanese political features with the need to establish an explanation based on uniquely Japanese factors. Gerald Curtis, for example, notes in his widely read textbook:

> This book is about the Japanese way of politics. Much of what it has to say will have a familiar ring, because there are many similarities in the way politics is

. . . aK}. If the maximization principle is not satisfied, the situation must be that the actor prefers ai to a_{i+1} for all i and ak to a1. This means that for any choice actually made there would have been some other action that was preferable but, for some external reason, it was not chosen. The task of observers, then, must be to investigate what that reason was. Such an investigation will necessarily be ad hoc and thus cannot produce systematic explanations. See Ferejohn, "Rationality and Interpretation," pp. 300–301, n. 6.

[14] The success or failure of the analysis depends on whether the observed outcome corresponds to the *unique* equilibrium of the logically reconstructed game. It is now well established that the concept of pure rationality alone often fails to select such an equilibrium out of many potential equilibria. Among the game theorists, this problem is generally referred to as the "Folk Theorem" (see Fundenberg and Maskin, "Folk Theorem in Repeated Games."

[15] The terms *auxiliary* and *thick rationality* are borrowed, respectively, from Simon, "Human Nature in Politics," and Ferejohn, "Rationality and Interpretation."

[16] See chapter 9 for the citation of these exceptions.

> practiced in any modern democracy, no matter how different the cultural contexts of those politics. Respect for civil liberties, competitive elections, responsible government, even the high cost of election campaigns will strike a chord of instant recognition. *But Japan has used the threads of democratic politics to weave through its social structure, constitutional order, political traditions, and value systems a distinctly Japanese pattern. A better understanding of this pattern should contribute to a deeper appreciation of this enormously vibrant, successful, and endlessly interesting country.*[17]

Although, as Curtis implies here, it may be true that many features of Japanese political systems and processes reveal a distinctive pattern, every country's political systems and processes are sui generis, and Japanologists are not justified in searching only for uniquely Japanese determinants.[18] In fact, those preoccupied with Japanese uniqueness violate the very elementary rule of comparative analyses articulated by John S. Mill one and a half centuries ago. According to Mill's "Method of Difference," the intellectual burden of identifying the cause of a unique phenomenon lies, not in the inclusion (into the list of explanatory variables) of factors unique to that phenomenon but rather in the exclusion (from the list) of other factors commonly observed across various phenomena.[19] Only after such an elimination process has been completed can one claim that the remaining factors are the true, and truly unique, causes.

The advantage of the microanalytic approach adopted in this study is that, built on general assumptions, it allows scholars to control for those "other factors" and thus to deduce causal inferences about the political phenomena observed. Japanese politicians, voters, and political parties are as self-seeking as those elsewhere, and there is no reason to believe that the application of these assumptions to the Japanese context is problematic. In this sense the persistent myth of Japanese uniqueness should not prevent one from searching for nonunique determinants of Japanese politics.

In addition, it is arguable that the application of the microanalytic approach to the Japanese context is desirable for the more general purposes of testing this approach and exploring its broad implications. According to standard case-selection rules, Japan provides an excellent vehicle with which to test the validity and generalizability of this approach, precisely because Japan has conventionally been described as a country with distinctive cultural, societal, and historical backgrounds. In this sense Japan presents a valuable "tough case" for theory confirmation/falsification; that is, if the analysis is successful in the Japanese case, the microanalytic approach is likely to succeed in exam-

[17] Curtis, *Japanese Way of Politics*, p. xii; emphasis added.

[18] For criticisms of various stereotypical misconceptions of Japanese uniqueness, see Reed, *Making Common Sense of Japan*.

[19] John Stuart Mill, *System of Logic*, as excerpted in Etzioni et al., eds., *Comparative Perspectives*, pp. 205–13.

ining other advanced industrial democracies whose culture, society, and history are (said to be) not so distinctive. Hence, although the primary purpose of this book is to establish a coherent and systematic account of the development of postwar Japanese parliamentary democracy, the analysis and conclusions drawn from this study will also have more general implications for the applicability of the microanalytic perspective to the field of comparative politics as a whole.

Framework, Argument, and Method in Brief

As noted earlier, the fundamental premise of the analytical framework adopted in this study is that observed political events and phenomena are the product of conscious decisions made by individual actors. My analytical task, then, is to interpret and reconstruct the events and phenomena in question as a series of decisions made by relevant political actors. More specifically, it is to reveal the processes through which the incentives of these actors, as well as their relative power and strategies, are reflected in the actual political outcomes.

Generally it would not be a novel venture to highlight such concepts as individual incentives, bargaining power, and strategic interactions for the analysis of party competition in a democratic context. Since Joseph Schumpeter made his famous discussion on "Another Theory of Democracy" more than a half century ago, it has become widely accepted to define democracy as fundamentally a competitive process and to regard individual politicians and political parties as agents struggling for votes and legislative influence.[20] In discussing the evolution of Japanese parliamentary democracy, however, it is particularly worth repeating and emphasizing the Schumpeterian notion of competition. Although some observers claim that there has been little meaningful competition under the LDP's long and remarkable one-party dominance, the rarity of power transition in the *outcome* does not necessarily imply the total absence of competition and strategic bargaining during the *process* of each election or each government formation.[21]

The central argument of this study can thus be put simply: in Japan, as in any other modern democracy, individual politicians and political parties are engaged in serious competition in which they struggle for votes and legislative influence. I demonstrate that such competition existed during the early post-

[20] Schumpeter, *Capitalism, Socialism and Democracy*. For example, Schumpeter's insights were crucial for Anthony Downs in developing his spatial theory of voting (see Downs, *Economic Theory of Democracy*). Downs, in fact, explicitly acknowledges this: "Schumpeter's profound analysis of democracy forms the inspiration and foundation for our whole thesis, and our debt and gratitude to him are great indeed" (p. 29, n. 11).

[21] See, for example, Masumi Ishikawa's remark in Curtis and Ishikawa, *Doken Kokka Nippon* [Construction state Japan]: "Japanese politics, which has not experienced power transition for a long time, must be called a 'half' democracy" (p. 163; translation by Kohno).

war periods, when the basic frameworks for party competition was created, when coalition governments were formed one after another, and when the ongoing partisan realignment led to the creation of the LDP and the JSP in 1955. I also demonstrate that, even after the LDP's parliamentary dominance became a semipermanent feature, the competitive and strategic interactions among individual politicians and between political parties caused the gradual and evolutionary changes in the nature of the Japanese party system and in the pattern of the LDP's intraparty politics. Finally, I demonstrate that such interactions also brought about the dramatic ending of the LDP's long-lasting regime in 1993. In essence, then, this study advances an argument for the competitive nature of politics and an analysis of how competition has shaped the postwar evolution of Japanese parliamentary democracy.

In order to advance the above argument and analysis effectively, various methods are employed throughout this study. I rely on detailed case studies to explain counterintuitive decisions and to uncover the reasoning beneath the apparently irrational behavior of individual political actors. In these case studies I make a conscious effort to use counterfactual explorations, because many of the decisions and phenomena analyzed below are one-time events and thus not suitable for other (regular) hypothesis-testing methods.[22] I also use available statistics on general elections in order to substantiate my arguments and to test my hypotheses. Occasionally, for the same purposes, I resort to survey data, especially large-scale public opinion polls conducted by major Japanese newspapers.

More generally, and perhaps most important, throughout this study I adhere to an organizational format in which I compare my explanations with the other existing interpretations. I adopt such a format to counter the anticipated criticism that what I offer is simply one possible way of "telling the story" about Japanese politics. Of course there are always numerous ways to interpret the same events and phenomena, and I do not claim that my version represents the only plausible account of the evolution of postwar Japanese party politics. What I do assert, however, is the *relative* advantage of my explanations both individually (developed in each chapter) and collectively (advanced in the study as a whole) over the existing ones. The purpose of the exercise, in other words, is not only to show that my version makes sense but to convince the reader that it reveals and accounts for more of the story than any other previous interpretation.

Organization

This book highlights the contrast between those interpretations of postwar Japanese party politics based on the conventional theoretical approaches and

[22] For an excellent essay that discusses the utility of counterfactual analyses in the study of political phenomena, see Fearon, "Counterfactuals and Hypothesis Testing."

those based on a microanalytic framework. Chapter 2 therefore begins by advancing a general critique of the three existing approaches.

The first three substantive chapters, 3, 4 and 5, focus on the first decade of the post-World War II period and examine the nature of multiparty competition that eventually led to the establishment of the Liberal Democratic Party in 1955. Chapter 3 investigates the politics of electoral reform during 1945–47. Because the electoral system sets the fundamental "rules of the game" that shape the patterns of party politics in any democratic country, I endogenize and explain this important institutional choice by highlighting the incentives and relative bargaining power of relevant political actors.

Chapters 4 and 5 draw on insights from contemporary coalition theories and present detailed case studies on the formation of two important governments during this period. Chapter 4 analyzes the establishment of the Socialist-led coalition government in 1947. Chapter 5 examines the government formation negotiations that eventually led to the merger of the two existing conservative parties and the creation of the LDP in 1955. In both these chapters I demonstrate the inadequacies of the existing socio-ideological explanations and argue that competitive and strategic behavior of political actors determined the course of the bargaining process as well as the final outcome.

The next two chapters turn to the post-1955 evolution of Japanese party politics. Chapter 6 focuses on intraparty politics within the ruling LDP and examines the determinants of the organizational changes that took place over the period of its long one-party dominance. Chapter 7 focuses on the changes in the framework in which the LDP competed with the opposition parties over these years. Both these chapters illustrate that the conventional political-culture and socio-ideological perspectives fail to provide fine-tuned explanations for the observed changes.

In chapter 8, the last substantive chapter of this study, I focus on the political process that led to the LDP's breakup and the demise of its enduring one-party dominance in 1993. This chapter again highlights the incentives of individual political actors and their competitive and strategic behavior as the key determinants of the political change.

Finally, chapter 9 summarizes various implications and concludes this study with suggestions for further research.

2

QUESTIONING CONVENTIONAL APPROACHES

OVER THE PAST few decades a vast literature has accumulated, both in and outside Japan, to describe various features of Japanese politics and to document their development during the post-World War II period. The Liberal Democratic Party in particular and the Japanese party system generally have become the focus of books and articles, as the LDP's parliamentary dominance continued for a long period. The majority of these books and articles, however, are either anecdotal observations made by journalists or memoirs written by politicians themselves, with more emphasis given to describing the pattern of the postwar party politics in Japan than to analyzing its causes and consequences.

This chapter focuses on the existing *scholarly* work, as distinguished from journalistic and autobiographical writings. I attempt to establish a typology of currently available theoretical approaches and to evaluate critically their intellectual foundations and basic arguments. Although many Japanologists do not make explicit efforts to associate themselves with a particular theoretical tradition, three orientations can be identified: the political-culture approach, the historical approach, and the socio-ideological approach. As indicated below, although their specific claims differ, these three approaches all emphasize macrostructural factors as the key determinants of contemporary Japanese party politics.[1]

The Political-Culture Approach

The political-culture approach to Japanese politics posits that the political systems and processes in Japan reflect the cultural attributes of the Japanese people, that is, their values, traditions, and behavioral norms. In explaining various aspects of postwar parliamentary democracy in Japan, those adhering to this approach focus on the hierarchical human relations and conservative attitudes toward political participation among the Japanese.

The intellectual underpinnings of the political-culture approach can be found in the early work on Japanese society published by anthropologists, psychologists, and sociologists. These scholars observed the apparent homo-

[1] This literature survey is not intended to be exhaustive but rather is organized to highlight the ways in which postwar Japanese party politics is explained and its determinants identified. For this reason, the survey is limited to those studies that advance positive claims.

geneity of Japanese society in terms of language, ethnicity, and religious beliefs, and suggested that such homogeneity was the source of the uniquely Japanese cultural attributes.

The most influential work was anthropologist Chie Nakane's monograph on the "vertical society." In this book Nakane argued that, despite Western influence and the pressure of modernization, the Japanese retained a cohesive sense of social unity embedded in their traditional human relations. According to Nakane, the sense of unity formed the foundation for the behavioral patterns of the Japanese, such as their tendency to avoid conflicts, to work in a familylike group, to form loyalty toward the group, and to respect those occupying superior positions. Nakane suggested that these patterns were in turn reflected in the hierarchical nature of social institutions such as the lifetime employment systems within, and the Keiretsu groupings among, Japanese business firms.[2]

The distinctive group-oriented behavior of the Japanese was also highlighted in several other studies. A social psychologist, Takeo Doi, argued that such behavior is characterized by a sense of dependence, *amae*, that is formed through child-rearing processes, especially Japanese mothers' indulgent and nondisciplinary practices toward their children.[3] The importance of the parent-child relationship and the lack of individualism were stressed by many anthropological textbooks on Japan.[4] The most ambitious of these was probably a collaborative volume written by Yasusuke Murakami, Seizaburo Sato, and Shumpei Kumon, which popularized the idea that the concept of *ie*, or the samurai-style hierarchical corporate family originating in the eleventh century, was the key to understanding the entire development of premodern and modern Japanese civilizations.[5]

While these anthropological, psychological, and sociological studies had a tremendous influence on Japanese studies generally, some of the early works on Japanese politics also highlighted its cultural foundations. In the case of Nathaniel Thayer's classic book on the LDP one can even detect a flavor of Oriental mystique, as he describes the evolution of an LDP faction:

> Take, for example, the Kono faction . . . The drive for membership in the faction started with a series of banquets in Mukojima, a geisha district . . . to which Kono's lieutenants invited Dietmen who, they thought, would rally to Kono's cause. The site was carefully chosen. It was far enough outside the usual haunts of the Dietmen so that any guest would not have to explain his attendance to other Dietmen, but not so distant that the invitees would have to make an undue

[2] Nakane, *Tate-Shakai no Ningen Kankei* [Human relations of vertical society].

[3] Doi, *Amae no Kozo* [The structure of dependence].

[4] See, for example, Lebra, *Japanese Patterns of Behavior*, and Befu, *Japan: An Anthropological Introduction.*

[5] Murakami, Sato, and Kumon, *Bunmei to Shite no Ie Shakai* [Family society as civilization].

effort to attend. . . . The Dietmen ate, drank, joked with the geisha, listened to the raconteurs, and at the end of the evening, signed a book to commemorate the occasion. . . . Kono's only factional membership list was the banquet books, and the only yardstick of factional loyalty was the distance the Dietmen were willing to travel to eat and drink with him. . . . In this period, any faction could be defined as a group of politicians who travelled to the resorts and hot springs for seminars and met for an occasional meal in Tokyo.[6]

Since the 1970s Japan has been increasingly recognized as the nation that has completed the process of modernization, and the portrayal of Japan as an exotic and mysterious country has disappeared below the surface. However, in the midst of the behavioral revolution in social science, proponents of the political-culture approach to Japanese politics became more sophisticated, equipped with statistical techniques and large-scale survey data.

Especially among those studying Japanese attitudes toward voting and political participation, the political-culture approach gained significant momentum and became the dominant mode of explanation.[7] Even in the 1980s some of these scholars still adhered to the view that values and attitudes embedded in the traditional Japanese society play an essential role in determining Japanese political behavior. Bradley Richardson and Scott Flanagan, for example, note in their widely read textbook on Japanese politics:

American textbooks on politics in other Western democracies, such as England, France, or Germany, rarely introduce cultural themes to explain political phenomena. Because the Western nations all share a common cultural heritage, the cultural context of politics in these nations is an assumed constant, and cultural differences are minor enough that their impact on political behavior rarely warrants detailed attention. These assumptions cannot be made in the Japanese case. Japan's cultural heritage and traditional values and beliefs, which are strikingly different from the Western experience in many important ways, have a great impact on Japanese political behavior. Consequently, a knowledge of some of the major outlines of Japan's traditional culture and contemporary patterns of social relations is important to our understanding of Japanese politics.[8]

Accordingly, with regard to the electoral fortunes of the LDP, Richardson and Flanagan claim that this conservative party up until the early 1970s made "effective use of the traditional symbols of power and authority . . . [manipulating] its distributive, please-all policies to create a sense of obligation and indebtedness." Certain segments of the Japanese society "continue to take

[6] Thayer, *How the Conservatives Rule Japan*, pp. 22–23.

[7] See, for example, Richardson, *Political Culture of Japan*; Nakamura, ed., *Gendai Nihon no Seiji Bunka* [The political culture of contemporary Japan]; Watanuki, *Politics in Postwar Japanese Society*; and Ward and Kubota, "Family Influence and Political Socialization."

[8] Richardson and Flanagan, *Politics in Japan*, p. 117.

their cues from local notables" who are regarded as a legitimate ruling class and "these deferential attitudes," they argue, "are more pervasive among the older, rural, and less educated elements of the population, and among women and those employed in the more traditional sectors of the economy." These elements and sectors coincide with the electoral stronghold of the LDP.[9]

Ronald Hrebenar also emphasizes the deferential and apolitical nature of Japanese electoral behavior in explaining the long-lasting LDP's one-party dominance. According to Hrebenar, "for many Japanese, voting is not so much a political activity as it is a part of general social behavior. Citizens are encouraged to vote as a function of their responsibility to the social unit to which they belong."[10] Hrebenar suggests that the Japanese generally have little interest in politics and do not strongly identify with political parties. Thus he asserts: "One reason the LDP remained in power for so many years is that the Japanese electorate is essentially conservative and resistant to change."[11]

The claims made by Richardson and Flanagan and Hrebenar are based on, and consistent with, various empirical findings accumulated by other scholars since the late 1960s. Some comparative analyses, for example, have shown that party identification among Japanese voters is weak relative to other nations.[12] In survey after survey Ichiro Miyake and others have found that Japanese voters emphasize the district-level candidate factors, as opposed to national policy issues or party choices, in casting their ballots.[13] Anson D. Shupe, observing the apparent gap between Japanese attitudes toward voting and toward other modes of political participations, has concluded that voting in Japan is a "passive act" that fits with the traditional value of avoiding overt political action.[14] Gerald Curtis's documentation of an electoral campaign has also illustrated how the presence of local elites and personal networks within the community play a decisive role in mobilizing votes.[15] These survey results and reports have amplified the image of a localized, deferential, and conserva-

[9] Ibid., 72, pp. 177–78.

[10] Hrebenar, "Changing Postwar Party System," p. 15.

[11] Ibid., p. 22.

[12] Richardson, "Party Loyalties and Party Saliency"; Verba, Nie, and Kim, *Participation and Political Equality*.

[13] See, for example, Miyake, "Seito Shiji no Ryudosei to Anteisei" [Fluidity and stability in party support]; Miyake, *Seito Shiji no Bunseki* [An analysis of party support]; and Miyake, Kinoshita, and Aiba, *Kotonaru Reberu no Senkyo ni okeru Tohyo Kodo no Bunseki* [The analysis of voting behavior at various levels]; and Watanuki et al., *Nihonjin no Senkyo Kodo* [The Japanese electoral behavior]. For qualifications and reservations made recently regarding the thesis of weak party identification, see White, *Migration in Metropolitan Japan*; Kabashima, "Yukensha no Ideorogi" [Ideologies of the electorate]; and Richardson, "Constituency Candidates versus Parties."

[14] Shupe, "Social Participation and Voting Turnout."

[15] Curtis, *Election Campaigning Japanese Style*.

tive electoral process in Japan, and have thus facilitated the political-culture explanations for the LDP's persistence.

Having summarized the basic tenets of the political-culture approach, what, then, are its weaknesses? One empirical problem is that, in so far as it emphasizes the cultural and behavioral foundations of the LDP's conservative hegemony, it cannot explain the intense multiparty competition that took place in Japan during the first decade of the postwar period. The lack of attention to this earlier period is problematic especially since, as I demonstrate in chapter 5, the LDP itself evolved out of interactions and bargaining under the previous multiparty framework. The proponents of this approach either entirely ignore this decade or treat it simply as an aberration.

The political-culture explanations are also problematic in light of the fact that the electoral support for the conservative party underwent a significant change over the long period of its governance. Throughout the 1960s and 1970s rapid industrialization and sweeping urbanization eroded the LDP's original stronghold among farmers and small business owners. During these two decades, seemingly in response to such erosion, popular support for the LDP has declined continuously. But there was a turnaround in the late 1970s and support for the LDP started to resurge gradually. This development was puzzling. If the LDP's electoral fortune was the product of the traditional Japanese attitudes toward voting and political participation, the continuing industrialization and urbanization in Japan would lead one to expect a further decline in LDP support.

The most famous response to this puzzle has been Yasusuke Murakami's hypothesis of the emerging "New Middle Mass."[16] According to Murakami, the resurgence in the LDP support did not reflect a revival of "tradition-oriented conservatism," but rather the rise of a new "interest-oriented" conservative majority in Japan. He suggests that the LDP was successful in converting itself from a party of rural loyalists to an interest-oriented catch-all party:

> Recent elections were decided not so much by the choice of parties as by the choice of whether or not to vote. When the majority is threatened, those of the

[16] The basic thesis was originally presented in Murakami, Sato, and Kumon, "Datsu 'Hokaku' Jidai no Torai" [The arrival of the post-"Conservative-progressive" era]. In this article the authors used the term *New Middle Class* [*Shin Chukan Kaiso*], which caused great controversy because of its ambiguity. It was criticized in particular for potential confusion with the conventional sociological term *Shin Chukan-so* which means "white collar workers" in Japanese (see Yamaguchi, "Seiji Tenkan to 'Chukan-so Mondai'" [Political change and the "middle-class problem"]; and Sugiyama, "Hoshuka Shakai-ron no Sai-Kento" [Rethinking the conservative society thesis]. Murakami therefore changed his terminology to *New Middle Mass* [*Shin Chukan Taishu*] in his later article "Shin Chukan Taishu Seiji no Jidai" [The age of new middle mass politics], in his book-length treatment of the subject, *Shin Chukan Taishu no Jidai* [The age of new middle mass], and in his translated version, "The Age of New Middle Mass Politics."

> interest-oriented NMM [New Middle Mass] return to vote for their immediate choice, the LDP. . . . The wider variation of election outcomes compared to opinion poll results, the increasing sensitivity of voters to minor issues, and the strong opposition to any change in the existing regime are all evidence of the change in the nature of the LDP toward an interest-oriented catch-all party.[17]

Thus Murakami's work can be seen as an attempt to supplement the original version of the political-culture interpretation: there appeared a new kind of conservative political culture in Japan, from which the New Middle Mass had emerged and on which the LDP's continuing dominance was based. In this sense Murakami does not depart from the logic that Japanese politics is a reflection of the underlying attitudinal and behavioral attributes of Japanese culture.

The real challenge to Murakami's thesis came in the early 1990s when the LDP's conservative regime started to crumble because of sweeping political distrust resulting from a series of scandals involving high-profile politicians. The LDP failed to obtain a majority in the July 1993 general election and was thus forced to hand over its power to a non-LDP coalition government.[18] Although Murakami focuses on the beginning of "the age of New Middle Mass politics," nothing in his original analysis predicts the decline of the LDP. In this sense his argument seems to have been falsified on empirical grounds.

Even more critical, the internal logic of Murakami's claim has flaws. Although it may be true that the Japanese political culture underwent a major change in the late 1970s, nothing is offered in his analysis to make a causal link between such a change and the comeback of the LDP. Murakami takes it for granted that the LDP was the "immediate choice" of the New Middle Mass, but no elaboration is offered as to why other political parties were not as attractive.[19] Murakami, in fact, tries to bypass this question by arguing that it was the LDP, which became the "catch-all party," that successfully attracted the votes of the new conservative population. But then the explanatory emphasis shifts to the change in the LDP's electoral strategy, and one can only conclude that the rise of the New Middle Mass had little to do with the party's resurgence.[20]

[17] "The Age of New Middle Mass Politics," p. 63.

[18] See chapter 8.

[19] This is indeed puzzling because Murakami also indicates that the New Middle Mass has ambivalent, pro- and antisystem tendencies and that "the NMM will not necessarily support the existing conservative party, say the LDP" (Murakami, "New Middle Mass Politics," p. 46).

[20] If Murakami meant to say that it was the LDP's strategy rather than the rise of the new conservatism that explained the LDP's comeback, then another puzzle arises: Why did the change in the LDP's strategy not take place much earlier? Murakami indicates (correctly) that the expansion of social welfare programs, new policy priority on employment rather than industrial profits, and the LDP's cultivation of grassroots party organizations all took place in the first half of the

In sum, the political-culture approach emphasizes Japanese attitudinal and behavioral attributes in explaining the postwar party politics dominated by the LDP. As Japan's modernization continues, the characterization of Japan as a mysterious Oriental nation has all but vanished, at least within the scholarly literature. In light of the electoral development since the late 1970s in particular, Murakami's New Middle Mass thesis has been offered as an attempt to supplement the original political-culture explanations, but its internal logic and empirical claims are problematic, leaving important questions unexplored.

The Historical Approach

The historical approach to Japanese politics posits that the contemporary Japanese political systems and processes are the product of the legacy from earlier historical periods, especially the pre-World War II era and the experience of the American occupation during 1945–51. In explaining various aspects of Japan's parliamentary democracy, the proponents of this approach emphasize especially the underdevelopment of the Japanese socialist movement and leftist political parties before the war, and the preservation of the bureaucratic structure during the occupation.

The intellectual origins of the historical approach go back to the early work of Japanese political scientists in the late 1950s and early 1960s. Having experienced the war, foreign occupation, and sweeping political and social reforms, these scholars were engaged in an intense debate over the changes and the continuity between pre- and postwar Japan—the constitutional framework, administrative processes, and structure of the state bureaucracy. In some instances, the debate took on a highly ideological and political tone, as was the case between the so-called Rounou-ha and Kouza-ha schools among the Marxist historians.[21] There were, however, exchanges of scholarly views that embodied pioneering analyses of Japanese political history.

A book edited by Yoshitake Oka in 1958, in particular, had a significant impact on the development of the historical approach to Japanese politics.[22] Because this book was a collection of articles to which many scholars contributed, it is difficult to distill from it a single coherent message. However, the most dominant and unambiguous theme of the book, which was strongly advanced by Oka's lead article and Kiyoaki Tsuji's article on Japanese bureau-

1970s and "the net result was to strongly attract those parts of the voting population not previously wooed by the LDP" (p. 63). If these changes were made for the LDP's electoral purposes, they could have arguably occurred some time in the 1960s when the LDP was actually losing its popular support in one election after another. Murakami needs to account for this apparent delay in converting the LDP's electoral incentives into policy changes.

[21] For a balanced review of these competing Marxist views, see Ohishi "Sengo Kaikaku to Nihon Shihonshugi no Kozo Henka" [Postwar reforms and the structural changes of Japan's capitalism].

[22] Oka, ed., *Gendai Nihon no Seiji Katei* [Political process of contemporary Japan].

cracy, was the peculiarity of the process of Japan's democratization as compared with the experience of other Western nations.

More specifically, Oka highlighted the unusual international pressure that influenced the evolution of democracy in Japan. He emphasized not only that Japan's democratization was originally brought about by external military force, but also that it was carried out when the international environment surrounding Japan was rapidly changing with the beginning of the Cold War. According to Oka, these external influences often resulted in ad hoc and drastic changes in the direction of reform, such as the sudden banning of general strikes, the hyperdeflationary "Dodge economic plan," and the significant changes in constitutional interpretation especially of the peace clause, all of which left lasting effects on the Japanese postwar political development.[23] The historical "illegitimacy" of Japanese democracy strongly implied in Oka's article was expressed by other contributors to the volume as well[24] and shared more generally by Japanese intellectuals at the time.[25]

Tsuji's article focused on the causes and consequences of one particular aspect of Japan's democratization, namely, the preservation of the state bureaucracy. According to Tsuji, Japanese bureaucrats inherited most of their power from the prewar period because of the popular illusion about their political neutrality. Tsuji also stressed that the Allied Occupation Forces adopted "indirect rule" and left the bureaucratic institutions intact during the occupation in order to carry out their reforms. The inevitable consequence was that Japanese public policy making had to rely heavily on the knowledge and expertise of these bureaucrats to whom other political actors, such as individual politicians, political parties, interest groups, and even the national Parliament were subordinate. It was in this characteristic of the Japanese state that Tsuji observed significant continuity between pre- and postwar Japanese polities.[26]

Tsuji's views on the bureaucracy were embraced almost in their entirety by American writers, most notably Chalmers Johnson. In his famous monograph on the Ministry of International Trade and Industry, Johnson characterizes Japan as a "developmental state," attributing much of its postwar economic success to the expertise and competence of the Ministry's officials to formu-

[23] Oka, "Gendai Nihon Seiji ni okeru Gaiatsu, Hannou" [Foreign pressure, reactions in contemporary Japanese Politics], pp. 1–50.

[24] See, especially, the chapter by Kyogoku on the changing Japanese attitudes toward politics ("Seiji Ishiki no Henyou to Bunka" [Transformation and diversification of political consciousness].

[25] See Maruyama, *Gendai Seiji no Shiso to Kodo* [The ideologies and movements of contemporary politics]; Ishida, *Kindai Nihon Seiji Kozo no Kenkyu* [A study on modern Japanese political structure]; and Ishida, *Sengo Nihon no Seiji Taisei* [Postwar Japan's political system].

[26] Tsuji, "Kanryo Kiko no Onzon to Kyoka" [The preservation and strengthening of bureaucratic institutions]," pp. 109–25. See also Tsuji, *Nihon Kanryo-sei no Kenkyu* [A study of Japanese bureacracy].

late the industrial policy. Parallel to Tsuji's argument, Johnson finds the origins of the Ministry's jurisdiction and influence in the prewar and wartime legislation as well as in the institutional structures that had survived the American occupation.[27]

The Tsuji-Johnson line of argument became the established analytical paradigm, often referred to as the "bureaucracy-dominant" model of Japanese policy making. Since the late 1970s this paradigm has been under attack from "pluralists" who claim, based on various case studies and survey analyses, that the Diet, individual politicians, political parties, and interest groups do influence Japanese public policies.[28] Although often construed otherwise, the question, "whether or not the bureaucratic influence has declined," is not a theoretical dispute but simply an empirical question. The recent accumulation of evidence in favor of pluralists' claims, therefore, does not negate the core logic of Johnson's (and Tsuji's) historical argument that the bureaucracy had inherited their power and influence from the earlier periods.[29]

In fairness to Johnson, he surely recognizes that the influence of politicians and political parties grew especially since the Tanaka cabinet established in 1972. But, he concludes, "the alleged ascendancy of party over bureaucracy during the early 1970s has probably been exaggerated." And he notes: "The LDP's persistent internal factionalism is also significant in causing the LDP to devote more attention to internal political competition than to political leadership, thereby leaving the field open for and making the party dependent upon the bureaucracy for policy leadership."[30]

The problem of the bureaucracy-dominant model, as has been suggested by its critics, is that it is too narrowly focused on policy making to constitute a general explanation of Japanese politics.[31] Johnson's argument provides few clues to explain why the existence of a strong state bureaucracy necessarily led to the existence of a single dominant party. It is one thing to claim, as Johnson does, that the ruling party could afford to engage in the internal factional strife because of the efficient and competent bureaucracy. It is another to explain why only the LDP, and not other political parties, could take advan-

[27] Johnson, *MITI and the Japanese Miracle*. The legacy of the prewar structure of Japan's political economy has also been a topic of recent studies among economists. See, for example, Okazaki and Okuno, eds., *Gendai Nihon Keizai Sisutemu no Genryu* [The origins of the contemporary Japanese economic system]; and Noguchi, *1940-nen Taisei* [The 1940 system].

[28] For the increasing role of the Diet, politicians, parties, and interest groups in Japanese policy making, see, respectively, Mochizuki, "Managing and Influencing the Japanese Legislative Process;" Muramatsu and Krauss, "Bureaucrats and Politicians in Policymaking"; Sato and Matsuzaki, *Jiminto Seiken* [The LDP's rule]; and Otake, *Gendai Nihon no Seiji Kenryoku, Keizai Kenryoku* [Political power and economic power in contemporary Japan].

[29] For a sophisticated treatment of this debate, see Yakushiji, *Seijika vs Kanryo* [Politicians vs bureaucrats].

[30] Johnson, "Japan: Who Governs?" p. 15.

[31] See Muramatsu, "Seisaku Katei" [Political process].

tage of such a bureaucracy and thus sustain a long and continuous dominance in Parliament.

More recently a different line of historical argument has been formulated to explain the LDP's persistent rule.[32] Instead of claiming categorically that the Japanese political parties and Parliament are underdeveloped, this argument highlights a set of historical reasons to explain why the opposition parties, especially the Japan Socialist Party, failed to become an electoral alternative to the LDP. There are at least two different versions within this historical perspective, and they are not mutually exclusive. First, Seizaburo Sato and Tetsuhisa Matsuzaki, among other Japanologists, advance a kind of "learning" hypothesis, claiming that Japanese voters had learned important lessons from the devastating consequences of the coalition government led by the Socialist leader Tetsu Katayama during 1947–48.[33] Second, T. J. Pempel takes an even longer-term perspective and emphasizes the effects of the late introduction of popular suffrage and the underdevelopment of the leftist and labor movements during the prewar period.[34] Thus, unlike Tsuji and Johnson who are concerned with abstract "state structure," these new analyses advance more specific claims about the historical sources of the LDP's strength relative to the opposition's.

These new claims, however, are also problematic. Like the political-culture explanation, these claims generally ignore the earlier postwar period of the multiparty competition. Describing the JSP and leftist forces as chronically weak does not reveal much about why the Socialist-led government was established in 1947. A careful look at the development of the Socialist Party after the collapse of the coalition government also reveals inconsistencies. It is true that the Socialists suffered a major defeat in the 1949 general election, but the available aggregate data of the election indicate that the Socialist votes did not go to the conservative camp but to the leftist opposition, the Japan Communist Party.[35] Not only did the Socialists make a quick electoral recovery, but they also expanded their popular support and parliamentary share through-

[32] This second historical argument was largely a product of a joint project on the one-party dominant regimes (cosponsored by the Social Science Research Council and the Japan Society for the Promotion of Science), in which many Japanese and U.S. scholars participated. The scholars from the United States were led by T. J. Pempel, who later edited the book *Uncommon Democracies: The One-Party Dominant Regimes*.

[33] Sato and Matsuzaki, *Jiminto Seiken*, p. 17; Tani, "The Japan Socialist Party before the Mid-1960s," pp. 80–85.

[34] Pempel, "Introduction. Uncommon Democracies," esp. pp. 24–29. See also Richardson and Flanagan, *Politics in Japan*; and Masumi, *Gendai Seiji* [Contemporary politics].

[35] By comparing the results of this election with the previous one, Masumi Ishikawa advances this interpretation in his *Deeta Sengo Seijishi* [A data history of postwar politics], p. 20. Aggregate data as such, of course, constitute only circumstantial evidence to show how voters "move" from one party to another. More microlevel evidence is presented by Babb in his "Statics and Dynamics of Japan Socialist Party Ideology."

out the 1950s and even maintained such popularity and share at least until the late 1960s. None of these trends can be explained by either the voters' "learning" or the prewar legacy hypothesis.

Having identified the empirical shortcomings of the historical approach, let me turn to its methodological problem. Even if it is true that a previous historical period provides lessons and directions for the contemporary era, it is extremely difficult to specify, *ex ante*, how long the legacy from the past continues to impact the shaping of current political outcomes. As a result, historical explanations are rarely presented in a positive and falsifiable manner. For example, Pempel suggests that the continuation of the LDP's one-party dominance itself has been an indication of the lasting historical effect because the LDP, in using its incumbency advantage to its full extent, successfully created what he calls a "cycle of dominance."[36] Such an argument cannot explain why, in other parts of the world, numerous incumbent governments have failed to create a similar cycle. Moreover, the absence of prior specification of "how long" leaves Pempel's argument unfalsifiable; one can only falsify his claim when the LDP's one-party dominance actually ended, but that means that the legacy also ended and that the cycle was somehow broken, thus leaving his basic causal argument intact.

In sum, the historical approach explains postwar Japanese politics in terms of Japan's earlier political development. Even aside from methodological weakness, the claims made by this approach with regard to the LDP's one-party dominance are problematic. While Tsuji-Johnson's bureaucracy-dominant model fails to explore why the existence of a strong bureaucracy may have led to the LDP's one-party dominance, more recent arguments that focus on the chronic weakness of the opposition are also inadequate to provide fine-tuned predictions for either the pre- or post-1955 development.

The Socio-Ideological Approach

The socio-ideological approach to Japanese politics posits that the contemporary Japanese political systems and processes are shaped by underlying societal and ideological cleavages. In explaining the pattern of postwar party politics, the proponents of this approach highlight the fundamental socio-ideological shift that led to the creation of the so-called 1955 system, or the party system entrenched in the underlying progressive-conservative cleavage formed during the late 1940s and early 1950s. They argue that the subsequent remarkable political success of the LDP can be attributed to the rigid and extremely polarized nature of the Japanese socio-ideological cleavage that prevented the leading opposition party, the JSP, from becoming a viable alternative.

[36] Pempel, "Introduction. Uncommon Democracies"; and Pempel, "Conclusion. One-Party Dominance."

The concept of the 1955 system was originally popularized by Robert Scalapino, Jun'nosuke Masumi, Jiro Kamishima, and other Japanese political scientists.[37] More generally, however, the socio-ideological approach owes much of its intellectual debt to Seymour Lipset and Stein Rokkan's seminal analysis of European party systems. In this classic work Lipset and Rokkan argued that the European cleavages were created as a result of the complex process of alliance/power-struggle between establishment elites and opposing forces. They presented a typological scheme with which to understand the varying pattern of translating the cleavages into actual party alignment. Thus, despite their ambitious aim of explaining almost the entire sociopolitical development of modern Western Europe, the specification of the fundamental causal direction in Lipset and Rokkan's model was simple: social variables (i.e., cleavages) explain political outcomes (i.e., party systems).[38]

Parallel to Lipset and Rokkan's analysis, those who regard 1955 as a landmark year in Japanese political history argue that the distinct socio-ideological cleavage had emerged through a series of salient political events that had a revolutionary effect on postwar Japan. These events included the adoption of a new democratic Constitution in 1947 and the conclusion of the Japan-U.S. Security Treaty in 1952. In the Japanese case, it is argued, the cleavage was clear-cut. Those on the one side of the cleavage, the conservative camp, were eager to revise the Constitution and to defend the treaty. Those on the other side, the progressive camp, were eager to defend the Constitution and to abolish the treaty. The party system called the 1955 system was seen as a reflection of this diametrically opposed ideological configuration.

The concept of the 1955 system, however, is a source of analytical confusion.[39] Contrary to the stable and static image implied by the term *system*, Japanese party politics in fact underwent a gradual but considerable change even during the period when the LDP remained in power. By the end of the 1960s the two centrist parties, the Democratic Socialist Party and the Clean Government Party, had entered the electoral race for the House of Representatives. In light of this, some analysts tried to redefine the 1955 system as a system of conservative hegemony, but such a reconceptualization is nothing more than an example of "conceptual stretching" and a post hoc justification.[40]

[37] Masumi "1955-nen no Seiji Taisei" [The political system of the year 1955], pp. 55–72; Scalapino and Masumi, *Parties and Politics in Contemporary Japan*; and a collection of articles in Nihon Seiji Gakkai, ed., *55-nen Taisei no Keisei to Houkai* [The formation and decline of the 1955 system]. Various scholars have later attached different normative nuances to the notion of the 1955 system. For a concise survey, see Yamaguchi, "Sengo Nihon no Seiji Taisei to Seiji Katei," [The political system and process of postwar Japan], esp. 83–85.

[38] Lipset and Rokkan, "Cleavage Structures, Party Systems, and Voter Alignments."

[39] Yasushi Yamaguchi also points to the ambiguity of the concept (see "Sengo Nihon no Seiji Taisei to Seiji Katei").

[40] See, for example, Ide, "Hoshu Choki Seiken-ka no Tochi" [The administration under the conservative extended rule], esp. 12–13.

Probably the most sophisticated contemporary defender of the socio-ideological approach is Hideo Otake. By carefully examining politicians' diaries, autobiographies, and news releases, Otake attempts to demonstrate that the political and economic ideologies prevailing in Japan shifted around the late 1940s. More specifically, according to Otake, the establishment of the coalition government led by the Socialists in 1947 represented a fragile social-democratic consensus that had existed among the Japanese public and the "New Dealers" within the U.S. occupation forces. The failure of the Socialists' policy experiments, especially the devastating consequences of the nationalized coal and mine productions, broke this consensus and gave rise to economic liberalism, which subsequently became the dominant conservative ideology under the leadership of Shigeru Yoshida.[41]

With regard to the LDP's persistent rule, Otake emphasizes the exceptionally rigid nature of the Japanese cleavage that prevented the leading opposition party, the JSP, from adopting more "social-democratic" policies, like those of the SPD in West Germany. According to Otake, the rigidity is owing partly to the historical fact that the cleavage originally formed at a time when intense public debate was taking place over highly ideological issues—the Constitution, postwar settlement, security ties with the United States, and Japanese rearmament.[42] He also acknowledges that the Japanese conservatism, championed by Yoshida, had a distinctive "reactionary" element, that made the JSP nervous and overly cautious in dealing with the LDP's policies, especially its educational policies. This, in Otake's words, was the "origin of the JSP's tragedy," and another important reason why the JSP failed to become a viable alternative to the LDP.[43]

Despite the sophistication Otake added to the original notion of the 1955 system, the socio-ideological approach that highlights the importance of the underlying cleavage still contains many critical problems. First, as is also the case with the two other approaches, this approach cannot account for the development of the Japanese party politics before 1955; that is, it treats the earlier period of intense multiparty competition merely as a transitional era in Japanese political history, awaiting more solid Japanese social and ideological foundations to be established.

Second, the socio-ideological approach simply assumes, rather than proves, a causal relationship between socio-ideological factors and party systems, without explaining how, and exactly when, the new cleavage replaced the old. In fact, scholars seem to be in disagreement about these points. The original proponents of the notion of the 1955 system argue that the cleavage was

[41] Otake, *Adenaua to Yoshida Shigeru* [Adenauer and Shigeru Yoshida].

[42] Otake, "Defense Controversies and One-Party Dominance"; Otake, "Rearmament Controversies and Cultural Conflicts in Japan."

[43] Otake, "Nihon Shakai-to Higeki no Kigen" [The origins of the Japan Socialist Party's tragedy]; see also Otake, *Sai-Gunbi to Nashonarizumu* [Rearmament and nationalism].

formed through a series of events, such as the adoption of the democratic Constitution and the conclusion of the San Francisco Peace Treaty. Otake and more recent defenders of the approach emphasize, more specifically, the collapse of the Socialist-Democratic coalition governments and the landslide victory of Yoshida's Liberal Party in 1949. In either case, it is not readily clear why it took some time before the change in the socio-ideological cleavage eventually led to the realignment in the party system. What explains the delay, and why was it in 1955 in particular that the conservative parties successfully merged?

Third, even with regard to the post-1955 development, the socio-ideological approach leaves many questions unanswered. For example, if the underlying cleavage were as polarized as suggested, why was the JCP electorally unsuccessful relative to the JSP? Furthermore, the socio-ideological approach provides very few clues to explain the fragmentation of the opposition camp or why two new centrist parties entered the electoral competition during the 1960s. Some authors, influenced by Ronald Inglehart's work,[44] suggest that the social and ideological foundations of the 1955 system have actually eroded over the years and that this erosion explains the fragmentation.[45] Such a claim, however, simply begs the key question: If the "erosion" had occurred, why did it not occur symmetrically, the other side of the cleavage (the conservative camp) also becoming fragmented as well?

In sum, the socio-ideological approach regards the underlying cleavage structure as the main determinant of the Japanese party system. Otake, in particular, provides a sophisticated interpretation in this theoretical tradition, arguing that the rigid and polarized nature of the Japanese cleavage benefitted the LDP in preventing the JSP from becoming a viable electoral alternative. Nevertheless, the socio-ideological analysis is problematic, treating the period before 1955 as simply a precursor to the formulation of a more solid cleavage as well as failing to predict many aspects of the post-1955 political development.

Absence of Micro-Level Politics

My discussion up to this point has concentrated on empirical and methodological criticisms of the three approaches in an attempt to demonstrate their lack of predictive power and their inherent operational problems. What should be emphasized even more is the common theoretical shortcoming of these conventional perspectives, namely, the absence of microlevel politics.

The three existing approaches to Japanese politics are all macrostructural theories in that they treat the political arena in Japan as simply a mirror reflecting the underlying structure, be it Japanese culture, history, or socio-

[44] Inglehart, *The Silent Revolution.*

[45] Flanagan, "Electoral Change in Japan."

ideological cleavage. As a result, they overlook competition and strategic interactions among individual voters, politicians, and political parties. One can even argue that the conventional views reject the notion of *independent* political actors because, in their frameworks, Japanese voters, politicians, and political parties are defined by the structural variables themselves. As such, these approaches all entail overly deterministic explanations for political outcomes: to the extent that Japanese political actors are the "prisoners of the underlying structure," no matter what power, incentives, and strategies each relevant political actor has, the Japanese political systems and processes would have evolved the way they actually did.

Given their deterministic nature, the only logical way for the conventional approaches to explain "changes" in Japanese political outcomes is to identify the changes in the underlying structure itself. Thus, for example, Murakami tries to highlight the change in the Japanese political culture as the determinant for the LDP's electoral turnaround in the late 1970s. For Otake and other adherents of the socio-ideological approach, it is the shift in the cleavage structure that explains the evolution of the 1955 system. Such a formulation, however, would necessarily force scholars to take another step to specify the conditions under which the cultural and societal backgrounds change over time. Such an exercise would involve immensely macroscopic theorization, and thus, by definition, would move further away analytically from the sphere of politics and the specific political phenomenon, the starting point of the original investigation. In fact, as I demonstrate throughout the rest of this study, a number of important changes have occurred in postwar Japanese party politics that cannot be adequately accounted for by structural changes at such a macrolevel. Even if in some cases political changes could be associated with the macrostructural causes, these causes alone cannot predict the exact pattern with which the political events have actually unfolded in those cases.

None of these criticisms deny that macrostructural factors matter in deriving behavioral outcomes in Japanese politics. Culture, history, and ideology all constitute an important background for political interactions in Japan, as in any other society. Macrostructural factors, however, are likely to be mediated by more specific institutional arrangements under which individual political actors have to interact. It is only by focusing microanalytically on such interactions that one can establish more fine-tuned predictions.

In sum, the conventional approaches have not adequately taken into account the role of individual political actors in bringing about important changes in postwar Japanese party politics. What is needed is a new perspective that explores microfoundations of Japan's parliamentary democracy in order to "bring politics back" into the analysis of Japanese politics.

3

THE POLITICS OF ELECTORAL REFORM, 1945–1947

IN THE AFTERMATH of World War II Japan began the task of building a democratic polity and institutions under the occupation of U.S. military forces. In late August 1945, only two weeks after Japan accepted the Potsdam Declaration, the Supreme Commander of the Allied Powers, Douglas MacArthur, arrived at the "GHQ," general headquarters of the occupation forces in Tokyo, to supervise sweeping postwar reforms. This does not mean, however, that Japanese political actors were irrelevant in determining the course of Japan's democratization. The basic direction and guidelines for reform were set by the GHQ, but some important structural details of the new institutions were left to the Japanese to decide. Thus, from the very beginning, the bargaining and negotiations took place between the GHQ and various domestic political actors, as well as among the Japanese actors themselves, who had their own visions and preferences for the design of these institutions.

In the fall, in anticipation of the arrival of an era of true parliamentary democracy, several political parties were established. One of the major issues to be settled immediately was the new electoral system, which would be used to elect a fresh assembly of representatives and to replace the existing Parliament carried over from the war. In the course of the next two years, two decisions were made with regard to the House of Representatives, the more important lower house. In late 1945 the government, led by Prime Minister Kijuro Shidehara, adopted a system that consisted of varying-sized multimember constituencies with each voter casting one to three votes depending on the size of the district. This complicated system was abandoned in early 1947, after only one general election, and the old system that had existed since 1925 was restored under the Liberal government of Shigeru Yoshida. This system, which lasted until 1993, provided for medium-sized multimember districts with each voter casting a single nontransferable vote.

This chapter examines the process through which these two decisions were made. In conventional analyses of Japanese party politics, the electoral system is often taken for granted as an exogenous "given," and the actual political bargaining that led to the postwar electoral reform is rarely subject to extensive scrutiny. In this chapter I endogenize this important institutional choice and reconstruct the decision-making process in a manner that highlights the basic incentives and relative bargaining power of relevant political actors. More specifically, I demonstrate that, in both 1945 and 1947, the final outcome reflected the preference of the dominant incumbent party as well as its strategy for coping with the GHQ's basic reform philosophy. I also argue that the subsequent survival of the electoral system was, at least in part, a product of the incumbent party's tendency to prefer the status quo in the electoral arrangement.

The chapter begins with a critical examinination of the conventional interpretations of Japan's early postwar electoral reform. I then reconstruct the interparty bargaining processes that led to the 1945 and 1947 decisions, respectively, and move on to discuss the system's survival after 1947. The chapter concludes with a summary of the implications presented here.

Conventional Interpretations

Given that the peculiar electoral system adopted in 1947 prevailed over the next four and a half decades, it is understandable that many scholars have addressed the institutional effects, or "the political consequences of the electoral law," in relation to the long-lasting conservative dominance.[1] Few studies, however, have focused on the question of the institutional design of the system. The origins of the Japanese electoral system have been taken for granted because, as discussed in the previous chapter, much of the analysis in the existing literature treats the pre-1955 period as an anomaly in the history of postwar Japanese party politics. The conventional wisdom is simply that the postwar electoral reform was largely influenced by unusual historical circumstances, namely, the presence of foreign occupation forces that had significant clout over the fate of Japan's democratization.[2]

Certainly some aspects of the electoral reform, which came as part of the GHQ's democratization package, were colored by ideas then alien to the Japanese, such as the extension of suffrage to women. With regard more specifically to the choice of the electoral system for the lower house, however, the "foreign pressure" hypothesis is not sufficiently fine-tuned to explain the actual reform process that allowed one system to be adopted in 1945, only to be replaced by another two years later. It is difficult to explain such a zigzag

[1] See Lee, "Shuugiin Senkyo de no Seito no Tokuhyo-su to Giseki-su [Political parties' votes and seats in the House of Representative elections]"; Lijphart, Pintor and Sone, "The Limited Vote and the Single Nontransferable Vote;" Cox and Niou, "Seat Bonuses under the Single Nontransferable Vote System"; Christensen and Johnson, "Toward a Context-Rich Analysis of Electoral Systems"; and Cox, "Is the Single Non-Transferable Vote Superproportional?"

[2] See, for example, Ishikawa, *Deeta Sengo Seiji-shi* [A data history of postwar politics], p. 5. Ishikawa does refer to an alternative interpretation advanced by some historians that the electoral reform was initiated by the Japanese government and that the GHQ was actually dissatisfied with the content of the proposed plan. Ishikawa, however, disputes this minority view by arguing, for example, that the introduction of a limited vote in 1945 was an idea foreign to the Japanese but consistent with the common practice in Western countries.

course of events based solely on the GHQ's ideology and commitment to democratization.

Although scholars fail to analyze the political process that led to the postwar electoral reform, they often point out that the system adopted in 1947 was the same as the one that had been in effect during the prewar period. This, along with the fact that the 1947 system subsequently survived for so long, reinforce the prevailing perception that the adoption of the varying-sized multimember constituencies with a limited vote in 1945 was an "experiment" engineered by the GHQ; naturally the failure of that "experiment" led to the restoration of the old system familiar to Japanese voters. Captivated by the structural resemblance between the prewar and postwar electoral systems, some studies have further explored the decision-making process by which the system was originally established in 1925. These studies generally concluded that the decision to adopt such a system was the result of political bargaining among the three incumbent parties allied at the time—the Kenseikai, the Seiyukai, and the Kakushin Club. Haruhiro Fukui, for example, notes:

> Of the three allied parties in government, the Kenseikai, which had been the second-ranking party more frequently than the first-ranking party in the Diet, and the Kakushin Club, which was a much smaller party than either of its two partners, both preferred a multi-member system; on the other hand, the Seiyukai, which had until early 1924 been by far the largest party, pressed for a single-member system. A medium-sized, multi-member system of between three and five members per constituency was apparently a logical compromise solution.[3]

It is difficult to believe, however, that postwar Japanese decision makers operated in a political vacuum and simply copied the 1925 system for the sake of its familiarity. Just as the adoption of the electoral system in 1925 was a result of interparty bargaining, the readoption of that system in 1947 must have been a product of the equally self-seeking behavior of political actors. The electoral system sets the fundamental "rules of the game" in a democracy, defining the formula for translating societal preferences into a choice of national government and public policy. It is therefore reasonable to assume that the political stakes involved in choosing one system over others are too high for any political party to overlook.

This is not to deny that the GHQ's pressure or the historical precedent from the prewar era had anything to do with the fate of the postwar electoral reform. The GHQ clearly limited the range of available options, and the 1925 precedent served as an important "focal point" in the debate and political bargaining over this issue. As reconstructed below, however, the presence of the GHQ and the availability of a historical precedent never undermined the basic

[3] Fukui, "Electoral Laws and the Japanese Party System," p. 130. For a similar view, see Akiyama, *Senkyo* [Elections], p. 75; see also Soma, *Nihon Senkyo Seido-shi* [The history of Japan's electoral systems].

competitive and strategic behavior of the Japanese political actors, who were seeking to further their own incentives.

Incentives, Power, and Japanese Electoral Reform

Assuming that political parties are rational in a standard Schumpeterian/Downsian sense and act "solely in order to attain the income, prestige, and power which come from being in office,"[4] their incentives in revising the electoral system seem straightforward: each party seeks to change the system in such a way as to maximize its own representation in Parliament.

This does not mean that whenever a new party (or a new coalition of parties) forms a government, it is likely to change the electoral system. On the contrary, the incumbent party may not want to change the current electoral system, given that its mandate to form a government was provided by that very system. As Kathleen Bawn puts it, "An important aspect of the stability of institutions is that the individuals who have the power to change them generally receive that power because of success in the existing institutional framework."[5] Hence there is a built-in tendency for the incumbent party to opt for the status quo, which is consistent with empirical findings that in any democratic country revisions of electoral laws are less frequent than changes in government.

It seems reasonable to hypothesize, then, that the dominant party seeks to change the electoral system if, and only if, it perceives that a new system is likely to be even more beneficial than the status quo. In what follows I demonstrate that the two cases from the early postwar electoral reform in Japan support this hypothesis: both the Progressive Party in 1945 and the Liberal Party in 1947 agreed to revise the electoral system precisely because they thought that the change would further their own electoral ends.[6]

The 1945 Reform

The process toward postwar electoral reform started in October 1945 when Kijuro Shidehara, a veteran diplomat, was chosen as Japan's new prime minister.[7] Shidehara replaced Norihiko Higashikuni, a member of the Imperial

[4] Downs, *Economic Theory of Democracy*, p. 28.

[5] Bawn, "Logic of Institutional Preferences, p. 987.

[6] In reconstructing the decision-making processes below, I have used numerous sources, including Shinobu, *Sengo Nihon Seijishi* [Political history of postwar Japan]; Kinoshita, *Katayama Naikakushi-ron* [On the history of the Katayama cabinet]; and Fukunaga, "Sengo ni okeru Chu-Senkyoku-sei no Keisei Katei [The formation process of the medium-sized district system in the postwar era]." In the interest of simplicity, I will specify sources only for quotations and in cases where I believe the arguments depend heavily on the author's speculation.

[7] Shidehara's nomination was recommended to the Emperor by Kouichi Kido, the Emperor's most trusted attendant.

family, who had refused to implement the GHQ's directive that required, inter alia, the liberalization of political discussion about the emperor.[8] Shidehara was the architect of harmonious relations with the United States in the 1920s and was therefore thought to be more suited for handling the GHQ's pressure.[9]

From the outset Shidehara adopted a different strategy from his predecessor in coping with the GHQ. Although he was a conservative politician, Shidehara recognized the futility of the then prevalent slogan "Preservation of the National Polity" [*Kokutai Goji*] and did not question the GHQ's determination to pursue a drastic transformation of Japanese political institutions. Instead, Shidehara tried to keep the control of the reform initiatives in his own hands and thus to preempt direct intervention from the GHQ. His aim in doing so was obviously to make his reforms a fait accompli so that the scope of democratization would be limited and its overall impact minimized.

It was in this context that the Shidehara government took the initiative in reforming the electoral law. On October 11, the day Shidehara was scheduled to meet with MacArthur, the cabinet approved the decision to extend the suffrage to women and to lower the minimum voting age to twenty. MacArthur heralded this decision as a harbinger of other reform measures to come, but the Shidehara government clearly had a political agenda:

> Domestic Affairs Minister [Zenjiro] Horikiri's sponsorship of women's suffrage had an internal security consideration in that women would not vote for the extreme left or the extreme right and their incremental progressiveness "could well be relied upon in such a turbulent period as today." The same was the case with the lowering of the voting age. Horikiri hoped that women and the younger generation were still influenced by the feudalistic family system and by their militaristic education and that their votes would help the continuation of conservative forces.[10]

With regard to the electoral system for the lower house, the government proposed a system of large constituencies, which it hoped would "undermine the basis of [emerging] political parties" and thus "contain the momentum for democratization within the [established] structure of the bureaucratic state."[11]

[8] Prince Higashikuni, the Emperor's uncle, became prime minister on August 17, two days after Japan accepted the Potsdam Declaration, which formally ended World War II. It was speculated that Higashikuni was chosen to suppress the militant group in Japan still insisting on the continuation of the war. It was on October 4 that the GHQ publicized what is known as its Civil Liberties Directive. This called for the release of more than two thousand political prisoners, the abolition of limits on freedom of speech and assembly, and the dismantling of the Home Ministry and secret police. The next day the Higashikuni cabinet resigned.

[9] Shidehara was foreign minister during the 1920s and early 1930s when Japan, the United States, and other countries concluded a series of arms reduction treaties concerning naval forces.

[10] Shinobu, *Sengo Nihon Seijishi*, 1:185 (translation by Kohno).

[11] Ibid.

TABLE 3.1
Proposed Categories of Districts

Category	*Number of Seats*	*Number of Votes*
(1)	5 or less	1
(2)	10 or less	2
(3)	11 or more	3

More specifically, the proposal divided electoral districts according to prefectural boundaries and allocated the seats based on population without substantially changing the total number of representatives.[12] The government further proposed to classify all districts into three categories based on their number of seats and to introduce a "limited vote" system whereby a voter would cast one to three votes depending on the size of the district (see Table 3.1).[13]

Because the Shidehara cabinet was formally a nonpartisan government chosen by the Imperial Old Guard, it was inevitable that the governmental proposal would be contested by political parties, which had reemerged one after another by the end of the fall.[14] The government convened an extraordinary session of Parliament in late November and presented the draft bill for deliberation on December 1. Both the Socialist Party and the Liberal Party demanded that the proposed bill be revised to make the electoral system even closer to a true proportional representation system.[15] The Socialists, for example, requested that the division of the electoral districts strictly coincide with the prefectural boundaries and that the vote be a single transferable vote. The Progressive Party, which was most conservative of all major parties at the time, also proposed its own revision, demanding that the number of assigned votes be two across all districts with fewer than eleven seats.

The reaction of these three parties vis-à-vis the proposed bill was clearly consistent with their respective electoral strengths and incentives. As one can see from Table 3.2, both the Socialists and Liberals were smaller in terms of the number of incumbent parliamentarians. Thus, compared with the Progressive Party, these two parties had no choice but to nominate a fresh group of

[12] According to the government proposal, seven prefectures with large populations (Hokkaido, Tokyo, Niigata, Aichi, Osaka, Hyogo, and Fukuoka) would each be further divided into two districts.

[13] Shugiin and Sangiin, eds., *Gikai Seido Shichiju-nen-shi*," [Seventy-year history of parliamentary institutions], pp. 279–80.

[14] Three major parties—the Japan Socialist Party, the Japan Liberal Party, and the Japan Progressive Party—were established on November 2, November 9, and November 16, 1945, respectively.

[15] Kinoshita, *Katayama Naikakushi-ron*, p. 3. For details of other aspects of each party's proposal, see Fukunaga, "Chu-Senkyoku-sei," pp. 409–10.

TABLE 3.2
Lower House Seat Distribution in 1945[a]

Party	*Seat*
Progressives	274
Liberals	46
Socialists	17
Others	72
Vacant Seats	57
Total	466

Source: Sato and Matsuzaki, *Jiminto Seiken* [The LDP's rule], p. 180.

[a]Each entry corresponds to the number of politicians belonging to each political party at the time of its creation. Although there were minor changes in these numbers during the period in which the parliamentary session was held, these changes were inconsequential to the following course of events and are thus ignored.

candidates who had less well-established reputations among voters. Although the proposed large constituency could work in their favor, the limited vote system, under which votes would be cast for individual candidates, was likely to be disadvantageous for these smaller parties.

For the dominant Progressive Party, the most preferred system would have been a single-ballot plurality system with smaller constituencies. It was well understood, however, that the GHQ would not approve such a system because it would favor and preserve the old establishment. The bill proposed by the government, on the other hand, although not ideal was still acceptable: even though the large constituencies would encourage the entry of new candidates with various social backgrounds as the GHQ preferred, the limited vote would still retain the dominant party's advantage because the dominant party already had many established incumbents.

As noted earlier, the only minor revision the Progressives proposed was to increase the number of votes from one to two in districts with fewer than six seats, thus merging categories 1 and 2 in Table 3.1. This proposal was consistent with their electoral incentives. If each voter had only one vote, the Progressive candidates might split the votes among themselves. Since the Liberals and Socialists were unlikely to nominate more than a few candidates in these smaller districts, Progressive candidates could lose to the candidates from these two rival parties. If each had two votes, the negative effect of the vote-splitting would be reduced, and the Progressives might retain a majority of the seats in these districts.

Given the nonpartisan nature of the Shidehara government, why was it that the bill the government presented, in its original form, was already acceptable to the Progressives? For one thing, Shidehara personally shared much of the Progressive Party's conservative ideology. This is evident in that he later joined the party and became its president after the 1946 election. More important, however, is that Shidehara knew that any proposal the Progressives opposed would not pass Parliament. Because his overall aim was to preempt the GHQ's intervention in this matter, he did not want to waste time in a legislative debate, which would only delay his electoral reform effort. Based on the Progressive Party's overwhelming majority, Parliament passed the bill amended by the Progressives' proposal on December 15.[16] Shidehara then moved quickly: his government dissolved the lower house on December 18, and the general election was scheduled for January 22.

In sum, the Japanese political actors involved in the 1945 electoral reform were acting strategically to further their own incentives in a competitive electoral environment. Prime Minister Shidehara took the initiative in electoral reform in an attempt to preempt the GHQ's direct intervention. Because the smaller parties, the Liberals and the Socialists, were opposed to the proposed system of large constituencies with a limited vote, the bill's passage reflected the preferences and power of the dominant Progressive Party.

Before moving on to the analysis of the next round of the postwar electoral reform, it should be noted that Shidehara's strategy did not ultimately pay off because the GHQ became suspicious about Shidehara's (and the Progressives') intention to hasten the process of electoral reform. Thus on December 20 the GHQ postponed the date of the election. Furthermore, although the GHQ did not challenge the newly established electoral law, on January 4, 1946, it declared a large-scale purge from public offices of prewar political leaders claimed to be responsible for the war.[17] This new development damaged the Progressive Party severely: of its 274 initial members, 260 were disqualified from running in the election.[18] Thus, in the election on April 10, the Progressives lost their majority while the Liberals won the most seats.[19] Shidehara initially tried to remain prime minister with support from the Pro-

[16] Before it became law, the upper house, the then House of Lords, further revised the bill and decided that a voter could cast only one vote in electoral districts with three or fewer seats. For practical purposes, this revision was inconsequential because the only district affected was in Okinawa where the United States retained all administrative control and Japanese electoral law did not apply. For this reason the Progressive Party agreed to the revision.

[17] For details of the discussion held within the GHQ on the electoral reform, see Fukunaga, "Chu-Senkyoku-sei," pp. 416–19.

[18] The Liberals lost 19 members out of 46, and the Socialists 11 out of 17 respectively (Shinobu, *Sengo Nihon Seijishi*, 1:263).

[19] See Table 3.3. I do not intend to claim here that the GHQ's purge was the only source of the Progressives' electoral defeat, although very few studies thus far have shown the degree to which the Japanese voters at this early stage had actually moved away from those candidates associated with the prewar regime (cf. Reed, "The People Spoke").

gressive Party, but he was forced to hand over his office to Shigeru Yoshida, the new leader of the Liberal Party. Yoshida eventually formed a coalition government with Shidehara's Progressive Party; under this government the next phase of the reform took place.

With the benefit of hindsight, one might argue that the political incentives of domestic actors, especially Shidehara, were eventually overshadowed by the exogenous factor, namely, the presence of the U.S. occupation forces. MacArthur's authority was significant enough to offset the electoral advantage that the dominant Progressive Party thought the reform would bring about.

Without the benefit of hindsight, however, the behavior of the Japanese political actors was clearly consistent with their own incentives. No one could have foreseen that MacArthur would intervene to purge as many politicians as he did. Although the reform did not result in an electoral victory for the Progressives, as they had intended, the final outcome should not obscure the fact that they clearly dominated the interparty negotiation and their preference prevailed in the bargaining process, as described above.

The 1947 Reform

The revision of the 1945 electoral law was high on the Yoshida government's agenda when MacArthur made a public statement in early February 1947 urging that a new general election be held soon. Because the new Constitution had already been publicized and was scheduled to become effective in May, the government decided that the lower house election, as well as the upper house and gubernatorial elections, would take place in April.

On February 14 the parliamentary session was reconvened to pass laws and to establish a legal framework in accordance with the new Constitution that was to be enacted.[20] Before the session resumed, Yoshida had shuffled his cabinet and appointed Etsujiro Uehara as the new Minister of Domestic Affairs. Uehara had stated at a press conference that he did not favor the existing system of large districts and suggested that medium-sized constituencies be adopted. In Parliament, however, Uehara did not propose a change in the electoral system, although he began to draft a government bill to revise other aspects of the 1945 law.

It was not until March 12 that this bill was presented to Parliament for deliberation. The next day the Liberal Party proposed an amendment to the government bill, which would replace the existing electoral system with a system of medium-sized constituencies and a single nontransferable vote. It was later reported that Yoshida had initially asked Uehara to draft a similar bill as a government proposal, but Uehara had rejected the request because the GHQ had discouraged the introduction of such a system. Yoshida, having

[20] Parliament had been in recess because a general strike was scheduled for February 1. The GHQ eventually intervened and prevented the strike.

consulted directly with MacArthur and apparently having obtained his personal approval for the system, had then arranged that the amendment would be presented as his own party's proposal.[21]

The sudden presentation of the amendment surprised and angered the opposition, especially since only two weeks remained before the end of the parliamentary session. The opposition parties thus lined up to confront the Liberal Party's proposal. The Communists insisted on the introduction of a proportional representation system with a single, nationwide constituency. The Socialists proposed a proportional representation system with the existing large districts and a transferable vote. The National Cooperativists also publicly denounced the Liberal Party proposal.[22]

Amid the confrontation between the Liberals and the opposition, the role of mediator in the interplay bargaining was played by the Progressives, the Liberals' coalition partner. On March 17 they presented a compromise to the Socialists to retain the medium-sized districts but to increase the number of votes from one to two. When the Socialists rejected the offer, however, the Liberals hardened their stance and returned to their original proposal. The Progressives later prepared another proposal increasing the number of seats in each district from three to five seats to four to seven seats with each voter casting two votes, but again they failed to reach a compromise with any opposition party.

As was the case in the previous round of electoral reform, the actions and reactions of different political parties documented here can be explained in terms of the parties' respective electoral incentives and relative bargaining power. Consider, for example, the Liberal Party's decision to propose the system of medium-sized districts. In the 1945 reform process the Liberals had insisted on a proportional representation system, but their electoral strength changed after winning the most seats in the 1946 election owing to the GHQ's large-scale purge. The number of Liberal seats in Parliament was nevertheless far from a majority (see Table 3.3). For that reason they now wanted to overturn the 1945 system of large constituencies, which had promoted the entry of various small parties. It was speculated that Yoshida, in particular, wanted to wipe out the Communists by introducing the single-ballot plurality system.[23]

Just like Shidehara two years earlier, however, Yoshida knew that such a system would be a difficult proposition to "sell" vis-à-vis the GHQ. Furthermore, he was concerned that the system of small constituencies would pit the candidates from the Liberal Party against those from the Progressive Party and, in light of the approaching election, proposing such a system might un-

[21] See Shinobu, *Sengo Nihon Seijishi*, 2:508–9.

[22] The National Cooperativist Party was established on March 8, following the amalgamation of the Cooperative-Democratic Party and the National People's Party.

[23] Shinobu, *Sengo Nihon Seijishi*, 2:507; Fukunaga, "Chu-Senkyoku-sei," p. 429.

TABLE 3.3
Lower House Seat Distribution in Early 1947[a]

Party	*Seat*
Liberals	148
Progressives	110
Socialists	96
National-Cooperativists	78
Communists	6
Others	28
Total	464

Source: Ishikawa, *Deeta Sengo Seiji-shi* [A data history of postwar politics], p. 115.

[a]Each entry represents the number of politicians belonging to each political party as of the last day of the previous parliamentary session in October 1946, except for the National-Cooperativist Party, the entry for which was computed by adding the number of politicians from the Cooperative-Democratic Party and National People's Party. Other minor changes resulting from party switching from October 1946 to March 1947 were inconsequential to the following course of events and are thus not reflected in the above entries.

necessarily amplify the conflict within the governing coalition.[24] In this sense the medium-sized district system was a good compromise: while allowing both the Liberal and Progressive candidates to be simultaneously elected in a district, it would undermine parties like the Communists, as long as the district size was kept sufficiently small.

The reactions of the Communists and the Socialists were also consistent with their respective electoral incentives. Clearly a smaller party like the Communists would have benefitted most from a pure proportional representation system in which "wasted votes" could be minimized. In fact, the Communists were severely penalized in the previous election, being awarded a much smaller share of seats than the vote share (see Table 3.4).

As one can see from this Table 3.4, proportional representation would also have benefitted the Socialists more than the two conservative parties. Unlike the Communists, however, the Socialists were not penalized under the large constituency system. In fact, under the existing system, the party had signifi-

[24] Indeed the Liberal-Progressive partnership had not been so smooth, especially since December 1946 when there surfaced a series of (unsuccessful) attempts to include the Socialists in a coalition government. The process of interparty bargaining to build alternative coalitions is well documented in Kinoshita, *Katayama Naikakushi-ron*, pp. 47–68.

TABLE 3.4
Seat/Vote Ratio in the 1946 Election[a]

	Lib	*Prog*	*JSP*	*JCP*
Seat Share (S)	31.8	23.6	20.6	1.3
Vote Share (V)	25.4	20.3	18.2	3.9
S/V Ratio	1.25	1.16	1.13	0.33

Source: Ishikawa, *Deeta Sengo Seiji-shi* [A data history of postwar politics], p. 115.
[a]Each entry is adjusted for the postelection party switching and thus represents the situation as of the last day of the parliamentary session in October 1946.

cantly increased its parliamentary share. Furthermore, at the time, the Socialists and the Communists were engaged in an intense battle for ideological leadership in the evolving Japanese labor movement. It is arguable, therefore, that the Socialists had reason not to endorse a pure proportional representation system preferred by the Communists.

Compared with the other parties, the behavior of the Progressive Party, which acted as the mediator, is perhaps the most difficult to analyze. This is partly because of the lack of reliable information about the negotiations within the governing coalition. Even though the proposal to revise the 1945 system came in the form of the Liberal Party's amendment to the government bill, the Progressives were presumably fully informed of the Liberals' plan in advance. This suggests that the proposal had been approved by the Progressive Party; as argued earlier, under the proposed system, the Liberal and Progressive candidates could both be elected in the same district.

In the course of negotiations with the opposition parties, the Progressive Party repeatedly explored the possibility of increasing the number of votes from one to two. This can be seen as a reflection of the relative weakness of the Progressive candidates vis-à-vis the Liberal candidates. In other words, if the two parties were going after the same pool of conservative voters, and if the Liberal candidates were perceived to be better candidates, it is reasonable to suggest that the Progressives wanted each voter to cast two votes in order to improve their candidates' electoral chance.

To substantiate this claim, I have investigated the relative electoral vulnerability of the candidates from the two parties based on data from the previous election.[25] At the aggregate level, the Liberal candidates were undoubtedly stronger than the Progressive counterparts. As shown in Table 3.5, the

[25] Because the proposal would have changed the size of the districts, data from the previous election might not provide a good indicator for this analysis. It should be noted, however, that this was also the only information available to the leaders of the political parties to assess their candidates' electoral vulnerability at the time.

TABLE 3.5
Partisan Competitiveness in the 1946 Election

Party	*Number of Candidates*	*Number of Seats*	*Success Ratio(%)*
Liberal	485	140	28.87
Progressive	376	94	25.00
Socialist	331	93	28.10

Source: Ishikawa, *Deeta Sengo Seiji-shi* [A data history of postwar politics], p. 115.

success ratio of the Progressive candidates was in fact worse than that of the Socialist candidates.

This evidence is consistent with the following two sets of microlevel findings about the competitiveness of individual candidates. Table 3.6 compares the average rank of the top candidates from the Liberals and the Progressives across the three categories of districts. This table indicates that, on average, the Liberal top candidates ranked consistently higher than their Progressive counterparts regardless of the type of districts. Table 3.7 compares the ranking of the two top candidates from the Progressive Party with the ranking of the two top candidates from the Liberal Party. This table suggests that the Progressive second-ranked candidates were much less likely to beat the Liberal first-ranked candidates than the Liberal second-ranked candidates were to

TABLE 3.6
Average Rank of the Top Candidates for Each Party in the 1946 Election

	District Category		
	(1) *N = 6*[a]	*(2)* *N = 31*[b]	*(3)* *N = 14*
Progressives	2.67	4.45	10.21
Liberals	2.00	3.45	2.29

Source: Shuugiin Jimukyoku, *Dai Nijuni-kai Shuugiin Giin Sosenkyo no Kekka* [The results of the twenty-second House of Representative election].

[a] I excluded the Tokushima district as a deviant case because no candidate from these two parties was elected in this district.

[b] I excluded the Miyazaki district as a deviant case because no candidate from these two parties was elected in this district.

TABLE 3.7
Comparison of Top Two Candidates

	District Category		
	(1)	*(2)*	*(3)*
% of cases where	*N = 6*[a]	*N = 31*[b]	*N = 14*
P1 > L1	33.3	45.2	0
P2 > L2	33.3	35.5	0
L2 > P1	16.7	38.7	57.1
P2 > L1	0	16.1	0

Source: Shuugiin Jimukyoku, *Dai Nijuni-kai Shuugiin Giin Sosenkyo no Kekka* [The results of the twenty-second House of Representatives election].

Note: "P1 > L1" refers to the situations where the Progressives' first-ranked candidate was ranked higher than the Liberals' first-ranked candidate.

[a]I excluded the Tokushima district as a deviant case because no candidate from these two parties was elected in this district.

[b]I excluded the Miyazaki district as a deviant case because no candidate from these two parties was elected in this district.

beat the Progressive first-ranked candidates. Thus the Progressives naturally perceived that their candidates were more vulnerable electorally than their Liberal counterparts.

Despite the difference between the Liberals and Progressives in the preferred number of votes, the governing coalition had to railroad the government bill and the Liberal amendment through Parliament because the session was coming to an end. Both the committee and floor deliberations evoked precedent-setting confrontations between the government and the opposition parties. With the police surrounding the Parliament building, ready to enter in the event of a riot, the Liberals and Progressives, based on their majority, were eventually successful in revising the 1945 electoral law. On March 31, immediately after the adoption of the new system, Yoshida dissolved the lower house and called a general election.

In retrospect, the medium-sized electoral system did not benefit Yoshida's Liberal Party, at least in the short run, because the Socialists became the largest party after the election in April 1947. The Liberal defeat, however, cannot be attributed simply to Yoshida's miscalculation regarding the effect of the medium-sized districts; it had more to do with the party alignment that was taking place at the same time as the electoral reform. On March 31, the day Parliament revised the electoral law, the Progressive Party absorbed some members of the National-Cooperativist Party and a handful of defectors from the Liberal Party to create the Democratic Party. The aim of Shidehara and other Progressive leaders was to shed their party's conservative and "reactionary" image. The most significant development was the participation of centralist Hitoshi Ashida, a former Liberal, who eventually became the new party's president. The Democrats were thus successful in placing themselves in the center of the ideological spectrum, leaving Yoshida's Liberals as the most conservative party just before the election.[26]

In sum, the 1947 electoral reform process involved political parties that were acting in accordance with their own electoral incentives. The outcome of this process reflected the relative bargaining power of the Liberal Party. The Liberal leader Yoshida refrained from introducing a single plurality system not only to avoid an anticipated veto by the GHQ but also to maintain the existing coalition with the Progressive Party. The behavior of the opposition parties was also consistent with their own incentives, although their call for a proportional representation system was destined to fail given the parliamentary majority held by the two governing parties.

Post-1947 Survival of the Electoral System

Given that the legislative process of the 1947 electoral reform was tense to the point of a physical confrontation, it is rather surprising that this controversial electoral system survived for the next four and a half decades. A simple explanation for this institutional stability may be found in what is often called the "path-dependency" argument. As one scholar puts it: "Institutions may persist because in a world of imperfect information, altering established routines will be costly and time consuming and the consequences of change cannot be fully predicted."[27]

Although the political uncertainty was no doubt pervasive during the early postwar period, the path dependency argument alone is not sufficient to account for the survival of the 1947 electoral system. More specifically, it does not account for the Socialists' inconsistent behavior. As documented above, the Socialists, who won a plurality in the general election, had in the past consistently been in favor of a proportional representation system with large constituencies. Why, then, did they not pursue a third round of electoral reform?

It is always more difficult to analyze why something did not happen than why something actually did. Nevertheless one can speculate on a set of factors

[26] It is possible to claim, although extremely difficult to prove, that this partisan alignment in the conservative camp was itself driven by Yoshida's electoral reform initiative. To substantiate such a claim would require more detailed and lengthy analyses of the electoral incentives of those politicians who left the Liberal Party and the National-Cooperativist Party to join the new party.

[27] Krasner, "Sovereignty," p. 85. For the classic discussion of this topic, see David, "Clio and the Economics of QWERTY." See also North, *Institutions, Institutional Change and Economic Performance*.

TABLE 3.8
Lower House Seat Distribution in April 1947[a]

Party	*Seat*
Liberals	131
Democrats	124
National-Cooperativists	31
Socialists	143
Communists	4
Others	33
Total	466

Source: Ishikawa, *Deeta Sengo Seiji-shi* [A data history of postwar politics], p. 116.

[a]These numbers represent party affiliations immediately after the election. There was some party switching thereafter, but it was inconsequential to the following course of events and is thus ignored.

that prevented the Socialist Party from initiating another round of electoral reform.

First, even though the Socialists had won the most seats in the lower house, their parliamentary share was only marginally higher than that of each of the other two major parties (see Table 3.8). As a result, they had to form a coalition government with two other parties, the Democrats and the National-Cooperativists.[28] Under such circumstances it was difficult for the Socialists to take the lead in discussing further electoral reform; such a discussion would have revealed the inherently conflicting visions and preferences regarding the electoral system among the three allied parties, and thus might have undermined the very basis of the coalition government.

Second, when the Socialist-led government was established, there was no prospect that the next general election would be held in the near future. Now that the April 1947 election was conducted under the newly established democratic Constitution, MacArthur had no legitimate justification for ordering another general election. Nor was an election on the Socialists' immediate political agenda. From the outset their government had to deal with the imminent economic crises, including persistent high inflation, low industrial production, and food shortages.

Third, before the election, the Socialist leaders had no expectation that their party would become the largest party. They had no reason, therefore, to call an early election, as they were surprised and felt "lucky" about the electoral

[28] I elaborate on this coalition formation in the next chapter.

results.[29] The Socialists had indeed won more seats under the 1947 system of medium-sized constituencies than under the 1945 system of large constituencies.[30] It is possible, then, that after the surprising electoral victory in 1947 the Socialists changed their order of preference and began to perceive that they could do well under the 1947 system.

In any case, the Socialist-led coalition government did not last long, largely because of its failure to establish a policy consensus among the governing parties. Retaining the same composition, the coalition was then led by the Democrats, but this government also collapsed in less than a year, following the political scandals involving Prime Minister Hitoshi Ashida himself. Subsequently Yoshida formed a caretaker government and called an election in January 1949, the result being a landslide victory for his Liberal Party and the formation of a majority government. The Liberals' rule continued until 1955 when the revived Democratic Party, under Ichiro Hatoyama, won the most seats in the election. The Liberals and Democrats subsequently merged to create the Liberal Democratic Party which prevailed for the next four decades.[31]

The system of medium-sized constituencies with a single nontransferable vote survived throughout these years. This does not mean, of course, that the LDP did not attempt to revise the system. In fact, as early as 1956, Hatoyama, the first president of the LDP, tried to change the electoral system by introducing a single-ballot plurality system. His initiative, however, ultimately failed because the proposed reform bill (and the attached redistricting plan) was blatantly designed to favor not only the LDP vis-à-vis other parties but also his own faction within the party, thus invoking both external and internal opposition. Another famous attempt to revise the 1947 electoral system was undertaken in the early 1970s by Kakuei Tanaka, who also was forced to abandon his initiative in the face of similar opposition. That these reform efforts ignited resistance within the LDP reflects the built-in mechanism that encourages incumbents generally to opt for the status quo in the electoral system.[32]

[29] See, for example, Party Secretary Suehiro Nishio's remark that appeared in *Asahi Shimbun*, April 28, 1947. All the preelection forecasts were in favor of the Liberals (see Kinoshita, *Katayama Naikakushi-ron*, p. 85).

[30] All other things being equal, the latter should have been more beneficial to the Socialists in so far as their candidates were less well established among voters than the conservative candidates. In 1945, however, other aspects of the general electoral environment nullified the advantages of the larger constituencies, such as the short campaign period and the ongoing inflation that had increased campaign costs (see Shinobu, *Sengo Nihon Seijishi*, 1:296).

[31] I elaborate on this merger process in chapter 5.

[32] Given the incumbents' incentive to preserve the status quo, one can speculate that the LDP leaders who pursued electoral reform were using this as a means to increase their share of seats and thus the power of their own factions within the party rather than as a means to compete vis-à-vis other political parties. With regard to Hatoyama's reform initiative, for example, a common

In the meantime, that the Socialists failed to return to power for a long time under the 1947 system does not mean that they miscalculated the effect of that electoral system. It is impossible to speculate what would have happened had the Socialists revised the system in 1947. Only in hindsight do the Socialists appear to have missed a unique opportunity to revise the system when they were in power in 1947. As argued above, however, it is not clear whether the Socialists had the desire or the capability to change the system. Even if the Socialists had revised the system, such a revision might not have prevented the subsequent formation of conservative governments. Furthermore, the Liberal (or the LDP) government could have reverted back to the medium-sized district system or even to a single-ballot plurality system with smaller constituencies.

In sum, the results of the April 1947 election provided a disincentive for the Socialist Party to pursue another round of electoral reform. Although the Socialists were the largest party, they held only a marginal advantage in the parliamentary share and were thus constrained by the need to maintain the governing coalition. The subsequent long-term survival of the 1947 system was a product of the built-in mechanism by which the incumbent government tends to opt for the status quo in the electoral arrangement. In other words, once the Liberals returned to power in 1949, the Socialists, operating under this mechanism, lost the opportunity to change the system to one of proportional representation, a system they had originally favored.

The above reconstruction of the political process that led to the 1945 and 1947 decisions reveals that the prevailing notion that the course of the postwar Japanese electoral reform was determined by unique historical circumstances, that is, the presence of foreign occupation forces, is false. It is true that the GHQ set the basic direction of the electoral reform, but the institutional details of the new electoral law were debated and contested by various domestic political actors.

The choice of the electoral system involves high stakes for political parties that are competing for legislative seats to form a government in any democratic country. As I have demonstrated in this chapter, in early postwar Japan

---

argument has been that his underlying motive was his nationalistic desire to revise the Constitution, which requires a two-thirds majority in Parliament. As indicated, however, Hatoyama's reform bill was written deliberately to favor his own faction. If Hatoyama's primary concern had been a two-thirds majority at the interparty level, he could have proposed a bill far more acceptable to his colleagues (but not to the opposition parties). In this regard it should be noted that Hatoyama's presentation of the reform bill took place in March 1956, before he was formally elected as the first LDP president in April. As I discuss in chapter 5, at that time the LDP was still internally divided between the former Liberals and the former Democrats over the issue of the presidency. It is difficult to believe, therefore, that Hatoyama's initiative was driven simply by his commitment to constitutional reform.

it was widely understood that the choice of the electoral system would significantly affect the fate of each political party and of individual politicians. Accordingly, the unusual historical circumstance did not prevent the domestic actors involved in both the 1945 and the 1947 processes from acting strategically to further their own incentives. The final outcomes of these reform processes reflected the bargaining power of the dominant party vis-à-vis other opposition parties, the coalition partners, as well as the GHQ.

Based on the "rules of the game" thus established, postwar Japanese party politics began to evolve in ways familiar in any parliamentary democracy, such as coalition formation, party realignment, and internal factionalization. I now turn to the analysis of these patterns.

4

COALITION BUILDING UNDER THE PRE-1955 MULTIPARTY SYSTEM

THE DIVIDED results of the April 1947 election, the first election held under the new democratic regime, clearly indicated that Japan's parliamentary democracy had entered an era of multiparty competition. As summarized in Table 4.1, the pattern of Japanese party politics during this early period was characterized by several political parties competing fiercely for legislative seats and taking turns forming coalition and minority governments. It was through the course of this intense party competition and fluid partisan alignment that the momentum toward a conservative merger finally resulted, in 1955, in the creation of the Liberal Democratic Party.

This chapter examines the nature of party competition under the early postwar multiparty system, a subject largely neglected in the conventional literature on Japanese politics. For those fascinated by the cultural and behavioral foundations of the post-1955 conservative hegemony, the preceding period of multiparty competition represents merely an aberration. Similarly, for the proponents of the historical and socio-ideological approaches, the political history before 1955 is seen as a period of transition from the aftermath of war to a party system built on more distinct underlying cleavages. In this chapter I present a case study on coalition government formation during this period in order to highlight the basic logic of competition and strategic bargaining that governs the interactions of political parties. More specifically, I focus on the interparty negotiation process that led to the establishment of the Socialist-led government in 1947. I seek to establish that much of the behavior of the parties involved in this process can be interpreted as a product of consciously made decisions under the given institutional constraints.

Of all coalition and minority governments formed under the pre-1955 multiparty system, the formation of this so-called Katayama government deserves particular consideration. In addition to being the first government formed under the new democratic Constitution, the April 1947 election was also a landmark in the sense that it was held under the revised electoral system. Moreover, the final product of the coalition negotiations, namely, the three-party coalition led by the Socialist Party, appeared the most "unusual"; all other governments formed during this period were led either by the conservative or centrist party. Finally, as I elaborate below, the formation of the Katayama

TABLE 4.1
Pre-1955 Government Formation

Date	Name	Government Type (headed by italicized party)
46.5	Yoshida I	Coalition (*Lib* + Prog = 51.3%)
[general election]		
47.5	Katayama	Coalition (*Soc* + Dem + Coop = 65.9%)
48.3	Ashida	Coalition (Soc + *Dem* + Coop = 56.7%)[a]
48.10	Yoshida II	Minority
[general election]		
49.2	Yoshida III	Coalition (*Lib* + Dem = 72.7%)
[general election]		
52.10	Yoshida IV	Majority (Lib = 51.9%)
[general election]		
53.5	Yoshida V	Minority (Lib = 43.3%)
54.12	Hatoyama I	Minority
[general election]		
55.3	Hatoyama II	Minority (Dem = 39.6%)

Source: Masumi Ishikawa, *Deeta Sengo Seiji-shi* [A data history of postwar politics], pp. 115–20.

[a]The decrease in the parliamentary share of the governing coalition was the result of the split of the Democratic Party.

government provides the key to understanding the political development of the rest of the early postwar period.

The chapter begins with a brief summary of the formation of the Katayama government in 1947. I then go on to evaluate critically the conventional interpretation of this government. An alternative interpretation, consistent with the basic logic of party competition and strategic interactions, is then advanced. Next, I draw some general theoretical insights from the analysis and discuss the long-term consequences of the Katayama government. The chapter concludes with a summary of the broader implications of this case study.

Facts

The bargaining and negotiations after the April 1947 election that resulted in the establishment of the coalition government led by the Socialist leader Tetsu Katayama was long and extremely complex.[1] The process involved lobbying on the part of many individual politicians at both inter- and intraparty levels. It

[1] The documentation of the following events and bargaining processes is based primarily on two sources: Shinobu, *Sengo Nihon Seijishi* [Political history of postwar Japan], vol. 2; and Kinoshita, *Katayama Naikakushi-ron* [On the history of the Katayama cabinet].

TABLE 4.2
Lower House Seat Distribution in April 1947

Party	*Seat*
Liberals	131
Democrats	124
National-Cooperativists	31
Socialists	143
Communists	4
Others	33
Total	466

eventually took more than a month for the Socialists to form the coalition government with the National-Cooperativist Party and the Democratic Party. The results of this election are shown in Table 4.2, borrowed from chapter 3.[2]

There was no formal rule or procedural agreement as to how to form a government when there was no majority winner. Nevertheless, the major parties seemed to have a general consensus that some form of coalition government was desirable to deal with imminent economic issues facing the war-torn nation. The questions were these: Which parties should participate in the coalition, and who should lead it?

Soon after the election the two smaller parties, the Cooperativists and Communists, endorsed a coalition government led by the Socialists. The Socialists themselves discussed the possibility of taking the initiative in forming the government. Most of the newly elected Socialists were in favor of either a Socialist-led, three-party coalition excluding the Communists and Liberals or a Socialist-led, four-party coalition including the Liberals.[3]

Subsequently, a series of meetings took place among the Socialists, Cooperativists, Democrats, and Liberals. On May 9 the leaders of the four parties made a public statement that they had agreed to form a four-party "grand" coalition to deal with the nation's economic crisis. They were, however, conspicuously silent as to who would lead the coalition.

On May 15 the Socialists made a surprising announcement that the left-wing element of the Socialists had no connection with the Japan Communist Party and its ideology. It was speculated that this announcement was intended

[2] Although the upper house election was held at the same time, the lower house election was by far the more important one because of the institutional importance given it under the new Constitution. Article 67, in particular, stipulates that if the two houses choose different nominees in the selection of prime minister, the candidate nominated in the lower house will ultimately become the prime minister.

[3] Some leftist members, such as Kanson Arahata, insisted on forming a minority government, but their opinions did not prevail (Shinobu, *Sengo Nihon Seijishi*, 2: 554).

to counter criticism from the Liberals: Liberal leader Shigeru Yoshida, a staunch anticommunist, was demanding huge policy concessions in exchange for his participation in any coalition that included the Socialists. Socialist leader Katayama and the chief negotiator Suehiro Nishio, both from the right-wing faction of the party, appeared eager to include the Liberals in the coalition. In the early morning of May 20, the day the new Diet session was to start, Katayama told Yoshida that the Socialist Party was prepared to exclude its left-wing members from occupying cabinet positions. Yoshida, however, declined the Socialists' request to participate in the coalition.

Owing to the slow coalition-building process, the Diet session had to be recessed in the afternoon. On the following day, May 21, Kijuro Shidehara, the leader of the conservative faction within the Democratic Party, asked Yoshida to reconsider his decision not to participate in the coalition.

On the evening of May 21 the lower house finally decided to elect its speaker and vice speaker.[4] The Socialists and Democrats jointly nominated a Socialist, Komakichi Matsuoka, for the speaker and a Democrat, Man'itsu Tanaka, for the vice speaker. The Liberals, on the other hand, nominated their own candidates for the two positions. The Liberals' apparent retreat from the coalition had a complex impact on the Democratic Party, which was internally divided. Upon the Liberals' new move, the Shidehara faction started to pursue a two-party coalition with the Liberals. The Liberals' departure also had an impact on the centrist group led by Hitoshi Ashida, who was trying to play a pivotal role in coalition building by placing himself between the Socialists and Cooperativists, on the one hand, and the Liberals and the Shidehara faction, on the other. Ashida, however, did not give up the idea of establishing a Democrat-led coalition headed by himself and, at the afternoon meeting of party delegates, he managed to forge a consensus that the Democratic Party would still pursue the four-party coalition.

On May 23 the Socialists suggested to the other parties that the election of the prime minister be held as soon as possible. The Liberals agreed that they would vote for the Socialist leader Katayama even if the Democrats might not agree to the Socialist-led coalition. The Democrats also agreed to vote for Katayama on the condition that the Liberals be included in the coalition. That evening Katayama was elected prime minister by an overwhelming majority, receiving 420 out of 426 votes in the lower house.

On the following day, May 24, Douglas MacArthur at the General Headquarters of the Allied occupation forces made a statement welcoming the choice of Katayama as Japan's new leader. MacArthur's endorsement seemed finally to have solved the question of who would lead the coalition. However, negotiations over which parties would participate continued. On May 27, despite repeated requests from the Socialists and Democrats, the Liberals stub-

[4] The upper house speakers were elected at the same time.

bornly declined to participate in the coalition. Within the Democratic Party, Shidehara insisted on pursuing a four-party grand coalition. Shidehara's resistance, however, did not pay off, and the Democrats finally decided on May 30 to participate in the three-party coalition. Two days later, on June 1, the Katayama cabinet was established. The Socialists and Democrats each occupied seven ministerial positions, and the Cooperativists had two.[5]

Conventional Interpretations

The existing literature on contemporary Japanese politics fails to account for the development of the multiparty system during the first decade of the postwar period. The formation of the Katayama government is but one of these early political events that begs for an explanation. References to this government in the literature have largely been limited to those that characterize it as the only Socialist-led government ever formed in Japan (before 1994) and those that focus on how its policy failures contributed to the long-term stagnation of the Socialists. Accordingly, the interpretations offered thus far regarding the formation of this government are unsophisticated and even misleading.

For example, the concept of the "1955 system," as discussed in chapter 2, has amplified the image of discontinuity in Japanese political development before and after 1955. The concept implies that the underlying socio-ideological cleavage that sustained the post-1955 conservative dominance is significantly different from the cleavage that existed before 1955. In this vein, Hideo Otake argues that the establishment of the coalition government led by the Socialists reflected a fragile social-democratic consensus that had existed among the Japanese public and the "New Dealers" within the U.S. occupation forces. According to Otake, the failure of their centrist policy experiments, especially the devastating consequences of the nationalized coal and mine productions, broke this consensus and gave rise to an economic liberalism that subsequently became the dominant conservative ideology under the rule of Yoshida's Liberal Party.[6]

Such a view is too macroscopic to provide any fine-tuned prediction for the formation of the Katayama government. True, judging solely from the *outcome*, the Katayama government does appear to have been a product of a social-democratic consensus. Otake, however, cannot account for many puzzling questions about various aspects of the *process* leading up to that outcome. If there was an ideological consensus for social-democracy, why did it take such a long time for the Socialists to form the coalition with the other two

[5] One other portfolio was distributed to a member of *Ryoku Hu Kai*, an independent group in the upper house.

[6] Otake, *Adenaua to Yoshida Shigeru* [Adenauer and Shigeru Yoshida], esp. pp. 226–29.

centrist parties? Why did the Socialists initially make a series of attempts to include the conservative Liberals in a grand coalition? Why did the Liberals vote for Katayama? And why did the Democrats, in voting for Katayama, attach the strange condition that they would participate in the coalition only if the Liberals were included?

Another naive interpretation widespread in the conventional literature is the view that the chief beneficiary of this coalition-building process was Shigeru Yoshida and his Liberal Party, neither of which took part in the Socialist-led coalition. Satomi Tani expresses this view: "Yoshida, knowing that the Socialists were not ready to manage the government, thrust them into power with the hope that they would discredit themselves. Insisting that the 'rule of constitutional government' demanded the leading party to take power, he rejected a role for his Liberal party in a coalition government."[7] There is no reason to believe, however, that Yoshida's apparent rejection represented his sincere desire to be out of the coalition rather than his strategy in the interparty negotiation. Nor is there any indication that the Liberals could somehow foresee the future policy fiasco of the coalition government. Only with the benefit of hindsight can one claim that the Liberal decision to become the opposition in 1947 laid the foundation for the Liberal hegemony after 1949.

In what follows I offer an alternative, more forward-looking interpretation of the Katayama government formation. Based on a microanalytic framework, I highlight the bargaining and strategic interactions among political parties that were seeking to further their own incentives under the given institutional constraints.

Institutional Constraints, Intraparty Politics, and the 1947 Coalition Formation

The existing positive literature on coalition governments is not monolithic; rather, several competing models exist built on different assumptions.[8] In the following analysis I adopt Robert Axelrod's model and assume that, although parties seek primarily to maximize their share in the cabinet, a coalition can-

[7] Tani, "The Japan Socialist Party before the Mid-1960s," p. 83.

[8] In his pioneering theoretical work on the subject, *The Theory of Political Coalition*, William Riker described coalition bargaining as a game of dividing the limited number of cabinet portfolios among political parties. Recently, this "office-seeking" paradigm has been challenged empirically as well as theoretically by those who emphasize parties' policy-seeking incentives. The major problem with Riker's "minimum winning coalition" model is that it cannot explain minority and surplus majority governments. For this criticism, see Strom, *Minority Government and Majority Rule*; and Crombez, "Minority Governments, Minimum Winning Coalitions and Surplus Majorities." For "policy-driven" models, see Laver and Shepsle, "Coalitions and Cabinet Government"; Laver and Shepsle, "Government Coalitions and Intraparty Politics"; and Baron, "A Spatial Bargaining Theory of Government Formation."

Figure 4.1: Location in Ideological Space of the Five Main Parties. This figure represents the approximate share of parliamentary seats for each party.

not be made between parties whose policy preferences widely diverge.[9] Axelrod's assumption is appropriate for the Japanese case, especially because the policy space in which Japanese political parties competed in 1947 was distinctively unidimensional (see Figure 4.1).[10]

Based on the above, let me reexamine in some detail the interparty negotiation process that led to the establishment of the coalition government in 1947. For the sake of clarity, I have divided the process into several stages based on key actions taken by the individual parties.

Two Smaller Parties Support the Socialists

One striking aspect of the process leading up to the formation of the Katayama government was that both the Cooperativists and the Communists endorsed the Socialists and/or a Socialist-led coalition almost immediately after the general election. They attached no preconditions or qualifications in expressing their support for the Socialists. How can one explain the behavior of these two smaller parties?

The Communist Party's endorsement of the Socialists appeared puzzling, given that these two parties at the time were engaged in an intense battle for leadership in the evolving labor movement in Japan. Especially since the failure to organize a general strike in February 1947, the ideological division between the two parties had been surfacing in a number of individual firm-based unions and inter-union associations.

From Axelrod's model of "minimal winning connected coalition," however, the Communists' endorsement of the Socialists was no surprise; only by forming a coalition with the Socialists would the Communists occupy any cabinet positions. This is why, despite the ongoing ideological rivalry, the Communists endorsed the Socialist-led government without any hesitation; as a small party located on the edge of the ideological spectrum, the Communists simply had no choice.

[9] Axelrod, *Conflict of Interest.*

[10] In addition, consistent with many recent coalition studies, I make two general assumptions regarding the environment in which political parties must operate. First, the interactions of political parties are constrained by the Constitution, laws, and other institutional arrangements that affect their activities. Second, the results of each election are exogenous and political parties are only concerned with the current period of coalition formation.

For the Cooperativists, the story was more complicated because, at least on the surface, they had the option of siding with the Democrats. The Cooperativists knew that any majority coalition would include the Democratic Party, given the electoral results and the ideological location of each party. Furthermore, even though the Socialists were the largest party, their number of seats was only marginally greater than the Democrats or Liberals, and it was unclear whether the Socialists had the formal mandate to form the coalition. Given all this, it is not readily evident why the Cooperativists endorsed the Socialist government even before the interparty negotiations started.

A closer examination of the situation, however, reveals that the Cooperativists also had no choice but to support the Socialist-led government. In order for the Socialists to form a majority coalition, they needed to include the Democrats; the combination of the Socialists and Cooperativists, even with the Communists, would not have been enough to form a majority. Therefore, by virtue of being sandwiched ideologically between the Socialists and Democrats, the Socialist-led coalition would by definition include the Cooperativists unless the Socialists were willing to form a minority government. In order for the Democrats to form a majority, on the other hand, there were two choices. The Democrats could side either with the Socialists or with the Liberals. In the former scenario, the Cooperativists would be a part of the coalition. In the latter, however, there was no reason to expect that they would be included; the combined force of the Liberals and Democrats would have been sufficient for a majority.

Hence, the Communists and Cooperativists endorsed a Socialist-led government because neither of these two smaller parties had a choice. It may be true that the public announcement of these two parties' endorsement added psychological momentum for the Socialists to take the initiative in starting interparty negotiations as early as they did. In the eyes of other parties, however, the behavior of the Cooperativists and the Communists was to be expected. Thus, although there were five parties on the political scene, only three were significant players in the coalition-building game; the two smaller parties were essentially inconsequential in the following course of events.

Socialist Call for a Grand Coalition

From the very beginning of interparty negotiations, the Socialists repeatedly proposed to form a four-party coalition including the most conservative Liberal Party. A grand coalition would have been a suboptimal outcome for the Socialists because they would have been left with a smaller share of cabinet portfolios and with less policy influence. What explains this apparently irrational proposal?

The key to understanding this puzzle lies in the absence of institutionalized rules regarding the coalition-building procedure under the circumstance of divided electoral results. The Socialists had won the largest number of seats, but there was no guarantee that they would be part of the coalition, let alone that their leader would be the prime minister. Although no other party objected to the Socialists taking the initiative in interparty negotiations, the possibility remained that other parties could cut a separate deal under the negotiation table. The most direct threat was the potential alliance between the Democrats and the Liberals, whose combined force would have been sufficient to form a majority. This threat, or the threat that the Socialists might be entirely excluded from the coalition, significantly affected their strategic calculations.

The Socialists had no credible way of binding the Democrats. Even if the Socialists offered the Democrats a "good deal" in terms of portfolio allocation or policy proposals or both, the Liberals could always outbid the Socialists. Put another way, for the Socialists, any deal made with the Democrats would not be credible because the Socialists had no way of preventing the Democrats from reneging *ex post* and allying with the Liberals. This explains why Nishio had to spend most of his bargaining efforts on the Liberals, not on the Democrats; given that the Democrats were ideologically in between the Socialists and Liberals, Liberal participation in a coalition would likely lead to policies closer to the preferences of the Democrats, thus mitigating the Democrats' incentives to secretly ally with the Liberals. For the Socialists, a grand coalition of which they would be part was a better choice than a Liberal-Democratic coalition of which they would not.

The Liberals, of course, had no illusions and knew that the Socialists' offer for a grand coalition was a strategic ploy to deter the Liberals from forging an alliance with the Democrats. The Liberals, however, were also constrained in what they could do. Even though their preference was the bilateral "cheap coalition" with the Democrats, their offer could be outbid by a Socialist counteroffer, just as the Socialists' offer to the Democrats could be outbid by theirs. Thus, in the absence of institutionalized rules regarding coalition building, there was a standoff. Both the Socialists and the Liberals, afraid of losing the prospect of being part of the coalition, had to agree on the suboptimal grand coalition, as they actually did on May 9.

Had the standoff been allowed to continue for a long time, the coalition-building process would probably have resulted in a minority government led by the Democrats. As indicated above, in such a three-way competition, the party in the middle would have overwhelming bargaining leverage over the two peripheral parties. Thus, for the Democrats, the best strategy was simply to wait and see which (the Socialists or the Liberals) would come up with a better coalition offer. For both the Socialists and Liberals, on the other hand, the longer they waited, the less bargaining power they had vis-à-vis the Democrats. That explains why these two parties subsequently tried to put an end to the standoff.

Liberals Retreat and Socialists Call for a Vote

Although the Liberals had once agreed to the four-party coalition, they soon made it clear that they would not be joining a grand coalition. They clearly signaled their intention to withdraw from the coalition when they nominated their own candidates for the speaker and vice speaker of the house. Overall, it was Liberal resistance that slowed down the interparty negotiations. What was the rationale behind the Liberals' behavior?

Given their policy and ideological preferences, the Liberals' obvious choice for a coalition partner was the Democrats. However, as long as the Democrats could turn to the left and ask for a Socialist counteroffer, the Liberals knew they would simply be squeezed by the Democrats in their bilateral dealings.

One can speculate, therefore, that in order to have a credible dialogue with the Democrats, the Liberals needed to make sure that their rivals, the Socialists, were "out of the game" of coalition building. This explains why the Liberals started to filibuster the interparty negotiation process by making unacceptable demands in exchange for their participation in the grand coalition, thus undermining the Socialist leadership in managing the negotiations. The Liberals' hope, in taking such a hard line, was probably that a sufficient delay in the process might make the Socialists give up their efforts to form a government and make the Democrats shift their focus to a two-party coalition with the Liberals.

This maneuvering on the part of the Liberals had a critical impact on the Democratic Party. The Democrats knew that they would most likely be included in any majority government that was formed. The issue at hand, therefore, was whether they could become the dominant partner of the coalition, and this intensified an internal division between the left and the right elements within the party. On the one hand was the centrist faction led by Ashida, who still hoped to be the dominant force in the coalition with the Socialists. On the other was Shidehara's conservative faction which started to negotiate, independent of Ashida's group, with the Liberals for a bilateral coalition. Thus Liberals' maneuvering had the consequence of splitting the Democratic Party.

The Socialists, as much as the Liberals, did not want the standoff to last. Upon the Liberals' apparent retreat, however, the range of their strategic options was limited. The Socialists could not take a hard line back to the Liberals, which would have simply prolonged the standoff. Their strategy instead was to call for a vote and seek to elect their leader, Katayama, as prime minister, even before the composition of the future coalition was decided. In contrast to the Liberals, the Socialists' strategy was to make sure that they themselves would be *in* the coalition-building game, rather than making sure that their rivals (the Liberals) would be *out* of it.

Of course there was no guarantee that Katayama would be chosen prime minister. No codified rules or conventions suggested that in a divided Parliament the leader of the largest party must be the first one asked to form the government. Going ahead with the vote, however, was a worthwhile gamble for the Socialists because they knew that the continuation of the standoff would only strengthen the bargaining leverage of the Democrats. The Socialists still had the largest number of parliamentary seats, albeit by a small margin. Thus, if no combination of the three parties could cut a separate deal and each party had to nominate its own leader for prime minister, the Socialists would have won the most votes. It was possibile that the Democrats and Liberals could come together at the last moment and vote for a joint candidate to beat Katayama, but, as long as the composition of the coalition remained undecided before the vote, the Shidehara-Ashida rivalry was likely to continue within the Democratic Party. The Socialists therefore gambled that the Democrats could not put forward a candidate with uniform party support.

Liberals and Democrats Support Katayama

In retrospect, the Socialists won the gamble. Their success, however, cannot be attributed simply to miscalculations on the part of the Democrats and Liberals. It is natural to assume that these rival parties understood correctly that the Socialists' May 23 call for a vote was aimed at electing Katayama in order to ensure the Socialists' inclusion in the coalition. Why, then, did the Democrats and Liberals not oppose the Socialists' call for a vote? And why didn't the Liberal Party or the Democratic Party nominate its own candidate, instead of allowing Katayama to receive overwhelming support?

The Liberals and Democrats did not oppose the Socialists' call for a vote for several reasons. First, the Socialists' proposal seemed legitimate, especially given that the Diet had been recessed for three days without accomplishing anything but electing the speakers of the two houses. Second, the Socialists had a formal justification for proposing an early vote: Article 67 of the newly adopted Constitution explicitly stipulated that the prime minister had to be designated by a resolution before any other matters could be discussed in Parliament. Furthermore, the Liberals and Democrats had reason to believe that there would be other rounds in the process of selecting a prime minister. According to Article 69 of the new Constitution, "If the House of Representatives passes a nonconfidence resolution . . . the Cabinet shall resign en masse, unless the House of Representatives is dissolved within ten days." Since the Socialists had the most seats and thus were not likely to call an early election, this constitutional provision gave the Liberals and Democrats a future opportunity to topple any coalition formed after the vote and to thus have another round of selecting a prime minister.

Once it had been decided that the vote would take place, the Liberals' options were limited. There was no point in nominating their own candidate, for without the Democrats' support a Liberal candidate would surely be defeated by Katayama. And the Democrats would not be inclined to vote for a Liberal candidate because it was likely that they did not simply want to participate in the coalition but to be the dominant partner. The Liberals' only hope, therefore, was for the Democrats to nominate a candidate; then, with the Liberals' support, that candidate could beat Katayama and a Liberal-Democratic coalition could be established. But with no Democratic candidate, the Liberals had no choice but to vote for Katayama.[11]

The Democrats' behavior was much more puzzling because, had they nominated a candidate, it was likely that the Liberals would have joined them, creating the prospect of a Democrat-led coalition with the Liberals. For the Democrats, a coalition with the Liberals was more desirable than one with the Socialists because in the former they were more likely to become the dominant partner than in the latter. Nevertheless, the Democrats did not nominate their own candidate; they voted for Katayama, attaching a strange condition that they would support the Socialist leader only if the Liberals were included in the coalition. Why?

There is of course no reason to believe that the Democrats wanted a four-party grand coalition. One can even speculate that because the Democrats were aware of their positional advantage being in the middle of the other two parties, their ultimate objective might have been to form a minority government by themselves. In any case, their conditional support for Katayama was not sincere but a strategic move intended to filibuster the interparty negotiations after the vote was taken. The Democrats knew that even if the Socialist leader were to be chosen as the prime minister in this first round of the selection process, they could always present a nonconfidence motion in the future, together with the Liberals, to overthrow Katayama. It is possible, then, that by declaring that their cooperation depended on Liberal participation, the Democrats were counting on the prospect of the Socialists facing difficulties and giving up their effort to form a government and that a second round of selection would take place.

With the benefit of hindsight, the Democrats' strategy was disastrous, as the prospect of a second round was shattered by an unexpected exogenous factor: MacArthur's May 24 announcement welcoming Katayama as the prime minister. It is not clear whether MacArthur was endorsing Katayama personally or whether he would have endorsed any nominee chosen through the newly established democratic process. What was evident was that MacArthur's endorsement, with his omnipotent authority as the head of the Allied Forces, in effect substituted for the lack of formal procedural rules about coalition building and put an end to the prime ministerial selection process. It was thus guaranteed that the Socialists would be in the coalition.

[11] The only other alternative was to abstain. However, there was still a chance, albeit remote, of a grand coalition, and the Liberals had nothing to lose by voting for Katayama in this first round.

Without the benefit of hindsight, however, the Democrats' behavior was not as unreasonable as it appeared. Because of the continuing rift between the conservative Shidehara and the centrist Ashida factions within the party, the Democrats could not nominate their own candidate. The Democrats' strategy of making their support contingent on Liberal participation was thus to ensure that the interparty negotiations after the first vote would reach a stalemate. This made sense because they had no reason to suspect *ex ante* that MacArthur would endorse the Socialist candidate, and especially because they knew that their candidate, once nominated, would likely receive Liberal support in a future vote. The Democrats essentially needed to buy time before they could put forward a candidate with a uniform party endorsement.

Although it is impossible to prove the motives behind the Democrats' strategy, as conjectured above, a closer examination of the behavior of the Shidehara and Ashida factions before and after MacArthur's announcement may shed light on the rationale behind their action. Before the announcement, when a future round was still possible, it was largely the centrist Ashida faction that pursued a four-party grand coalition, presumably in an attempt to filibuster any negotiations after the vote. After the announcement, which guaranteed that the Socialists would be in the coalition, it was the conservative Shidehara faction that demanded a grand coalition. There was thus a reversal in the filibustering roles within the Democratic Party. This indicates that both Shidehara and Ashida, the two principal players within the party, were acting strategically within the changing environment and that they were clearly projecting a future in which they themselves would be dominant in a coalition.

Once it was decided that the Socialists would lead the coalition, the rest was easy to settle. The Liberals knew that they had lost the chance of being a meaningful part of the coalition because the Socialists (and the Democrats) would have no reason to favor a surplus majority government. The centrist elements of the Democrats, Ashida and his followers, soon accepted the idea of a three-party coalition with the Socialists and Cooperativists, in which they would be better off than in a Socialist-led minority government. Shidehara attempted to resist the coalition with the left, relying on the previously attached condition for supporting Katayama, but his filibustering effort was destined to fail because MacArthur's endorsement had already nullified the credibility of that condition. Thus, with few further complications, the long process of interparty negotiations finally came to an end.

Theoretical Implications

The formation of the Katayama government, as reconstructed above, suggests that the behavior of political parties involved in this coalition negotiation were governed by the basic logic of party competition and strategic interactions. Nevertheless, it should be noted that the exact outcome of the coalition building—a government consisting of Socialists, Democrats, and Cooperativists—was not what Axelrod's original model would have predicted. The governing three parties were certainly "connected" in terms of their policy preferences (see Figure 4.1), but a Democrat-Liberal alliance was also connected and an even more efficient winning coalition, which would have occupied just over 50 percent of the legislative seats (see Table 4.2). Before moving on to discuss the long-term consequences of the Katayama government, this gap between the model's prediction and the actual outcome needs to be clarified.

The analysis in the previous section suggests that two factors, which are generally overlooked or underemphasized in the theoretical literature on coalition governments, were important in understanding the formation of the Katayama government. First, the lack of institutionalized rules governing the coalition-building process was important in explaining the apparently irrational behavior of the political parties. Although the institutional ambiguity was critical in explaining why both the Socialists and Liberals initially agreed to a suboptimal four-party coalition, it was MacArthur's statement, which in effect substituted for the institutional void, that preempted the Liberal-Democratic presentation of a nonconfidence motion and thus put an end to the prime ministerial selection process.

In many formal studies on coalition governments, a rule or convention that the largest party should be the first one asked to form a coalition is an assumption that drives the predictions of a unique coalition outcome.[12] The above case study suggests, however, that if there had been an unambiguous norm regarding who goes first in forming the government, each major party would have taken a different strategy. For example, the Socialists would probably have had no reason to propose a grand coalition in the early stages of negotiations, nor, in the later stages, to separate the issue of electing a prime minister from that of forming the coalition. The Democrats, on the other hand, would probably have been more closely united (presumably under the leadership of the centrist Ashida), and so, for the Liberals, a hard-line strategy might not have been as effective. Thus different types of institutional arrangements would likely have led to different coalition outcomes.

Second, the above analysis points to the importance of internal party politics in determining the final coalition outcome. In most contemporary coalition theories, including Axelrod's, political parties are treated as unitary actors and the impact of intraparty politics on interparty coalition bargaining is assumed away. In the above Japanese case, however, intraparty politics was the key to understanding the Democrats' puzzling behavior. Had there not been a split within the Democratic Party, nothing would have prevented the Democrats from nominating their own candidate at the May 23 vote, and, if they

[12] See, for example, Austen-Smith and Banks, "Elections, Coalitions, and Legislative Outcomes"; and Crombez, "Minority Governments."

had, the final outcome would probably have been a Democrat-Liberal coalition government.

The only attempt made so far to theorize about the interaction between intraparty politics and interparty coalition building is that of Michael Laver and Kenneth Shepsle, and, in their framework, the factions within a party are exogenously given and distinguished from one another based solely on their policy preferences.[13] To assume, however, that political parties are similarly divided according to common ideological dimensions is as unrealistic as to assume that all parties are unitary actors. The above analysis suggests, to the contrary, that the unity/disunity (or the "degree" of unity) of political parties is endogenous and thus a variable. True, as Laver and Shepsle would argue, the Shidehara-Ashida division within the Democratic Party was based on their ideological difference over policy preferences (and thus over the choice of coalition partners). But the same kind of internal division did not plague the Socialist Party although it was known for its history of internal ideological battles between the left and right wings. In fact, one of the most remarkable aspects about this coalition-building process was how little such ideological conflict surfaced to hinder the Socialists' bargaining position.

The presence of a significant conflict within the Democratic Party and the absence of such a conflict within the Socialist (and the Liberal) Party may yield a more specific hypothesis about the nature of the endogeniety of internal party politics. Although a centrist party, like the Democratic Party, may have a bargaining advantage in that it can play one peripheral party off against another, at the same time it may also be more susceptible to internal factional strife. Compared with the peripheral parties, whose primary concern remains *how to participate* in the winning coalition, the centrist party has a higher expectation that it will indeed be part of any majority coalition and thus is primarily concerned with *how to lead* the coalition; this, in turn, could aggravate any latent ideological divisions and facilitate the battle for leadership within the party. Yet looking back on the Japanese experience, the Democrats' internal rift might have been inconsequential had the Liberals not taken a hard-line strategy signaling their unwillingness to compromise their policy demands. Tentatively, then, one may conclude that the unity of a political party is a function of both the ideological location of the party itself and the bargaining strategy of other parties involved in the negotiation process.

The Long-Term Consequences of the Katayama Government

From the outset the Socialist-led coalition government established in 1947 had to confront major difficulties in forming a policy consensus. Katayama was thus forced to dilute the Socialists' original policy proposals for legislative

[13] See Laver and Shepsle, "Government Coalitions and Intraparty Politics."

purposes. The compromises Katayama had to make intensified the internal ideological battle between his right-wing faction and the frustrated left-wing elements within the Socialist Party. Katayama did pursue the nationalization of coal and mine production almost as a token to Socialist policies, but this in turn alienated the conservative Shidehara faction, which eventually left the Democratic Party.[14]

Faced with the growing opposition in and outside his own party, Katayama resigned in March 1948 and was replaced by Hitoshi Ashida, the leader of the remaining Democrats.[15] Ashida led the same three-party coalition until October 1948, when Ashida himself and other cabinet members were arrested for their involvement in bribery scandals. Two months later the lower house was dissolved under Yoshida's caretaker government. The landslide victory in this election laid the foundation for Yoshida's Liberal hegemony under which his party continued to govern until 1955.

As has been well documented in the literature, an important consequence of the failure of the coalition governments and the 1949 electoral defeat was a kind of "identity crisis" for Ashida and his Democratic Party, which eventually led Ashida to pursue the issue of Japan's rearmament as a way of appealing to Japanese nationalism. The outbreak of the Korean War also prompted the Democrats to decide that they would promote the policy of strengthening Japan's self-defense capability.[16] This raises an analytical problem as to whether the Democrats could still be characterized as "centrist" even at that point. Proponents of the socio-ideological approach would probably argue that the change in the Democrats' policy position is suggestive of the transformation of the underlying cleavage, that is, the diminishing of the ideological center and the consolidation of the conservative camp.

I am willing to accept that the Democrats (and their reincarnations as the National Democratic Party and the Reform-Progressive Party) should be referred to as a conservative party and that the Japanese political landscape underwent a major change around this time. It should be stressed, however, that what changed was the nature of the ideological/policy space itself, not the relative positions of the Democrats and other parties. Simply put, the Left-

[14] Shidehara's group was initially called the Partner Club [*Doshi Kurabu*]. It was then renamed the Democratic Club, which was later absorbed by Yoshida's Liberal Party. See footnote 15.

[15] As one would expect, the power transfer from Katayama to Ashida was hardly smooth. The Liberals approached members of the Democratic Club, remaining members of the Democrats, and independents, and tried very hard to nominate Liberal leader Yoshida as prime minister. Their maneuvering was unsuccessful because the Socialists finally decided to endorse Ashida. (This process is documented in Shinobu, *Sengo Nihon Seiji-shi*, 3: 733–47.) It was immediately after Ashida formed the coalition government that the Democratic Club joined the Liberals to create a new party, which was called the Democratic Liberal Party.

[16] See Miyazaki, "Nihon ni okeru 'Sengo Demokurashii' no Koteika" [Consolidation of "Postwar democracy" in Japan]; and Otake, *Sai-Gunbi to Nashonarizumu* [Rearmament and nationalism].

Right space no longer reflected an economic dimension in terms of government intervention (as it did in the 1947 coalition building) but instead reflected a foreign policy dimension measured by the preferred level of diplomatic closeness to the United States. As I demonstrate in the next chapter, the Democrats, subsequently revitalized under the leadership of Ichiro Hatoyama, were still clearly located between the Liberals and the Socialists on this dimension.[17]

Another point often made in the conventional literature is that the failure of the Katayama-Ashida governments led to Yoshida's landslide electoral victory in 1949. A closer examination reveals, however, that the "lesson," if indeed there was one, that the Japanese voters had learned from the devastating experience of the coalition governments did not last long. Figure 4.2 summarizes the results of the four elections held between 1947 and 1955.

Three related points are illustrated in Figure 4.2. First, although the Socialists indeed suffered a significant defeat in 1949, they started to recover their parliamentary share as early as the next election in 1952. This quick recovery was all the more remarkable given that the party was divided organizationally in 1951 between the Right Wing and the Left Wing, and each competed as a separate party in the election.[18] Second, although the Liberal government started with a comfortable majority in 1949, its surplus majority diminished gradually and consistently as the party went through more elections. In the February 1955 election, the Liberal Party finally lost its majority and was forced to form a minority government.[19]

The third related point is that between 1949 and 1955 was essentially a period of adjustment for the voters in the aftermath of the Katayama-Ashida coalition experiment, and the results of the elections held during this time well reflected this. As one can see from the figure, the distribution of parliamentary seats after the 1947 election and that after the 1955 election were almost identical in terms of the respective shares of Socialists, Liberals, and the sum of non-Liberal conservatives and centrists. In this sense one can argue that the electoral results in 1952 and 1953 were a deviation from the "normal" distribution of parliamentary seats.

[17] Ichiro Hatoyama, who had been purged in 1946, returned to the political scene in 1951, together with his fellow powerful politicians Ichiro Kohno and Bukichi Miki. Because Hatoyama suffered a stroke immediately after the comeback, however, he had to abandon temporarily his initial plan to create a new party and thus joined Yoshida's Liberal Party. As he recovered, Hatoyama challenged Yoshida's long-standing leadership within the party. In November 1954 he was chosen to be president of the Democratic Party, which was created as the amalgamation of the anti-Yoshida forces within the conservative camp.

[18] The two wings of the Socialist Party started to engage in separate political activities in late 1951 as a result of their fierce ideological quarrel over the issues of postwar settlement and Japan's security arrangement with the United States.

[19] The establishment of Yoshida's last minority government therefore also involved fierce competition and bargaining among major political parties. For an insightful documentation of this process, see Miyazaki, "Nihon ni okeru 'Sengo Demokurashii' no Koteika," esp. pp. 181–86.

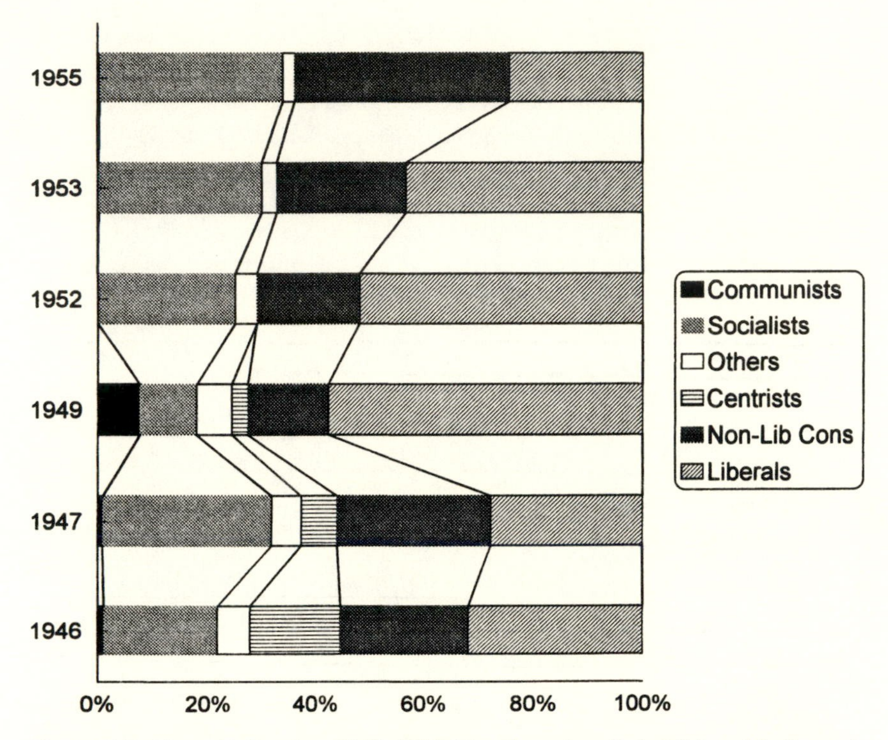

Figure 4.2: Electoral Results, 1947–1955. For the sake of simplicity, this figure is based on a dichotomous classification of the conservative parliamentarians, Liberals, and non-Liberals, thus ignoring the series of partisan realignments that led to the establishment of the Democratic Party in 1954. It also ignores the Socialist Party's split that lasted from 1951 to 1955. *Source*: Ishikawa, *Deeta Sengo Seiji-shi* [A data history of postwar politics].

The apparent resemblance between the electoral situation in 1947 and that in 1955 raises an important question: Why did two such similar legislative environments produce different final outcomes in government formation? Whereas the interparty negotiations in 1947 resulted in an ordinary coalition government made up of progressive and centrist parties, the negotiations in 1955 eventually took the form of a formal merger of two major parties on the Right. In this chapter I have dealt extensively with the 1947 case and have explored the determinants of the coalition formation. The next chapter is devoted to an analysis of the latter case, that is, the political process that led to the creation of the LDP in 1955.

Even though the formation of the Socialist-led coalition government in 1947 was the first experience of government formation under the newly established democratic regime, political parties involved in the negotiations were acting to further their own incentives in searching for a coalition. Thus Japanese party politics during the first decade of the postwar period cannot be characterized as a transitional era simply awaiting the one-party dominance of the LDP.

In particular, the analysis presented in this chapter challenges the conventional view that the underlying socio-ideological structure that has sustained the post-1955 dominance of the Liberal Democratic Party is significantly different from the socio-ideological cleavage that existed before 1955. True, the Katayama government was formed under "unusual" historical circumstances in that Japan was still under American occupation and the Japanese public was not yet accustomed to the newly established democratic process. As shown, however, the parties involved in the 1947 coalition formation were as self-seeking as those in other advanced industrial democracies. One should not overemphasize the idiosyncratic historical context in explaining the Katayama government: historical context mattered only in the sense that each political party had to operate under a lack of institutionalized procedural rules, and thus under pervasive uncertainty. This unusual environment influenced the range of options open to each party, but it never undermined the basic logic of party competition and strategic bargaining.

5

THE CREATION OF THE LIBERAL DEMOCRATIC PARTY IN 1955

THE LIBERAL Democratic Party in Japan was created in 1955, following the amalgamation of the two conservative parties, the Liberals and the Democrats.[1] Despite the LDP's subsequent remarkable one-party dominance (or perhaps precisely because of it), the interparty negotiation process leading up to the establishment of the LDP has rarely been the subject of systematic scholarly scrutiny. The joining of the conservative forces more than four decades ago is now often taken for granted and perceived simply as an inevitable course of events in Japanese political history.

In this chapter I reexamine the determinants of the 1955 conservative merger. Instead of relying on hindsight and regarding 1955 as the beginning of a new political era, I offer a more forward-looking interpretation and highlight the process of interparty bargaining and strategic interaction that led to the formation of the LDP. Like the 1947 case analyzed in the previous chapter, the process in 1955 started as a coalition government building, a phenomenon typically observed in a competitive multiparty system. The final outcome, of course, was drastically different from 1947 in that this time the process resulted in a formal merger of the two existing major parties.

The chapter begins with a brief description of the interparty bargaining process that led to the creation of the LDP. I then review the conventional interpretations associated with the notion of the 1955 system and the socio-ideological perspective. Next, I offer an alternative interpretation that highlights interparty bargaining and strategic interactions. After drawing some general theoretical insights from the analysis, I go on to discuss the post-1955 survival of the LDP as a unified party. The chapter ends with a summary of the implications that may be drawn from the material presented here.

[1] It is difficult to pinpoint the exact beginning of the process that led to the establishment of the LDP. For example, as discussed in chapter 4, the conservative faction of the Democratic Party (Kijuro Shidehara and his group) had joined the Liberal Party as early as 1948. When Shigeru Yoshida formed his third cabinet in 1949, he was successful in dividing the Democratic Party even further and eventually absorbed a group led by Ken Inukai. The latter incident, in particular, is often referred to as "First Conservative Merger" [*Dai Ichiji Hoshu Godo*], to distinguish it from the 1955 merger. For the present purposes, however, the series of small-scale partisan realignments preceding the reformation of the Democratic Party in November 1954 are of little significance and are thus ignored.

Facts

It was the 1953 general election in which the Liberal Party lost its majority that set the stage for an intense power struggle among the major political parties in Japan.[2] The Liberal leader, Shigeru Yoshida, formed his fifth cabinet but faced considerable opposition in Parliament, reflecting the inherent weakness of a minority government. Even within his own party, he had to deal with a growing number of dissidents who challenged his long-standing leadership. After a year of difficulties, Yoshida and his entire cabinet finally resigned when a nonconfidence motion was presented jointly by the Democrats and the Socialists in December 1954. The Democratic leader, Ichiro Hatoyama, then established a caretaker government on December 10 to hold a general election.

This development provided the momentum for the two wings of the Socialist Party to seek reunification.[3] Some leaders of the Right Wing Socialists, such as Suehiro Nishio, opposed the idea of reunification. The Left Wing Socialists, however, put together their proposal as early as December 12 and campaigned vigorously in its favor. At their respective party conventions in January 1955, both wings declared that they would reintegrate themselves into a single party after the next election, which was expected to be held in February.

Yoshida's decision to step down also had an impact on the interaction between the two conservative parties. On the one hand, the Liberal Party, under the new leadership of Taketora Ogata, expressed its renewed interest in joining forces with the Democrats. On January 5 Ogata stated at a press conference that if both parties failed to obtain a majority in the next election, the Liberals and the Democrats should coordinate their efforts and aim for a merger. On the other hand, the Democrats, who had just succeeded in overthrowing the Liberal government, seemed disinterested in the issue of a conservative merger. Hatoyama's booming popularity added to their confidence in the approaching election.[4] Thus Hatoyama responded cooly to Ogata's statement by remarking that it did not make sense for parties to seek unification immediately after a general election in which they would be competing against each other. Hatoyama's response was reinforced on January 17 by two

[2] In this section I have used various sources, including numerous reports and articles from *Asahi Shimbun*, to describe the events and bargaining during this period. In the interests of simplicity, I will only specify sources for quotations and in cases where I believe the article depends on editorial speculation.

[3] The two wings of the Socialist Party had been engaged in separate political activities since late 1951.

[4] Hatoyama's popularity was in large part a reaction to Yoshida's long-term reign. Hatoyama also attracted popular sympathy, being characterized as a "tragic" figure in Japanese politics for having been purged and for his poor physical condition.

TABLE 5.1
Lower House Seat Distribution after the 1955 Election

Party	*Seats (%)*
Liberals	112 (24.0)
Democrats	185 (39.6)
Right Socialists	67 (14.3)
Left Socialists	89 (19.1)
Communists	2 (0.4)
Others	12
Total	467

Source: Masumi Ishikawa, *Deeta Sengo Seiji-shi* [A data history of postwar politics], p. 120.

other powerful Democrats, Bukichi Miki and Ichiro Kohno, who flatly denied the possibility of a merger.

Thus, in contrast to the Socialists' preelection commitment to reunification, there was no significant Liberal-Democrat dialogue at this point. The situation changed drastically, however, when Hatoyama's Democratic Party failed to obtain a majority in the election (see Table 5.1).

Although it had the largest number of parliamentary seats, the Democratic Party had no choice but to explore legislative support from the Liberals and the Socialists. The Liberals rejected Hatoyama's request, saying they would not form a coalition or even a policy-based cooperative arrangement with the Democrats. Similarly, the Left-Wing Socialists expressed their determination to quash any attempts by the Democrats to lure the opposition into forming a majority. Hatoyama thus decided to form a minority government.

From the outset, the Hatoyama government suffered a number of major setbacks in Parliament. The first incident occurred when he attempted to nominate a fellow Democrat as the speaker of the lower house. Despite the prearrangement forged between the two parties, the Liberals reneged and joined the Socialists to nominate a Liberal candidate for speaker and a Socialist candidate for vice speaker.[5] Far more significant was the difficulty Hatoyama faced in the deliberations over the annual budget. The Liberals and Socialists stub-

[5] Initially the two parties had agreed that the Democrats would take the speaker's position, and the Liberals the vice speaker's. They had also agreed that they would distribute the positions of the lower house standing committee chairs among themselves. This deal outraged the Socialists. When the Democrats withdrew their original offer and proposed that the committee chairs be distributed proportionately to all major parties, this gave the hard-liners within the Liberal Party sufficient reason to renege. The Liberals and both wings of the Socialists voted for Liberal Hideji Masuya as the speaker and for right-wing Socialist Motojiro Sugiyama as the vice speaker of the house.

bornly refused to compromise, and both made many specific requests to revise the original proposal. Some important bills introduced by the government were not even discussed on the floor.

Frustrated with these legislative difficulties, Bukichi Miki, chair of the Executive Council of the Democratic Party, made a public statement on April 12 stressing the need for a conservative merger. Miki's remarks attracted widespread attention because they also hinted at Hatoyama's early resignation.[6] The Liberals nevertheless remained unyielding and refused to discuss the matter of unification, arguing that such discussions could not be held when Parliament was in session and still deliberating over the budget.

Within the Democratic Party, Hatoyama himself was reluctant to take further initiatives to facilitate the conservative merger. Occasionally Hatoyama even hinted at the possibility of dissolving the lower house if the legislative deadlock were to continue. Such a hard line intensified the Liberals' stance. They gradually began to regard Hatoyama's retirement as a precondition for their dialogue with the Democrats. Thus on May 7, when Democratic Party Secretary Nobusuke Kishi reiterated the need for the conservatives to join forces without mentioning the retirement issue, the Liberals again gave no reply.

In mid-May, as the stalemate continued in Parliament, the Democrats decided to pursue a coalition government with the Liberals. The Liberals rejected any such proposal if the government were to be led by Hatoyama. The Democrats' initiative, nevertheless, finally brought the Liberal leaders to the negotiation table. After a series of preliminary meetings between Miki and Banboku Ohno, the chair of the Liberal Party's Executive Council, the first official meeting to discuss the issue of conservative unification was held on May 23.

Thus negotiations between the two parties entered a new phase. The Liberals were still not convinced as to whether the Democrats' move was really meant to explore the joining of conservative forces or was simply a tactic to manage the legislative process of the current parliamentary session. Accordingly, the Liberals did not drop their guard in the budget deliberations.

When the two party leaders, Hatoyama and Ogata, finally met on June 4, Hatoyama asked Ogata to agree to support his government for the remaining period of the current session. Ogata, apparently convinced that the Democrats were not using the unification issue merely as a tactic, agreed in principle to pass the annual budget. This meeting between the two party leaders changed the nature of the subsequent negotiations in that the discussion moved from *whether* the two parties should join forces to *what form* the arrangement should take. On this issue, however, the two sides still heartily disagreed. The

[6] Hatoyama's age (seventy-two) and poor health (having suffered a disabling stroke in June 1951) had always been political issues.

Liberals insisted on a formal merger of the two parties, as opposed to the formation of an ordinary coalition. Within the Democratic Party, leftists such as Kenzo Matsumura and Takeo Miki vocally opposed such a merger.[7]

As the issue of form remained unresolved, the matter hung over the legislative interactions during the final stage of the budget deliberations. On June 23 the Liberals, together with both wings of the Socialists, presented a nonconfidence resolution against Agriculture Minister Ichiro Kohno.[8] When the Democrats complained, the Liberals withdrew their support for the resolution. The Liberals' maneuvering, however, apparently forced the Democratic Party to concede, and on June 29 the Democrats finally agreed to a formal merger. Two days later, on July 1, the annual budget was passed in Parliament.

Even after the issue of form was resolved, the two parties still had to discuss policy platforms and other details. On July 22 the joint policy committee approved the draft proposal that stipulated the mission and character of the new unified conservative party. On July 24, however, differences in opinion surfaced with regard to the exact timing of the merger. Liberal negotiator Ohno preferred that the merger take place some time before December. Democrats, on the other hand, hoped that it would not occur until the next spring. What complicated negotiations was that this issue was linked to the debate as to whether to extend the current parliamentary session. The Liberals preferred no extension and wanted instead to hold an extraordinary session in the fall. The Democrats, in contrast, wanted to pass all the important legislation, including a set of three bills related to sugar importation, within this session in order to avoid an extraordinary session.

Frustrated with this impasse, Agriculture Minister Kohno began to cultivate support from Socialists for the sugar importation bill. The Liberals were outraged by this move and threatened to nullify the entire merger. In the end the Democrats agreed to abandon the sugar bill in return for Liberal support for another bill related to national defense.[9] Because of all these complications, the Democrats lost the opportunity to extend the session, which ended on July 30.

The stage for negotiations over the conservative merger then moved outside the parliamentary buildings. The Liberals insisted that deliberations over the budget for the next fiscal year be undertaken by the new unified party, and therefore they pressured for an early merger. Hatoyama, on the other hand,

[7] The two were members of the former National-Cooperativist Party.

[8] Unlike nonconfidence motions provided for in the Constitution (Article 69), nonconfidence resolutions, targeted at individual ministers, have no legal authority. Nevertheless, as a convention, the passage of such a resolution often led to the minister's resignation.

[9] The Socialists then started to prepare another nonconfidence resolution against Kohno. When Kohno revealed that the Liberal Party was to benefit from the domestic sugar industries if the bill died, some Liberal members joined the Socialists to support the resolution. The resolution, however, was not presented after all because the chair of the House Management Committee, elected from the Democratic Party, made himself "unavailable," thus preventing the bill from being presented.

told reporters that he would not rush the merger and would not be pressured to make a decision about his own retirement. On August 4, at his Karuizawa villa, Hatoyama expressed his pessimism about the prospect of a merger and indicated that his own government would deal with the next year's budget in an extraordinary session, which he proposed be convened some time during November. Hatoyama's statement triggered immediate Liberal anger. On the same day Liberal Party Secretary Mitsujiro Ishii told reporters that his party, as the opposition, would become more confrontational in legislative dealings during the forthcoming parliamentary session. When Miki and Kishi made an apologetic explanation to Ohno the next day, the Liberals requested that the extraordinary session be held as early as October 10.

The Hatoyama government had to spend the rest of the summer dealing with important foreign policy matters, some of which became a source of new tension between the two parties. For example, there was the issue of postwar compensation for the Philippines. Although the Democrats had agreed informally to the amount demanded by the Filipino government, the Liberals were concerned that the amount was excessive. Another controversial issue was Japan's diplomatic normalization with the Soviet Union. Although Hatoyama had repeatedly expressed his enthusiasm for facilitating the bilateral negotiations, the Liberals remained firm and pressured the government not to compromise on the issues of territory and the deportation of Japanese still in Russia after the war. It was obvious that these diplomatic issues, in addition to the budget, would be linked with the unification discussions between the two parties in the forthcoming parliamentary session.

No sooner was the summer over than the two parties resumed their political posturing. On September 2 the Liberal leaders stated, upon their visit to the five economic organizations in western Japan, that they would reject any budget proposal if the Democrats were to continue their deflationary economic policies.[10] The Democrats, on the other hand, made it clear that the budget was an issue independent of the merger talks, and they began planning a draft budget proposal. The Liberals responded by saying that they would not agree in advance on the budget unless the two parties agreed that the draft would be drawn up by the new unified party.

What broke the stalemate between the two conservative parties was the unexpectedly quick progress made in the Socialists' reunification process. The final draft for the new Socialist policy platform was finalized on September 3, and even the skeptics within the Right-Wing Socialist Party, such as Suehiro Nishio, finally agreed to reunification. The two wings decided to hold a unified party convention in mid-October to adopt a platform and elect the new leader.

[10] The Liberals had been insisting on the issuance of public bonds for industrial investment in order to expand industrial production.

This development within the rival camp clearly revitalized the conservative negotiations. Democratic Party Secretary Kishi promised the Liberals that his party would make a formal decision regarding the procedure for unification by October 10. Arguing that priority be given to the timing of the merger, he made a two-point proposal: (1) that the merger take place under Hatoyama before the end of the year, and (2) that Hatoyama transfer the leadership to Ogata the following spring. Initially some objection to Kishi's new initiative arose within the Democratic Party. The party's Executive Council chairman, Bukichi Miki, for example, criticized Kishi's plan on the basis that the principle of selecting a new leader in an open election should not be compromised. Hatoyama himself still believed that the merger would be difficult unless the two parties agreed on key foreign policy issues. Nevertheless, when the self-appointed "coordinator" within the Democratic Party, Agriculture Minister Kohno, endorsed Kishi's plan, it became the prevailing and official party view.

While the Democrats thus managed to forge a consensus among themselves, the Liberals still considered unacceptable any deal that presupposed Hatoyama as president of the new party. The Liberals therefore rejected the Kishi-Kohno proposal, insisting that the new leader be openly elected. Even though the Liberals were far outnumbered by the Democrats within the lower house, the difference between the two parties in the number of total parliamentary members was only marginal (209 versus 207). When the Liberals turned down Kohno's request to meet with Ogata in late September, clearly the selection of the new leader remained as the final and most serious obstacle in the negotiations.

In light of the renewed standoff, Hatoyama took the offensive. On September 28, at a public speech in Tokyo, he reemphasized that the merger be "a means to implement policies" and cautioned against a merger simply for the sake of a merger. On September 29 at a press conference, he told reporters he would not trade his retirement for the success of the merger. When the Liberals expressed their objection to the Democrats' handling of the Philippines' postwar compensation, Hatoyama reiterated his determination to manage this issue and to draft the budget single-handedly. He also hinted at the possibility of a cabinet shuffle in the fall.

On October 10 Kishi, Kohno, and Miki agreed that the Democrats would stick to the Kishi-Kohno plan and aim for an early merger under Hatoyama. It was later reported that Miki had secretly met with Ogata and had become convinced that the Liberals would not walk away from the negotiating table even were the Democrats to insist on Hatoyama's leadership.[11] The Liberals, in fact, seemed to have softened their position. On October 17, contrary to his previous statement, Liberal negotiator Ohno told Miki that the Democrats' formal party decision would be acceptable to the Liberals without specifying

[11] *Asahi Shimbun*, October 12, 1955.

the voting procedure for the new presidential selection, as long as it did not personally endorse Hatoyama as the leader of the new party. Even after Hatoyama made a public statement on October 19, in which he expressed his pessimism about the prospect of the presidential election, the Liberals protested, but they agreed to delegate this issue to the joint "New Party Preparation Committee," which was scheduled to be convened within a week.

On October 25, just before this new committee was to meet for the first time, Liberal leader Ogata took the offensive. Declaring that he would definitely be running for the leadership of the new party, he stated that he would stand firm on the original Liberal foreign policies and that the Liberals were prepared to withdraw from the preparation committee talks unless a presidential election was guaranteed.

Despite Ogata's hard line, the committee met on October 27 and decided that the two parties would aim for a merger before November 10. When Kohno proposed that the new leader be selected not by a vote but through negotiations, the Liberals did not walk away from the committee discussion and the two parties began exploring a compromise regarding the selection procedure.

Subsequently, a series of public and private meetings were held but the parties failed to reach any compromise. On November 6 the committee members agreed that the merger would take place on November 15, but they could not come up with a practical proposal for the procedure. They therefore decided to delegate the task of engineering a new idea to a meeting of the powerful four—Kishi, Miki, Ohno, and Ishii—who were given carte blanche to decide on the issue of presidential selection.

It was from this meeting of these four men that the framework of collective leadership emerged, which postponed the selection of a new president. The basic idea behind this compromise was a division of labor: Hatoyama would remain prime minister but Ogata would be in charge of party affairs. They and Miki and Ohno would collectively preside over the party until the formal presidential election was held the following spring.[12] For the Democrats, this compromise was easy to accept because Hatoyama still remained prime minister. For the hard-line Liberals, on the other hand, it represented a surrender. On November 9, however, Ogata finally accepted the compromise and, as previously agreed between the two parties, the merger took place and the Liberal Democratic Party was established on November 15. Kishi was appointed the new party secretary, and Ishii became chairman of the Executive

[12] According to *Asahi Shimbun*, November 11, 1955, the powerful four found justification for postponing the presidential election and adopting the idea of collective leadership in the earlier statement made by Kohno pointing to the underdevelopment of conservative party organizations at the local level. Ideally, it was argued, the presidential election should be held not by parliamentarians but by delegates chosen from the local party caucuses; in the absence of such a process, any leadership choice would be tentative in nature.

Council. The extraordinary session was convened on November 22, and the third Hatoyama cabinet was formed.

This, of course, should not have been the end of the story, because the issue of presidential selection had not yet been solved. Hatoyama, as well as other former Democrats, began entertaining the idea that Hatoyama would govern at least until the fall. The former Liberals naturally opposed this view, and Ogata reiterated that he would be running for the leadership. Thus the seed for major internal strife had been planted in the new party. The story had to end here, however, because of an unexpected development: Ogata's sudden death on January 28. Hatoyama was therefore the only candidate left for president at the party convention held on April 5, winning 394 out of 489 votes. He continued to lead the LDP until the end of 1956. After achieving Japan's diplomatic normalization with the Soviet Union, he decided to resign, thus leaving the leadership contest to the next generation of party leaders.

Conventional Interpretations

As discussed in chapter 2, the socio-ideological perspective fosters the view that the emergence of the so-called 1955 system reflected a fundamental shift in Japan's underlying societal and ideological configurations. Accordingly, the creation of the LDP has been interpreted as a product of a basic demand within the Japanese society that transcended the accumulated mistrust between the two long-standing rival parties, the Liberals and the Democrats. However, although the socio-ideological factors may have been at work, such factors alone cannot account for the details of the actual process by which the LDP was created.

Some scholars argue, for example, that the merger of the Liberals and the Democrats was a timely response to the ideological consolidation of the progressive camp, or the "threat from the left."[13] According to this view, such a threat was evident both in the increasing electoral strength of the Left relative to the Right Wing within the Socialists and in the nature of the Socialists' negotiation process itself, which was driven largely by Left-Wing initiatives. Others emphasize the role of Japanese economic organizations in mediating and soliciting the conservative merger.[14] They argue that the Japanese business establishments, especially since Japan's economic recovery during the Korean War, craved the political stability necessary to expand their capitalist

[13] See, for example, Tomita, Nakamura, and Hrebenar, "The Liberal Democratic Party," esp. pp. 240–41. For a more general discussion of "crisis" during the pre-1955 period, though not necessarily in the context of partisan realignment, see Calder, *Crisis and Compensation.*

[14] See, for example, Shinobu, "Dokusen Shihon to Seiji" [Politics of monopolitic capitalism]; Tomimori, *Sengo Hoshu-to Shi* [History of postwar conservative parties], esp. pp. 69–71; and Yamaguchi "Sengo Nihon no Seiji Taisei to Seiji Katei" [The political system and process of postwar Japan], esp pp. 86–87.

activities. The Liberals and the Democrats were thus pressured to merge under the often quoted slogan, "Abandon small differences and concentrate on larger similarities."[15]

These conventional views are problematic in that they are too macroscopic to offer fine-tuned predictions for the interparty negotiations before the establishment of the LDP. First of all, until the very last stage it was uncertain as to whether the merger would even take place successfully. The negotiation process between the Democrats and Liberals was characterized by recurrent stalemates over various issues, including the form of the merger, its timing, and the procedure to select a new president. The Liberals repeatedly threatened to walk away from the negotiating table, and Hatoyama, as late as mid-October, expressed pessimism over the merger. Even after the two parties managed to merge in November, it was not clear whether the new party would survive another round of the internal power struggle expected to take place at the forthcoming presidential selection in the spring. It was only the unexpected death of Ogata that enabled the LDP to avoid such a struggle and thus remain unified. Hence the conservative merger was not a predetermined event in postwar Japanese political history, as the "societal demand" hypothesis suggests.

It is also difficult to view "the threat from the left" as being the major force that induced the merger. As documented in the previous section, the conservative camp was not ideologically cohesive enough to respond to such a threat. A clear policy gap existed between the Liberals and the Democrats. Their differences over the then dominating diplomatic issues, such as postwar compensation for the Philippines and relations with the Soviet Union, were so significant that the Liberals actually used them in their bargaining with the Democrats. Furthermore, it is odd to consider a "threat from the left," when the extreme left, the Japanese Communist Party, was a negligible legislative force with only two seats in the lower house. The Communists at the time were indeed going through a major organizational crisis just after embarking on ideological self-criticisms at the July 1955 "Roku Zenkyo" (the Sixth JCP Congress).[16] If the leftist threat were the driving force for the conservative merger, one would have expected to see the merger take place either when the Communists' influence was strong enough to organize a general strike, as in early 1947, or when they actually gained thirty-five seats in the lower house after the 1949 election.

Finally, it is problematic to consider Japanese business establishments as

[15] This famous statement urging for the conservative merger was made as early as October 4, 1952, as a joint statement from four of Japan's economic organizations: the Japanese Federation of Economic Organizations (Keidanren), the Japanese Federation of Employers' Associations (Nikkeiren), the Japanese Chamber of Commerce and Industry (Nissho), and the Japanese Committee for Economic Development (Doyu-kai).

[16] Goto, Uchida, and Ishikawa, *Sengo Hoshu Seiji no Kiseki* [The course of postwar conservative politics], esp. pp. 117–18.

the key facilitators of the conservative merger. True, the four economic organizations involved often made joint public statements urging a stable polity. These statements, however, were usually sent not only to the Liberals and Democrats but also to the Right-Wing Socialist Party.[17] Although the business circles undoubtedly wanted a stable government for the continuity and consistency of Japan's economic policies, there is no evidence suggesting that they had either the intention or capability to design a government specifically based on a merger of the two conservative parties.[18]

In sum, the establishment of the LDP was not simply a product of underlying societal demands. Such a view may account for the final *outcome* of the conservative merger, but it fails to explain any of the behavior of individual parties and politicians involved in the *process* that led to that outcome. Only with the benefit of hindsight can one regard the year 1955 as the beginning of a new political era. In what follows I develop an alternative, more forward-looking interpretation of the interactions among the political parties.

Credible Commitments, "Nested Game" and the Creation of the LDP

In the previous chapters I have focused on political parties as the central units of analysis. In the following analysis I extend the basic Schumpeterian/Downsian framework to define the utility of individual politicians within each party: they seek (1) to increase the chance of their own (re)election and, once (re)elected, (2) to pursue their promotion to more lucrative, prestigious, and powerful positions.[19] Based on these assumptions, let us reexamine in some detail the interparty negotiation process leading to the creation of the LDP in 1955. For the sake of clarity, I have divided the process into several stages based on key actions taken by the major players in the merger negotiations.

Preelection Behavior of the Major Parties

The formation of the caretaker government under Hatoyama, and therefore the increased prospects for a general election, had different effects on the various political parties. The two main conservative parties made no commitment to a coalition or merger, although the Liberal Party leader Ogata suggested the possibility of joining forces in case either party failed to obtain a majority. The two wings of the Socialist Party, on the other hand, decided to reintegrate

[17] Uchida, *Sengo Nihon no Hoshu Seiji* [Conservative politics of postwar Japan], p. 86.

[18] For a similar criticism, see Miyazaki, "Nihon ni okeru 'Sengo Demokurashii' no Koteika" [Consolidation of "postwar democracy" in Japan], esp. pp. 199–200.

[19] In addition, I rely on those assumptions specified in the previous chapter regarding the formation of coalition governments.

TABLE 5.2
The Relative Electoral Strength of the Left- and Right-Wing Socialists before 1955

	Left Wing		*Right Wing*	
Year	*Seat*	*Vote Share*[a]	*Seat*	*Vote Share*
1951	16		29	
1952[b]	56	9.80	60	12.84
1953	72	13.05	66	13.52
1955	89	15.35	67	13.86

Source: Ishikawa, *Deeta Sengo Seiji-shi* [A data history of postwar politics], pp. 26, 118–19.

[a]"Vote Share" refers to the percentage of partisan votes in the total number of votes cast in the election.

[b]The entries for the 1952 seat distribution refer to the numbers of parliamentary members at the time of the party split in October 1951.

themselves into a single party after the election, and they publicly announced their decision at their party conventions. What accounts for such variance in the preelection partisan behavior?

The Socialists' preelection commitment for reunification can be explained by the electoral strength of the respective wings and their strategy for coping with future interparty bargaining for government formation. First, consider the Left Wing. In the previous elections, namely, those in 1952 and 1953, the Left Wing had been more successful than the Right Wing in expanding their popular support and parliamentary seats (see Table 5.2).

The Left-Wing Socialists welcomed this trend to the extent that if they were to be reunited with the Right Wing, their influence would more likely dominate the organization and policy platforms of the unified Socialist Party. There was also a latent fear, however, that the frustrated Right Wing would seek a coalition with the Democrats independently, especially if the upcoming election were to accelerate this trend even further. This explains why the Left Wing took the initiative for the talks on reintegration *as soon as* the prospect for the next election became definite; before the formation of Hatoyama's caretaker government, the Left-Wing Socialists in fact had no consensus among themselves as to whether they should initiate reunification talks with the Right Wing.[20]

The Left Wing could have proposed other lower levels of partisan cooperation to the Right Wing, such as coalition governments or cooperative strategic voting in the upcoming prime ministerial selection, instead of formal reunification. However, if the aim of the Left Wing in initiating negotiations was primarily to prevent the Right Wing from exploring a liaison with the Demo-

[20] *Asahi Shimbun*, January 19, 1955.

cratic Party, then the proposal had to be for formal reunification.[21] Moreover, the only way to make the Right Wing's commitment for reunification credible was to make sure that the Right Wing would run an electoral campaign based on the prospect of reunification, thus increasing the "audience costs" vis-à-vis the Socialist supporters.[22] This explains why the proposal was made long before the election, even though the actual timing of reunification in the proposal was set to be after the election.

Whereas the behavior of the Left-Wing Socialists was thus understandable, that of the Right Wing was more puzzling. According to the preelection forecast, neither the Liberals, the Democrats, nor the combined Socialists were likely to obtain a majority. It was therefore possible that the Right Wing might have played a pivotal role in establishing a coalition government once the election was over. On the surface, there is no direct evidence that the Right-Wing Socialists actually explored the possibility of forming a coalition with the Democrats. Nevertheless, prominent Right-Wing leaders, such as Suehiro Nishio, openly opposed reunification with the Left Wing, presumably because they did not want to limit their options by committing to reunification. Furthermore, from a policy standpoint, the difference between the Right Wing Socialists and the Democrats was as little as, if not less than, the difference between the Democrats and the Liberals. Hatoyama's central foreign policy initiatives, particularly the normalization with China and the Soviet Union, were likely to require legislative support from the Socialists rather than from the Liberals.

Why, then, did the Right Wing agree to the Left Wing's proposal for reunification, thus apparently forfeiting its option of a coalition? Nishio, of course, could have resisted more vehemently had he believed that there was a realistic prospect for an alliance between the Right Wing Socialists and the Democrats. A closer examination of the electoral forecast available then, however, reveals that no such prospect existed. According to the *Asahi Shimbun* opinion polls taken before the election, for example, the Liberals, Democrats, and Socialists were in a three-way tie in terms of the level of party support. But this poll also indicated that even with the most favorable estimate and supposing that the Right Wing obtained exactly half the Socialists' support, the combination of the Right Wing and the Democrats appeared far short of a legislative majority[23] (see Table 5.3).

[21] In this context I discount yet another conventional wisdom, namely, that the Socialist reintegration was caused by a fear of constitutional reform. To prevent that possibility, the Socialists would have needed to maintain one-third of the Diet, but there was no reason for the two wings of the Socialist to "merge" for that particular purpose.

[22] The term *audience costs* is borrowed from Martin, "Credibility, Costs, and Institutions"; and Fearon, "Deterrence and the Spiral Model."

[23] Whether such opinion polls accurately reflected the actual distribution of voters is not important. What matters is that they were the only means the parties had at the time to judge their

TABLE 5.3
Opinion Polls before the 1955 Election

Party	*Definitely Support(%)*	*Probably Support(%)*	*Total(%)*
Liberals	19	4	24
Democrats	24	6	30
Socialists[a]	22	3	25

Source: Asahi Shimbun, January 20, 1955.
[a]The numbers represent the results of the poll for the left- and right-wing Socialists combined.

Whereas the prospect for a coalition with the Democrats was therefore rather unlikely, the polls revealed that support for the Socialists was relatively solid in contrast to the two conservative parties, presumably because of the Socialists' organizational ties with labor unions. One may speculate, then, that the Right-Wing Socialists, as well as the Left Wing, had good reason to commit to reunification. By so doing, the combined Socialists might have had a chance to become the largest parliamentary force (and thus form a government) especially if they could successfully coordinate their candidate nominations so as to maximize their representation. The two conservative parties, on the other hand, would have to run separate campaigns and their candidates would be competing for the same pool of voters in each district.[24]

Unlike the Socialists, the Liberals and Democrats both had less incentive to commit to a merger before the election. As long as the electoral results were expected to be roughly a three-way tie between themselves and the *combined* Socialists, there was no immediate need for them to join forces. The Liberal leader Ogata did make a remark before the election suggesting the possibility of working with the Democrats, but this was largely a reflection of Ogata's vulnerability as the newly chosen party leader. Because the number of Liberal seats had been decreasing over the past few elections, Ogata wanted to prevent the last-minute party switching of rank-and-file Liberals concerned with their

own relative electoral strengths. In this sense it is reasonable to expect that each political party took these opinion polls seriously in calculating its electoral prospects and in deciding its strategy in party competition.

[24] In retrospect, the preelection forecast turned out to be wrong. The actual seat distribution resulting from the election suggests that the number of newly elected Right-Wing Socialists was sufficient to establish a majority coalition government with the Democrats (see Table 5.1). This, should not lead one to conclude, however, that Nishio miscalculated. It is difficult to speculate what would have happened had the Right Wing chosen not to reunite with the Left Wing. It is possible that under such a scenario the Right Wing would not have obtained as many seats as it did because its candidates would have had to compete directly with the Left-Wing candidates during the election.

electoral chances.[25] As the election date approached, therefore, Ogata withdrew this suggestion and indeed his campaign rhetoric became much more confrontational with regard to the Democrats.[26]

Hence, although the electoral outcome was fundamentally uncertain, it is nevertheless possible to claim that the actions (or inactions) of the major political parties before the election were consistent with their own *estimated* electoral strengths. When the election was over, much of the uncertainty disappeared, and the parties involved had to interact within a different environment.

The Liberals' Hard Line and Hatoyama's Minority Government

What was left behind after the election was the prospect of Socialist reunification. This had a decisive impact on the incentives and strategy of the two conservative parties and on their postelection interactions. For the Democrats, who failed to win a majority, the prospect of Socialist reunification had practically sealed off their option to turn to the left for a coalition partner. Working with the Right-Wing Socialists, who had made a commitment to the electorate to reintegrate with the Left Wing, would have meant the formation of a huge surplus majority government. The Liberals, on the other hand, knowing that the Democrats' options were limited, were now able to take a hard line. They knew they were the Democrats' only viable ally for managing the upcoming parliamentary session. Thus, despite Ogata's earlier solicitation, the Liberals refused to make any cooperative arrangements with the Democrats.

In the short run, the Liberals' hard-line strategy did not work in that they failed to prevent Hatoyama from forming a minority government. The Democrats had the advantage of being located at the center of the ideological spectrum, although their parliamentary share was far short of a majority. Even had the Liberals tried to prevent Hatoyama from being elected prime minister, the only way to do so would have been to vote strategically for a unified Socialist candidate. But for the Liberals, Hatoyama was preferable to a Socialist prime minister, especially since the Socialist candidate was likely to come from the Left Wing. In the same vein, the Socialists were unlikely to support a Liberal candidate over Hatoyama, had there been one. Thus, as long as the Democrats had the plurality of parliamentary seats, the Liberals had no choice but to let Hatoyama be elected.[27]

In the long run, however, the Liberals' strategy was effective. Because of

[25] Although they had won a landslide victory in 1949, the Liberals had been losing their surplus majority in the past two elections and, according to opinion polls, their parliamentary share was likely to decrease even further after this election (see Figure 4.2 and Table 5.3).

[26] *Asahi Shimbun*, January 17, 1955.

[27] The logic developed here is consistent with recent comparative findings which suggest that parties located in the ideological center are more likely to form stable minority governments than those located at the periphery. See Crombez, "Minority Governments, Minimum Winning Coalitions and Surplus Majorities."

the significance of the obstacles and delays in the legislative process, the Democrats had no choice but to court the Liberals and to propose a coalition government, as they did in mid-May. The Liberals nevertheless remained unyielding because they believed that the Democrats' proposal was merely a strategy to manage the current parliamentary session. The Liberals' interests in pursuing a liaison with the Democrats were to gain their share of cabinet portfolios and policy influence in the government. Moreover, by offering their legislative support during the current period, the Liberals hoped that the Democrats would reward them in the future so that their leader Ogata would replace Hatoyama as prime minister. The Liberals' insistence on formal merger rather than on an ordinary coalition was thus aimed at making the Democrats' proposal credible and at preventing them from reneging. The Democrats, desperately needing to pass the budget, had to begin the merger discussions in late June, despite substantial opposition from the leftist group within the party.

It was in this same context that the Liberals insisted that the timing of the merger be earlier, while the Democrats favored a merger the following spring. The Liberals were again skeptical because, by spring, the next annual budget would have been passed and the Democrats might have been tempted to nullify their future endorsement of Ogata. The Liberals essentially had to complete the merger deal with the Democrats while they could use the next year's budget as a hostage for the negotiations. This calculation led the Liberals to oppose a further extension of the current parliamentary session, and indeed they forced it to end in late July.

Hence, by mid-summer, it was evident that the Democrats were losing badly in the bargaining game. The series of concessions made to the Liberals was clearly the high price Hatoyama had to pay as prime minister of a minority government. Even more important, as discussed below, it turned out that Hatoyama's legislative defeat also had a complex impact on the nature of his leadership role within the Democratic Party.

Division within the Democrats

Before and immediately after the February election, the Democratic Party seemed cohesive in dealing with the Liberals.[28] Under the Liberal offensive in Parliament, however, the Democratic Party became less and less monolithic. By the time the long and humiliating session had ended, it was obvious that the Democrats could no longer form a uniform opinion regarding the issue of a conservative merger.

At first the internal division within the Democratic Party reflected ideological and policy differences. The most vocal opposition to the merger option came from the former Cooperativist members on the left represented by

[28] Note, for example, that the statement Hatoyama made before the election in response to Ogata's remark was almost instantaneously confirmed by other influential party members.

Kenzo Matsumura and Takeo Miki. Subsequently, however, an even more critical rift emerged between Hatoyama and the rest of the Democrats. The initial symptom of such a rift surfaced when Hatoyama made his "Karuizawa statement" in early August. This statement upset other party leaders who obviously had not been consulted beforehand. Hatoyama continued to use various opportunities, throughout the month of September, such as press conferences and public speeches, to express his reluctance about the conservative merger. In contrast, Party Secretary Nobusuke Kishi began to take the initiative in facilitating the dialogue with the Liberals, putting together a two-step proposal: (1) that the merger would take place under Hatoyama during the year, and (2) that Ogata would replace him in the spring. When this plan was endorsed by another hopeful in the party, Agriculture Minister Ichiro Kohno, Hatoyama clearly lost his leadership role in the negotiations with the Liberals.

The growing discord between Hatoyama, on the one hand, and Kishi and Kohno, on the other, cannot be explained without exploring the different incentives of those individuals. Hatoyama's goal was simple: to remain prime minister at least for another year. Thus, for Hatoyama, a cooperative arrangement with the Liberals was simply a means to avoid the passage of a nonconfidence motion and to manage the present political situation so as to prolong his premiership. Hatoyama preferred coalition over a merger because in the latter he would inevitably have to face a leadership contest with the Liberal leader, Ogata. In such a case, his age and poor health might be an issue. In the former scenario, Hatoyama would likely continue to lead the coalition; furthermore, as soon as the next year's budget was passed, he could disband the coalition, call an election, and even seek another term.

Of course one might expect that such opportunistic behavior would, in the long run, lead the Liberals to retaliate. Hatoyama did not have to worry about such retaliation, as he would be ready to retire by then. Other party members, however, still had their own promotion incentives and therefore had reason to be concerned about future dealings with the Liberals. Aspiring politicians like Kishi and Kohno, who hoped to take over the party leadership, did not necessarily want to sacrifice long-term relations with the Liberals for Hatoyama's immediate legislative gains; that is, they did not want to inherit the consequences of Hatoyama's *ex post* "defection" when it was they who would be in charge of bargaining with the Liberals. This explains why Kishi and Kohno took the initiative in the negotiations.

Caught between Hatoyama and the next generation of party leaders was Bukichi Miki, recognized as "number two" among the Democrats. Initially Miki sided with his long-time friend Hatoyama and criticized Kishi's two-step proposal, but when Kishi was joined by Kohno, Miki started to endorse the proposal as well. This change in Miki's behavior can be attributed to his own incentive to remain influential in the party. Miki knew, as did other party members, that because of his age he would not become the party leader or prime minister. His aim, therefore, was to remain "number two" even after

Hatoyama retired. Since Kishi and Kohno represented the voice of rank-and-file members concerned with the future, Miki's support for the Kishi-Kohno plan was decisive in isolating Hatoyama within the party.[29]

In contrast to the Democrats, the Liberals retained their party's cohesiveness during most stages of the negotiations. United under their immediate goal of making their leader Ogata the next prime minister, there was no room for a comparable intergenerational division to emerge. True, the interests of Ogata and of others, especially Banboku Ohno, seemed to diverge toward the end, Ogata insisting on the principle of an open election of the new party leader and Ohno willing to compromise on this principle. This division, however, was of little consequence to the events that followed because, as discussed below, Ogata's hard-line stance had already lost credibility as a result of the development in the rival political camp: reunification of the Socialists.

The Democrats' Comeback

During the last stage of negotiations, the balance of bargaining power started to shift in the Democrats' favor. When the two parties agreed on the date of the merger, the question of the new party leader was postponed, as the Democrats had hoped. The final compromise also favored the Democrats because Hatoyama did not have to face a leadership contest immediately. Although it was called "collective leadership," Hatoyama, as prime minister, retained the formal power of appointing cabinet ministers and other influential government officials.

The Democrats' apparent comeback was influenced by the expected timing of the merger in relation to the schedule of other relevant political events. The Liberals had to take seriously the proposal put forth by the Democrats (i.e., Kishi-Kohno), in so far as it called for an early merger. As argued earlier, the Liberals could not wait too long to conclude the merger agreement because, according to convention, the next year's budget would have to be drafted by the end of December. Thus the Democrats knew that the Liberals would not walk away from the negotiating table even if they could not agree on the exact procedure for selecting the new leader.

Furthermore, the prospect that the Socialist reintegration would take place in October imposed a significant constraint on the Liberals' strategy. The united Socialists would surpass the Liberals as the second largest parliamentary force. This meant that, were the two conservative parties to fail in their negotiations and the Hatoyama government to fall, the Socialists' influence would likely increase in the next round of the government formation process, the worst case scenario for the Liberals.[30]

[29] Miki died in July 1956 before Hatoyama decided to retire.

[30] According to commentary in *Asahi Shimbun*, September 14, 1955, this was precisely the calculation that had led Kishi to engineer his two-step proposal, despite his senior party member

For this reason the Liberals softened their position *immediately after* the Socialists formally reintegrated themselves on October 13. Liberal leader Ogata continued to insist on an open election for the new party president and repeatedly threatened to walk out on the negotiations. The credibility of his threat, however, was undermined by the fact that the Liberals were no longer the largest opposition party in Parliament. The Democrats knew that the stakes involved in the success of the conservative liaison were now much higher for the Liberals.

When the Liberals agreed that the merger would proceed without the issue of the leadership being decided, it was clear that the Democrats would dominate the remainder of the negotiations. The Democrats' advantage over the Liberals continued after the merger took place, because they no longer had to be concerned with legislative difficulties over the next year's budget. Ogata's sudden death decisively disadvantaged the former Liberals within the new party. No other candidate within their camp was comparable to Ogata in experience and leadership. Their frustration was reflected in the fact that, although no former Liberal candidate was running against Hatoyama, many ballots were deliberately spoiled in the April election of the LDP president.

Hence the choice of Hatoyama as the LDP's first president was the product of two factors. First, the changing legislative environment, namely, the rise of the reintegrated Socialists as the second largest parliamentary force, had shifted the balance of bargaining power in favor of the Democrats. The second and more exogenous factor was the sudden death of Ogata, which left Hatoyama as the only viable candidate in the spring presidential election.

Theoretical Implications

In the positive literature on coalition governments, a political party is usually treated as a "given," and the outcome of the coalition is predicted on the basis of each party's parliamentary strength, which is defined exogenously by the results of the previous election. In the real world, however, political parties sometimes merge (and also split) between elections, creating new parties, changing the distribution of seats, and thus altering the basic legislative environment for party competition. The above case study on the process that led to the creation of the LDP in 1955 provides insight into this largely unexplored theoretical area.

On the surface, the partisan incentives for a formal merger can be considered similar to those for the formation of an ordinary coalition. In a parliamen-

---

Miki's objection. This commentary also notes that Kishi was concerned that a failure of the conservative merger negotiations would lead to an early election in which the newly integrated Socialists would win the most seats. Such a development would be detrimental to both the Liberals and the Democrats, thus strengthening their incentive to merge.

tary democracy, a political party without a majority has to search for a partner or partners to form a stable government and to pass the bills it proposes. This basic logic also applied to negotiations between the Liberals and Democrats: the starting point was clearly the legislative need for Hatoyama's minority government to pass laws, and especially to pass the annual budget.

Based on the analysis given in the previous section, however, critical differences can also be identified in the circumstances under which political parties prefer a merger to a coalition. The Liberals preferred a merger because it would require coordination of policy platforms, integration of party finances, and generally a long-term commitment from the Democrats. Without such a commitment, the Liberals' support for Hatoyama's government during the present period might not be appropriately rewarded by the Democrats in the future. The same was true for Socialist reunification. The Left-Wing Socialists proposed a formal reunification, as opposed to other lower-level cooperative arrangements, because they wanted to control the Right Wing's postelection opportunism and thus prevent its pursuit of a liaison with the Democrats. Thus a merger takes place in the "shadow of the future," that is, in the iterative context in which parties are expected to deal with one another again. If there were no concerns about the future, there would be no credibility problem, and thus no practical difference between a merger and coalition.

Contemporary studies on coalition governments have not adequately dealt with the issue of mergers between existing parties, as these studies typically assume that the game of coalition building is a single-shot game. One justification for this may be that, in so far as electoral results are analytically exogenous, a term of government can be identified simply as the period between elections. The above case study on the creation of the LDP suggests, however, that considerable political bargaining takes place even within one inter-election period. Because the incumbent government is responsible for drafting and implementing the national budget annually, it may have to engineer a legislative coalition frequently. Thus, regardless of the timing of elections, political parties repeatedly interact with one another and expect to deal with one another in the future.

Iteration, of course, was not the only factor that led to the successful merger of Japan's two conservative parties. Unlike the Left-Wing Socialists (vis-à-vis the Right Wing), the Liberals did not have the option of making the Democrats run an electoral campaign on the merger issue so as to increase the "audience costs" and thus the credibility of the rival party's merger offer. Although it would have been more difficult to withdraw from an already merged party than from a coalition, the Democrats could still have reneged on their offer to the Liberals once the merger was complete.[31]

[31] For example, when the idea of extending Hatoyama's term surfaced contrary to the Kishi-Kohno proposal, the former Liberals had no way of enforcing the original promise, although this problem became moot because of Ogata's death.

What, then, was the key that made the creation of the LDP possible? As illustrated above, the nature of the game in which the Democrats and the Liberals were engaged in 1955 was not only iterative but was also complex in that the interparty negotiations were "nested" with the intraparty power struggle.[32] If the Democratic Party had been cohesive under Hatoyama's leadership, the Liberals might have walked away from the negotiating table, convinced that the Democrats would renege anyway. Within the Democratic Party, Hatoyama himself vehemently opposed the formal merger fearing it might shorten his premiership. What overcame the Liberal suspicion was the internal division or perhaps the diverging interests between Hatoyama and the next generation of Democratic leaders. Driven by their own incentives to seek office and achieve a promotion, Kishi and Kohno, backed by Miki, in effect stole the leadership role in the negotiations from Hatoyama. For the Liberals it was critical that they knew Hatoyama was no longer running the show.

In the previous chapter, which analyzed the formation of the coalition in 1947, I raised the hypothesis that the centrist party, although having bargaining leverage over the peripheral parties, may be more prone to internal ideological conflicts. The notion of the nested game discussed here also questions the prevailing assumption and suggests yet another insight regarding the endogeneity of a party's unity; that is, in the iterative context, the incumbent party, like the Democrats, is more likely to be susceptible to intergenerational splits within the party. In the opposition parties, like the Liberals, on the other hand, the relationship between the current leaders and the next generation of leaders is likely to be cohesive precisely because the parties are not yet in power; only after their leader becomes prime minister does their internal strife surface and become analytically significant.

In sum, two theoretical implications can be drawn from the above analysis of the creation of the LDP. First, a formal merger of existing parties, as opposed to the formation of a coalition, results from a party's desire to increase the credibility of the incumbent party's offer to form a coalition. Second, the success of the merger negotiations depends, at least in part, on the "nestedness" of the game, which affects the likelihood of diverging incentives between the current leader and the next generation of leaders within the governing party.

Ogata's Death and Its Long-Term Consequences

As indicated earlier, an exogenous factor, namely, the sudden death of the former Liberal leader Ogata, was crucial for the immediate survival of the LDP as a unified party. Before the formation of the LDP, both the Liberals (under Yoshida) and the Democrats (under Hatoyama) had experienced the

[32] For a pioneering study on this concept and its applications, see Tsebelis, *Nested Games*.

legislative difficulties inherent in minority governments; thus both were motivated to opt for a stable majority government. It was also possible, however, that the leadership contest scheduled in the spring of 1956 could have torn the party apart, especially if Hatoyama had sought to extend his term beyond what had been offered in the Democrats' original (Kishi-Kohno) proposal. Clearly it was Ogata's sudden death that left no other option but to elect Hatoyama as the first LDP president, thus making this sensitive issue beside the point.

Ogata's death also had critical long-term implications for the LDP's fate. As originally specified in the Kishi-Kohno proposal, there was a consensus among party members that Ogata would replace Hatoyama as the next party leader. Although its exact timing left room for disagreement, the transfer of power from the former Democrat leader to the former Liberal leader was taken for granted. Essentially, then, the final compromise the two parties reached was based not so much on a division of labor as on the idea of a rotation between Hatoyama and Ogata. In other words, there was an implicit agreement that for the next few years first Hatoyama and then Ogata would form the Japanese government.[33]

Ogata's death prevented this rotation from occurring and, in the long run, rendered the original party division entirely irrelevant. By the time of Hatoyama's retirement, eight major factions had emerged within the party. These were initially based on the old partisan lines, as they were led by four former Liberals and four former Democrats.[34] The absence of a former Liberal contender to Hatoyama at the first presidential selection, however, made the post-Hatoyama leadership contest open to all aspiring leaders at once. In fact, during the party convention to elect the second LDP president held in December 1956, the above leaders began to form alliances beyond the old party lines. The newly chosen leader, Tanzan Ishibashi, was supported by former Democratic factions as well as former Liberals.[35] Subsequently, these factions became the LDP's distinctive organizational feature, but the strife among fac-

[33] Needless to say, the arrangement of rotation is not a phenomenon unique to the Japanese context. Political parties representing diverse interests often, as a convention, alternate party leaders with different regional, ethnic, and ideological backgrounds. For an insightful interpretation of a similar arrangement in early Stuart England, see Ferejohn, "Rationality and Interpretation."

[34] The eight politicians were former Democrats Nobusuke Kishi, Ichiro Kohno, Takeo Miki, and Tanzan Ishibashi and former Liberals Hayato Ikeda, Eisaku Sato, Banboku Ohno, and Mitsujiro Ishii.

[35] Initially three candidates ran: Ishibashi, supported by the Ishibashi, Miki, and Ohno factions; Kishi, supported by the Kishi, Kohno, and Sato factions; and Ishii, supported by the Ishii and Ikeda factions. In the first ballot, Kishi won the largest number of party delegate votes (223), Ishibashi the second largest (151), and Ishii the third largest (137). Based on a prior agreement between the Ishibashi and Ishii camps, Ishii's support was added to Ishibashi's on the second ballot. Thus, throughout this nomination process, the alliances were clearly made beyond the original Liberal-Democrat division.

tions within the LDP was not as colored by differences in ideology and policy preferences as it would have been had these factions inherited their original partisan mold. One might argue, then, that Ogata's death had an unforeseen impact in shaping the pattern of the LDP's internal political dynamics.

Of course the pattern of factionalization had to change over the thirty-eight years of the LDP's governance. The above factions competed for party leadership until the late 1960s, despite minor splits and realignments, but the last two decades of the LDP's rule witnessed a more significant change in this pattern. As I elaborate in the next chapter, however, this change had nothing to do with policy or ideological orientation. The original division between the Liberals and Democrats therefore never resurfaced throughout the LDP's one-party dominance.

The key to understanding the creation of the LDP lies in the basic logic of government formation under the competitive multiparty system. In the previous chapter I established that Japanese party politics during the first decade of the postwar period operated under such a system, and I examined the 1947 coalition building experience in detail. In this chapter I have analyzed the interparty bargaining process in 1955, with an attempt to account for the differences in the outcomes between those two cases. Regardless of the different outcomes, however, the above analysis reveals that political parties, as well as individual politicians involved in the negotiations, were acting strategically to further their own electoral and promotional incentives.

In reconstructing these events, I have attempted to explain the seemingly puzzling behavior of the major parties involved: Why did the Left-Wing Socialists propose reunification with their Right-Wing counterparts before the election? Why did the Liberals and Democrats not agree to the merger before the election? Why were the Democrats able to form a minority government? Why did the Liberals insist on a merger as opposed to a coalition, whereas the Democrats preferred the opposite? And how was it possible that the Liberals reached an agreement with the Democrats while Democrat leader Hatoyama was reluctant to enter a merger? These questions cannot be answered adequately by the conventional perspectives that view the creation of the LDP largely as a product of change in Japan's underlying socio-ideological foundations. Even though such a macrostructural cause may have been at work, the microanalytic focus certainly increases the scope and power of explanation, as demonstrated in the above analysis.

6

THE EVOLUTION OF THE LDP'S INTRAPARTY POLITICS

DURING ITS thirty-eight years of one-party rule, the LDP's intraparty dynamics were shaped by interactions among competing factions. As discussed in the previous chapter, soon after the inception of the LDP these factions began to take shape beyond original party divisions and became the central organizational units within the party. Over the long period of the LDP's reign, a series of attempts to dissolve factions altogether was undertaken internally, based on the recognition that intense interfactional struggle for party leadership led to excessive "money politics." Factionalism, however, persisted within the LDP and did not lead to the breakup of the party until 1993.[1] It is now widely believed that factionalism had positive effects in sustaining the LDP's predominant rule, as the change in party leadership (and therefore the prime minister) from one factional leader to another transformed the party's public image and usually enhanced the popularity of the LDP government.[2]

Although factions were thus unquestionably the distinctive organizational feature of the LDP, the pattern of factionalization was not static throughout the LDP's governance. Particularly over the last two decades of its rule numerous changes took place: the number of competing factions was reduced, their membership increased, and they became more formal political entities with well-defined functional branches. Moreover, there emerged within the LDP a new set of institutionalized norms that governed their interactions. A seniority rule regulated the promotion of individual politicians according to the number of times they had been reelected. Further, interfactional balancing principles, such as proportionality and separation of powers, affected the appointment of cabinet portfolios and of important positions within the party.

In this chapter I examine the determinants of the evolution of factional politics within the LDP. In the conventional analyses, the internal organizational attributes of the LDP were often explained in terms of Japanese traditional culture, psychology, and social behavior. It is difficult, however, for such conventional views to explain the developments that took place during the last twenty years of the LDP's rule. This chapter offers an alternative microanalytic explanation that highlights individual political actors seeking to further their incentives and their

[1] The creation of the New Liberal Club by a group of politicians who left the LDP in 1976 was not a result of interfactional strife. For a discussion of the 1993 situation, see chapter 8.

[2] See Ishikawa, *Deeta: Sengo Seiji-shi* [A data history of postwar politics], pp. 210–12.

competitive and strategic behavior under the given institutional constraints. More specifically, I argue that the pattern of factionalization within the LDP was primarily determined by the electoral incentives of two sets of rational actors, LDP politicians and LDP supporters, operating under such institutional constraints as electoral laws and political funding regulations. I also argue that the party's organizational norms originated in the promotional incentives of LDP politicians whose strategies were influenced by the uncertainty in the dynamics of the interfactional political process.

The chapter begins with a brief summary of the origins and development of the LDP factions and of the evolution of institutionalized norms within the party. The conventional approach is then evaluated and its inadequacy demonstrated. An alternative explanation is proposed based on the microanalytic framework. The chapter closes with a discussion of the implications of the analysis presented here and speculates on the post-1993 development of LDP factions.

The Evolution of the LDP's Factional Politics

Soon after the inception of the party in 1955, the LDP factions became the central units functioning as an important liaison between the party and individual Liberal Democrats. By the end of 1957 eight factions led by eight powerful leaders had emerged as a distinct organizational feature of the LDP. Despite minor splits and realignments, all of these factions competed for party leadership until the late 1960s.

After that, however, the pattern of factionalization in the LDP changed in at least three major ways. First, the number of major LDP factions was reduced to five and remained at that number. There were four relatively large factions and a fifth smaller faction. From 1972 to 1993 all of the Japanese prime ministers were selected from these five factions. Other minor factions that had often played a pivotal role in the selection of the new party leaders either disappeared or merged with others. Smaller groups tended to depart from the five factions when there was a change in factional leadership, but these defecting groups also tended to disappear eventually or merge with the major factions.[3]

Second, partly because they absorbed the members of the smaller groups, the major factions grew significantly in size. In 1972 the average number of LDP incumbents belonging to each of the five factions was about sixty-five; by 1989, the number had increased to eighty-two.[4] The number of Liberal

[3] For a detailed lineage of LDP factions, see Sato and Matsuzaki, *Jiminto Seiken* [The LDP's rule], p. 241. This tendency was finally broken in 1993 when the faction led by former prime minister Noboru Takeshita split into two groups, one of which, led by Tsutomu Hata, eventually left the LDP. See chapter 8 for an analysis of this process.

[4] It is extremely difficult to identify exactly who belonged to which faction and thus to determine the precise number in each faction. Although, technically, factional membership must in-

Democrats not belonging to these five factions, including nonaffiliated independents, was declining consistently (see Figure 6.1).

Third, even as realignment and expansion altered the external appearance of LDP factions, so their internal profiles changed as well. The LDP factions were transformed from groups of leaders with entourages into more formal political entities with permanent offices in Tokyo and well-defined functional branches.[5] In addition to the post of vice chairman (who is the counterpart of the party vice president), each of the five major factions established three important positions corresponding to the "Big Three" of the LDP: the Secretary-General, the chairman of the Executive Council, and the chairman of the Policy Affairs Research Council (PARC). Thus the formal structure of each LDP faction came to mirror that of the party itself.

As the organizational structure of the LDP changed, so did the mode of interaction between LDP factions and individual Liberal Democrats. Ad hoc summit meetings between factional leaders ceased to be the dominant mode of resolving disputes and adjusting conflicting interests. Instead, the management of interfactional politics became more dependent on a set of organizational norms or institutionalized rules and principles.

These norms dealt, in particular, with the issue of promotion within the party, that is, with the appointment of individual members to a limited number of important public positions. The best-documented of these is the seniority system, an institutionalized ladder of success that each LDP politician had to climb. To move up a step, a politician was required to win a certain number of elections (see Table 6.1).

This seniority rule was rigidly administered within the party until it handed over power to the non-LDP coalition in 1993.[6] Moreover, because each LDP politician usually advanced by specializing in a particular issue area, the institutionalized system of promotion contributed to the development of so-called policy tribes (*zoku*)—groups of politicians who developed skills and knowledge in their specialized fields. These policy tribes were said to exert significant influence on policy-making processes that had hitherto been dominated by powerful bureaucrats.[7]

Another important party norm dealt with the distribution of powerful positions among the five major factions. Two principles were in operation, one for the distribution of cabinet portfolios and the other for the distribution of important positions within the party. The central principle in the distribution of

---

clude only elected members of the Diet, there were always some who were temporarily out of office but were strongly affiliated with their factions. Even with the short-term fluctuations owing to such electoral turnover, however, the increase in the average factional membership was an undeniable trend.

[5] Iseri, *Habatsu Saihensei* [Factional realignment].

[6] See Sato and Matsuzaki, *Jiminto Seiken.*

[7] Muramatsu and Krauss, "Bureaucrats and Politicians in Policymaking"; Inoguchi and Iwai, *"Zoku Giin" no Kenkyu* [A study of "policy tribes"].

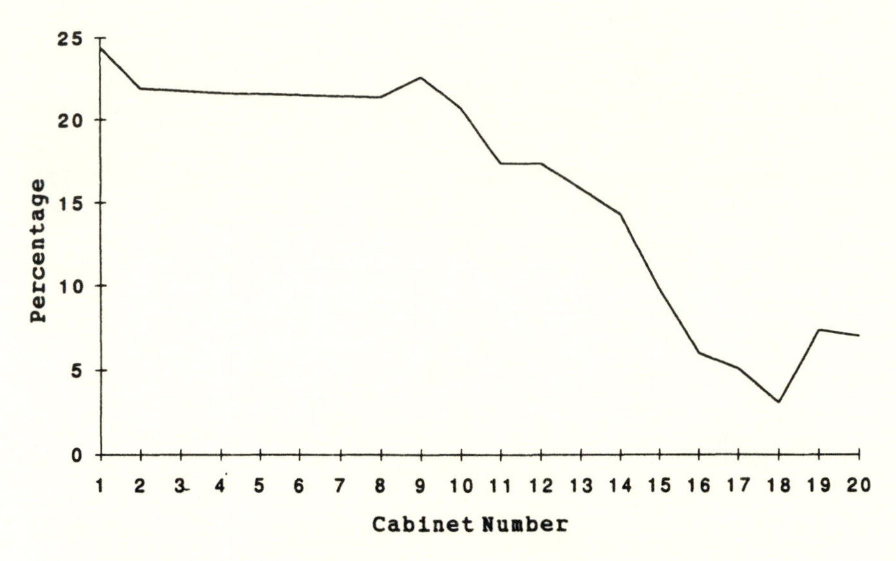

Cabinet #	*Date*	*Cabinet Name*
1	July 1972	Dai Ichiji Tanaka Naikaku
2	Dec. 1972	Dai Niji Tanaka Naikaku
3	Nov. 1973	Dai Niji Tanaka Kaizo Naikaku
4	Nov. 1974	Dai Niji Tanaka Sai-Kaizo Naikaku
5	Dec. 1974	Miki Naikaku
6	Dec. 1975	(vice ministers shuffled)
7	Sept. 1976	Miki Kaizo Naikaku
8	Dec. 1976	Fukuda Naikaku
9	Nov. 1977	Fukuda Kaizo Naikaku
10	Dec. 1978	Dai Ichiji Ohira Naikaku
11	Nov. 1979	Dai Niji Ohira Naikaku
12	July 1980	Suzuki Naikaku
13	Nov. 1981	Suzuki Kaizo Naikaku
14	Nov. 1982	Dai Ichiji Nakasone Naikaku
15	Dec. 1983	Dai Niji Nakasone Naikaku
16	Nov. 1984	Dai Niji Nakasone Kaizo Naikaku
17	Dec. 1985	Dai Niji Nakasone Sai-Kaizo Naikaku
18	July 1986	Dai Sanji Nakasone Naikaku
19	Nov. 1987	Takeshita Naikaku
20	Dec. 1988	Takeshita Kaizo Naikaku

Figure 6.1: Percentage of Liberal Democrats Not Belonging to the Five Factions. *Source*: Sato and Matsuzaki, *Jiminto Seiken* [The LDP's rule], p. 243; reports in *Asahi Shimbun* on each cabinet change.

TABLE 6.1
The LDP's Seniority System

Ladder of Public Roles	*Number of Reelections Required for Advancement*
House Committee Member or Vice Chair of a PARC Committee	2
Vice Minister	3
Chair of a PARC Committee	4
House Committee Chair	5
Minister	6 or more

cabinet offices was proportionality. Since the late 1960s, the number of ministerial positions assigned to each faction whenever the cabinet was re-formed or shuffled closely corresponded to the relative strength of the faction within the party, as measured by the number of affiliated LDP incumbents.[8]

The most vital positions within the party were distributed according to the principle of separation of powers. The president and the "Big Three" of the party were customarily chosen from four different factions. And the director of the party Treasury Bureau, in charge of the LDP's financial affairs, tended to be nominated from a faction other than that of the president or the secretary-general.[9]

Although these norms remained uncodified, they imposed substantial constraints on the political behavior of factions and individual Liberal Democrats. Thus, for example, when in 1972 Prime Minister Kakuei Tanaka deliberately violated the principle of proportionality in cabinet appointments by underrepresenting the rival faction of Takeo Fukuda and overrepresenting his own, Fukuda initially opposed having members of his faction take part in the Tanaka cabinet. Fukuda's resistance eventually paid off, and Tanaka restored the interfactional balance in his first cabinet shuffle. Facing similar opposition from other factions, LDP President Masayoshi Ohira was pressured in 1978 to abandon the idea of appointing his loyal disciple, Zenko Suzuki, as party secretary.[10] Both examples indicate that these norms had gained legitimacy within the party and were accepted as the standard mechanisms for avoiding and managing interfactional conflicts.

In sum, the 1970s and 1980s witnessed a manifold change in the organiza-

[8] Ishikawa, *Deeta: Sengo Seiji-shi*, pp. 219–21.

[9] Sato and Matsuzaki, *Jiminto Seiken*, pp. 71–72.

[10] Ohira eventually appointed Kunikichi Saito, a more senior member of his own faction. This appointment, however, should be seen as an exceptional face-saving compromise because Saito was respected by all Liberal Democrats for his earnest personality.

tion of the LDP. LDP factions were transformed in number, size, and structure. Moreover, the establishment of party norms generated highly regular and predictable appointments and promotions within the LDP. Such routinization had the important effect of stabilizing interfactional strife.

Conventional Interpretations

As discussed in chapter 2, one of the dominant theoretical approaches underlying much of the contemporary work on Japanese politics is the political-culture approach. Although Japanologists do not wholly ignore other explanatory factors, resorting to Japanese culture and social behavior to explain the organization of the LDP is ubiquitous in the literature.

For example, in his classic analysis of the LDP, Nathaniel Thayer argued that factions initially started as informal organizational units rooted in a kind of indigenous Japanese clientalism based on the value of personal trust and "long-term commitments" between bosses and followers. Thayer also attributed the factionalization of the LDP to the nature of Japanese social behavior and Japanese psychology:

> Japan has spent more than a century trying to catch up with the modern world. To be judged old-fashioned is the political death sentence. . . . But the Dietman feels a little uncomfortable in its glare; he talks new but thinks old, and continues to look to his faction for both comfort and support. . . . [The factions] have adopted the social values, customs, and relationships of an older Japan. . . . The old concepts of loyalty, hierarchy, and duty hold sway in them. And the Dietman (or any other Japanese) feels very comfortable when he steps into this world.[11]

The notion that LDP factions were the product of traditional attributes of Japanese society is still prevalent. In their textbook written in the mid-1980s, Bradley Richardson and Scott Flanagan note that "most explanations [for LDP factions] mention the importance of leader-follower relationships in Japanese history, and sometimes the factions are seen as an extension into the present of traditional *oyabun-kobun*, or patron-client relationships."[12] Richardson and Flanagan themselves do not describe contemporary factions as "purely traditional" entities, stressing various functional needs for their existence. However, they view LDP factions as "political clubs united around a core group of leaders," and thus they still perceive the role of patron-client bonds in sustaining and promoting factionalization within the LDP.

A similar view is also presented by Hans Baerwald. In predicting the continuation of the LDP factions, he argues that "factions and subfactions have been components of Japan's society for a very long time, much longer than the

[11] Thayer, *How the Conservatives Rule Japan*, p. 41.

[12] Richardson and Flanagan, *Politics in Japan*, p. 102.

period since the Meiji Restoration in 1868. . . . There have been the 'clan oligarchs' (*hanbatsu*), the 'militarists' (*gunbatsu*), 'family lineages' (*iegara*), 'higher school and university ties' (*gakubatsu*) *ad infinitum*." Baerwald continues: "Hence, to anticipate or wish that factionalism could or should be eliminated from the LDP . . . is to expect this political party to become something other than a Japanese organization."[13]

As is evident from this brief review, the political-culture approach, in explaining the LDP factions, emphasizes the continuity of Japanese traditional attributes. Such a view is problematic in so far as it plays down the impact of the dramatic and ongoing process of Japan's modernization/Westernization. Even more critical is that, as discussed in chapter 2, the political-culture approach is too deterministic to provide predictions; that is, it cannot adequately explain the evolution of the LDP's intraparty politics over the years.

With regard to the emergence of the LDP's organizational norms, for example, it is taken for granted that the seniority and interfactional balancing principles were the product of cultural factors, such as the system of conveying honor and respect embedded in the Confucian tradition and the consensus-oriented nature of Japanese social behavior. Gerald Curtis, for example, observes that the kind of norms that had emerged within the LDP exist in Japanese society more generally, and he analogizes the rule for promotion in the LDP with that in Japanese private firms.[14]

The organizational norms of the LDP, however, cannot simply be seen as the products of Japanese societal characteristics because those norms were not present in the party from its inception. The LDP's seniority system, for instance, was not an established mechanism of promotion in the early days of the party. As Seizaburo Sato and Tetsuhisa Matsuzaki point out, there were many examples of *batteki jinji* (leap-frog promotion) during these earlier years, whereby LDP representatives in the Diet became cabinet ministers with fewer than five terms in the House of Representatives or with fewer than two terms in the House of Councillors. The far-right column of Table 6.2 indicates the ratio of such promotions to the total number of LDP politicians who became cabinet ministers for the first time under each prime minister. Thus, as Sato and Matsuzaki conclude, it was not until the long reign of Prime Minister Sato (1965–72) that the seniority rule was established as the mechanism for promotion. And it was only during the 1980s that this system came to be rigidly implemented within the party.

The interfactional balancing principles were also relatively recent innovations. Proportionality, for example, was not in effect before the late 1960s. Until then, interfactional politics within the LDP did not reflect the "honorific system" or the "consensus-oriented" nature of Japanese culture and tradition.

[13] Baerwald, *Party Politics in Japan*, p. 17.

[14] Curtis, *Japanese Way of Politics*, pp. 88–89.

TABLE 6.2
Appointment of Cabinet Ministers[a]

Prime Minister	*Date Took Office*	*# of Cabinet Shuffles*	*# of First-Time Ministers Promoted*	*# of "Leap-Frog" Promotions*	*Percentage of Leap-Frog Promotions to All First-Time Ministerial Promotions*
Hatoyama	Nov. 1955	3	24	6	25.0
Ishibashi	Dec. 1956	1	13	4	30.8
Kishi	July 1957	3	21	3	14.3
Ikeda	July 1960	6	42	1	2.3
Sato	June 1965	7	46	0	0
Tanaka	July 1972	4	27	3	11.1
Miki	Dec. 1974	2	15	0	0
Fukuda	Dec. 1976	2	17	4	23.5
Ohira	Dec. 1978	2	28	2	7.1
Suzuki	July 1980	2	17	0	0
Nakasone	Nov. 1982	5	60	0	0
Takeshita	July 1987	2	21	0	0
Uno	June 1989	1	11	0	0
Kaifu	Aug. 1989	2	23	0	0

Source: Sato and Matsuzaki, *Jiminto Seiken* [The LDP's rule], p. 43; and *Asahi Shimbun*, July 23, 1986; November 7, 1987; December 28, 1988; June 3, 1989; August 10, 1989; and February 28, 1990.

[a]Excludes appointments of non-Diet persons.

The distribution of these positions clearly favored factions that were allied with the winner of the presidential selection both in quantity (the number of cabinet portfolios assigned to those factions; see Figure 6.2) and in quality (the "attractiveness" of the assigned positions).[15]

The principle of separation of powers was yet another party norm established only during the last two decades of the LDP's rule. From 1972 to 1993 Presidents Miki, Fukuda, Nakasone, Takeshita, Uno, Kaifu, and Miyazawa did not nominate a single person from their own factions for the "Big Three" positions; only one president, Tanaka, managed consistently to appoint the Secretary-General from his own faction. By contrast, during the 1950s and 1960s, LDP presidents selected at least one of the "Big Three" from their own factions.[16] Customarily the president nominated his right-hand man as the

[15] For the latter, see Leiserson, "Factions and Coalitions."

[16] The two exceptions were Ishibashi's appointment of party officials in 1956 and Ikeda's appointment in 1964. It is interesting that in both cases Takeo Miki was appointed as the secretary-general, and both Ishibashi and Ikeda became ill and resigned soon after making the appointments.

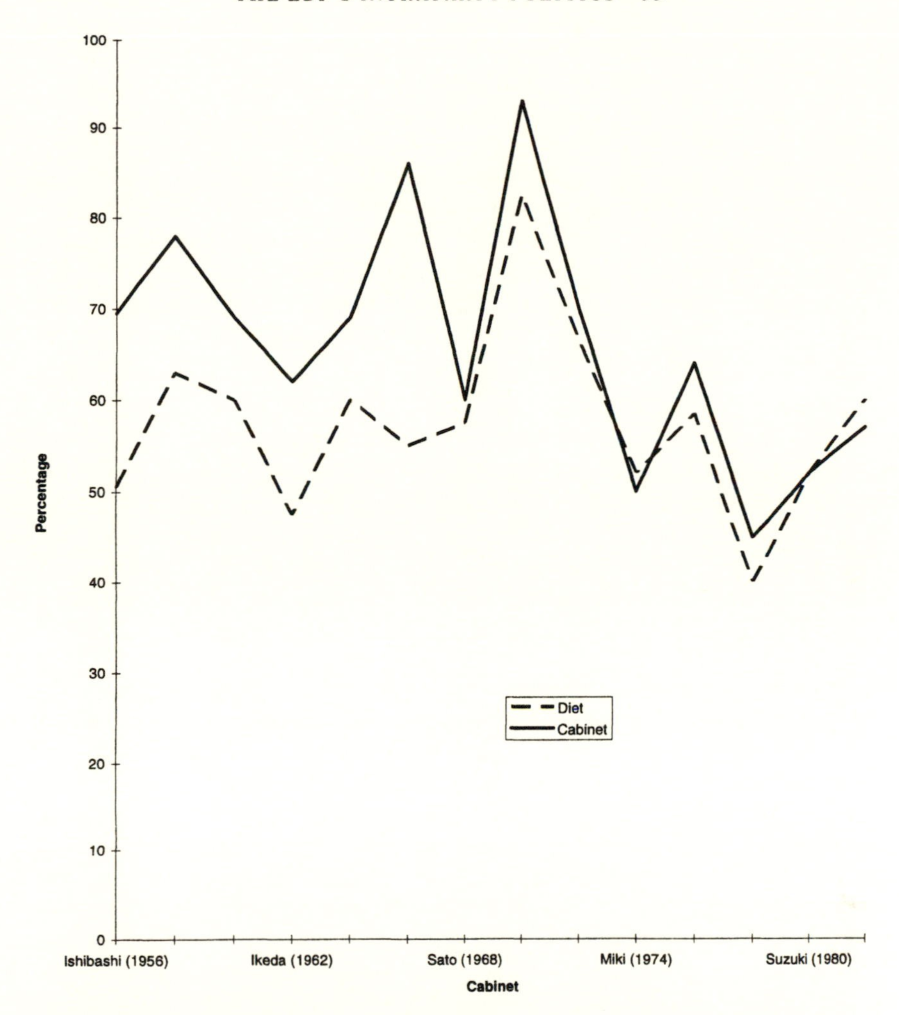

Figure 6.2: Distribution of Cabinet Portfolios and of Diet Seats for the "Mainstream" Factions Allied with the President. *Source*: Approximated from Sato and the Matsuzaki, *Jiminto Seiken* [The LDP's rule], p. 66, Figure 7.

Secretary-General; the secretary could then tend to internal party matters leaving the president, in his role as prime minister, free to concentrate on cabinet affairs. Similarly the rule of looking outside one's own faction for the director of the Treasury Bureau was established only during the last twenty years. Before 1974 this position was usually filled by someone from the president's (and the Secretary-General's) faction.

Thus the political-culture approach cannot explain the development of organizational norms within the LDP. That the seniority and interfactional balancing principles were once absent suggests that these norms did not derive from Japanese tradition and social behavior.

The political-culture approach is equally problematic with regard to the other important aspect of the LDP's intraparty politics: the pattern of factionalization. Some analysts argue that the changes in the number, size, and structure of LDP factions resulted primarily from the changes in Japanese political culture itself. Curtis observes that the patron-client bonds between bosses and followers played an essential role in maintaining factions in the past but these bonds became "much less evident in factional organization in the 1980s," as factions "evolved into less leader-dominated, more collegial structures." Curtis attributes this change not only to the progress of Japan's modernization in general but also to "generational change" in factional leadership: "All faction leaders today have inherited their factions, and there are few LDP politicians left who are cut out of the mold of the old-line political bosses who dominated the party's factional politics in early years."[17] With the disappearance of the party's founding fathers, the succession of leadership became the major source of conflict within each faction. Thus, according to Curtis, the dissolution of personal ties was the main cause for the regrouping of factions and for the organizational modernization to manage intrafactional strife.

This explanation, however, leaves important questions unanswered. Although it may be true that socioeconomic and demographic factors caused a decline of solidarity within each faction, it is not clear why these factors did not lead to the dissolution of all factions and thus to a complete transformation of the LDP's internal structure. Why, in particular, did five major factions survive the crises and not the others? Furthermore, although the political-culture approach may reveal the cause of the weakening of the old factional alignment, it does not explain why, and the extent to which, the remaining factions were able to expand and incorporate the members of the defunct smaller factions. Given the decline of personal bonds, what accounts for the entry of these members into other factions?

In sum, the conventional political-culture approach fails to explain the changes in the LDP that took place during the last twenty years of its governance. In the next section I offer an alternative microanalytic explanation.

Incentives, Institutional Context, and the LDP's Factional Politics

Consistent with the rest of this study, I assume in the following analysis that the two sets of political actors, politicians and voters, are rational in the stan-

[17] Curtis, *Japanese Way of Politics*, p. 81.

dard Schumperterian/Downsian sense. First, LDP politicians (like those affiliated with any other party) seek to increase the chance of their (re)election and, once (re)elected, they seek to pursue their promotion to more lucrative, prestigious, and powerful positions. Second, LDP supporters vote according to their "expected candidate differential" or the relative expected utility associated with different politicians' activities during their incumbency.[18]

Electoral Incentives and Factionalization of the LDP

Based on the above set of assumptions, let us reexamine some fundamental questions about the LDP: Why did factionalism persist? And why did the number, size, and structure of LDP factions change over the last two decades of its governance?

PERSISTENCE

The Japanese electoral system under the electoral law adopted in 1947 was known to be one in which it would be "relatively easy for any candidate to run" but would be "extremely difficult to win."[19] Suppose, for example, an LDP politician was ready to enter an electoral race for the first time. In order to run for office, the candidate was required to deposit only a relatively small amount of cash, which would be returned after the election if the candidate received approximately 5 percent of the votes cast. Thus, in entering an electoral race, there was no incentive to join any faction. However, in order to run an effective campaign and eventually win an election as an official LDP candidate, the incentive structure would be different. Several institutional constraints limited the range of options, and factional affiliation was almost a prerequisite for winning.

The incentive structure for individual candidates to affiliate with a major faction originated from two important characteristics of the 1947 electoral system. First, the law stipulated, with few exceptions, medium-sized districts

[18] This, of course, is a modified version of Anthony Downs's "expected party differential." Implicit in this modification is that the LDP supporters, because of their expectation that the party as a whole will win the largest number of seats, focus on the difference in the expected benefits associated with individual LDP candidates rather than on the difference at an interparty level. In addition, I assume that these actors seek to maximize their utility under two constraints: (1) a given set of institutional arrangements that affect the activities of political parties; and (2) the uncertainty involved in the dynamics of intraparty politics that influences actors' strategy of utility optimization. Implicit in the latter is that the impact of political dynamics at an interparty level is considered negligible and/or irrelevant as a source of the strategic behavior of LDP politicians and LDP supporters.

[19] Pempel, *Policy and Politics in Japan*, p. 36. For the political process through which this system was adopted, see chapter 3.

with three to five members in the House of Representatives.[20] Second, under this law, votes could not be transferred among the candidates from the same party (single nontransferable vote). In order to win a majority of seats, the LDP had to nominate two or more candidates in each electoral district because the house consisted of more than 500 delegates and the total number of electoral districts was 130. Since these candidates competed for the same pool of conservative voters, it would have been difficult for the party to develop a campaign for any particular candidate. Unable to rely on the party per se, the candidates were better off affiliating with the existing LDP factions for financial support and campaign expertise.

Candidates also had an incentive to join major LDP factions for the less tangible benefits associated with official party nomination, which were otherwise difficult to obtain. Under the system of medium-sized electoral districts and the single nontransferable vote, the LDP had to limit the number of candidates in each district in order to maximize its representation with the votes cast. As a consequence, the existing factions were always directly involved in determining party nominations to secure their "share" in the final list of nominees. Obviously this process favored incumbents, who were already affiliated with these factions; for new candidates this process provided an incentive to declare a firm and explicit commitment to some faction even before they knew whether they could run as official LDP candidates.[21]

Candidates might not have needed to rely so heavily on factional support and endorsement if the electoral environment were more generally such that smaller unknown candidates could compete efficiently with the veterans. But other institutional factors further amplified the disadvantage of being an independent Liberal Democrat or one with no factional affiliation.

The timing of elections under a parliamentary system is not periodic. Although the Japanese Constitution defines the maximum length of the inter-election period (four years), the exact timing of elections is determined by a host of factors such as pressure from the opposition, intraparty negotiations, and international events, as well as by macroeconomic considerations.[22] This advantaged factionally affiliated candidates over the independent Liberal Democrats even before an electoral campaign began: those who belonged to

[20] There was only one single-member district (in the Amami Island district). In the 1986 redistricting, one six-member district (Hokkaido) and four two-member districts (Ishikawa, Hyogo, Kagoshima, and Nigata prefectures) were created as exceptions.

[21] Because usually more candidates wanted to run for the LDP than the optimal number the party could nominate, the nomination process produced a strange phenomenon in many electoral districts: some candidates were running with support from LDP factions but without the official nomination of the party. Although this might split the conservative vote and thus work against the LDP, the net effect remained ambiguous. Should the officially nominated candidates lose and the unofficial candidates with factional support win, the LDP could (and did in fact) nominate the winners after the election in order to ensure its majority in the house.

[22] Kohno and Nishizawa, "A Study of the Electoral Business Cycle in Japan."

major factions and thus had frequent contact with influential senior members of the party were more likely to have inside information regarding the political schedule. Independents, in contrast, had to rely on newspapers and other public sources.

In addition to this asymmetry in access to political information, the independent Liberal Democrats were disadvantaged during the campaign period itself. Under a system of periodic elections it might be easier for less well-known candidates to run an efficient campaign by distributing their financial, personnel, and other resources to synchronize the peak of support with the predetermined timing of elections. An innovative campaign strategy might thus compensate for the lack of a bloc vote based on organizational support. In a country like Japan, however, strategy does not substitute for resources because no candidate can plan a sophisticated campaign schedule in advance to maximize the efficiency of resource allocation. In fact, precisely because of the uncertainty in the timing of elections, most candidates were likely to follow a similar conservative campaign strategy, waiting until the very last moment to launch a major offensive, by which time the election was already absolutely certain.

The relatively short Japanese campaign period is another institutional factor that worked to the disadvantage of Liberal Democrats running without factional endorsement. If it were longer, unknown candidates would have time to develop grassroots support, building up their reputations gradually and collecting political contributions along the way. According to the Japanese Constitution, however, a general election must be held within forty days of the date the House of Representatives is dissolved (Article 54). Candidates were thus limited to the resources at their disposal at the opening of the campaign; they could not rely on future political contributions.

In sum, electoral laws, nonperiodic elections, and the short campaign period constituted a set of institutional constraints. Factions persisted because they met the electoral incentives of rational LDP candidates; without factional affiliation, it was virtually impossible to win an election.[23]

[23] One can also argue that, from the perspective of LDP supporters, LDP factions had a rational foundation. Suppose a voter was calculating his "expected candidate differential" among two or more LDP candidates. The most important element in this calculation was his judgment about the relative ability of each local candidate to influence the central policy-making authority, such as high-ranking Japanese bureaucrats and/or influential members of policy tribes within the LDP. Whether his vote would be translated into tangible benefits depended almost entirely on this ability, which in turn depended on the candidate's background, especially her connections with the relevant ministries and bureaus, her relationship with senior LDP members, her experience, and her overall influence in the policy-making process. Obviously it would be extremely difficult and costly for the voter to collect such information for all candidates. The information might not have been available to the public, and even if it had been, it might not have been credible. The voter knew, however, that affiliation with a major LDP faction almost guaranteed the candidate a network of personal ties with the established elites and thus direct access to the policy-making

Optimal Size, Expansion and Structural Modernization

The tendency for LDP factions to persist, however, did not necessarily entail their expansion. In fact, LDP factions remained relatively constant in size throughout the 1950s and 1960s, which suggests the existence of an inherent optimal size of membership. What accounts for this optimality?

Because LDP factions, rather than the party itself, financed the campaigns of individual members under the 1947 electoral system, factional leaders were responsible for soliciting political funding from corporations and business associations. Some factional leaders may have been more effective fund-raisers of course, and it is therefore possible that some factions attracted more candidates than others and that the size of factions varied accordingly.[24] Obviously, however, the membership of an LDP faction could expand only to the limits of each leader's fund-raising capability. Such a point is a rationally induced equilibrium. Individual candidates could shop around until they found the faction that promised the best financial support; the size of a faction would thus have necessarily expanded up to this point and not beyond it.

In addition, there were sometimes clear disincentives for rational LDP candidates to join certain factions. If candidates were entering an electoral district that already had representatives of some factions, they would avoid affiliating with those factions. Even veteran candidates might want to change their affiliation from one faction to another if exogenous factors created similar disincentives.[25] Thus the Japanese electoral system generated two seemingly opposite dynamics. On the one hand, it encouraged an individual Liberal Democrat to join an LDP faction, thus promoting factional expansion. On the other hand, the system inhibited a particular LDP faction from expanding indefinitely, thus preventing a single faction from dominating the party.[26]

---

processes in important issue areas. In this sense, factional affiliation played a role similar to Downs's "political ideology": it helped voters make their voting decisions without knowing about every candidate specifically and in detail. See Downs, *An Economic Theory of Democracy*, pp. 96–113; and Ferejohn, "The Spatial Model and Elections."

[24] The Tanaka (and subsequently Takeshita) faction became the largest because of the leader's outstanding ability to raise political funds.

[25] There is ample evidence that these disincentives actually determined factional affiliation. A well-known example was the case of candidate Hayashi in Kochi prefecture. Hayashi had been an elected member of the House of Councillors, but he lost his seat in the July 1989 election (in which the LDP lost its majority in the upper house for the first time since 1955). In 1990 the House of Representatives was dissolved, and Hayashi decided to run in the February general election. Although he was originally a member of the Miyazawa faction, he knew that he would not receive factional endorsement because that faction already had representation in the lower house. Therefore, before the election, Hayashi left the Miyazawa faction for the Takeshita faction.

[26] Many examples of testimony by factional leaders during the 1950s and 1960s not only point to the existence of a certain optimal factional size but also confirm the basic logic of the explanation developed here. For example, Shojiro Kawashima, who led a minor faction, was once quoted as saying, "The appropriate size of a faction is about twenty five, given the financial constraints"

Given the optimality of membership size, what then explains the expansion of the factional membership during the 1970s and 1980s? Most directly, factional expansion was a consequence of the decrease in the number of viable factions from eight to five within the party. Because of "natural selection"—on which I elaborate in the next subsection—smaller factions disappeared during the last two decades. Individual Liberal Democrats who had been members of the smaller factions found that they were better off joining other factions than remaining independents. Thus the reduction in the number of factions changed the optimal size.

A more indirect but no less important factor was the 1975 revision of the political funding regulations. This revision came in the aftermath of the "Lockheed scandal," in response to sweeping public demand for reform of Japan's excessive "money politics." The revised law, with its many loopholes, had complex and pervasive implications.

On the one hand, the new law strictly limited political contributions from firms and business groups, thus making it more difficult and risky to attract large contributions at a party or factional level. On the other hand, it imposed no restrictions on political contributions from registered "political groups." Because there was no limit on the number of such political groups that could support a single politician, and because these political groups were exempt from filing a report on the original sources of contributions not exceeding a million yen per year, individual politicians had new incentives to raise political funds on their own. Tomoaki Iwai presents convincing evidence that LDP politicians tried to increase their financial autonomy by establishing many small political groups, thus diversifying their sources of political funding (see Figure 6.3).

In practice, however, the extent to which LDP politicians gained financial autonomy and the pace at which they did so varied. Although some veteran candidates became less dependent on factional support, other Liberal Democrats, especially those who were entering the electoral race for the first time, continued to rely on factions for financial support. This growing asymmetry in individual financial situations enabled factions to reallocate their resources for recruiting new candidates while spending less on maintaining the affiliation of their current members. In fact, each of the five major factions invested in modernizing its internal organizational structure in order to recruit new members more aggressively and more efficiently. New positions, such as the offices of secretariat and public relations, were specifically created within each fac-

(quoted in Sato and Matsuzaki, *Jiminto Seiken*, p. 61). Banboku Ohno, who led a major faction, is reported to have said that the optimal number was about forty. Beyond this number, he explained, factions would face three major problems: the possibility that members would have to compete within the same electoral district, the difficulty of soliciting sufficient contributions, and a shortage of cabinet and party positions for promotion (see Watanabe, *Habatsu:* [Factions], pp. 2–3).

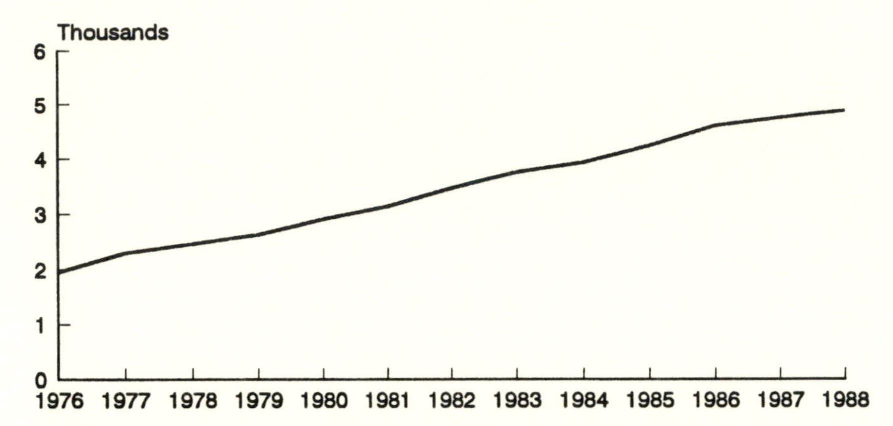

Figure 6.3: Political Groups Registered to the Ministry of Home Affairs. *Source*: Tomoaki Iwai, *"Seiji Shikin" no Kenkyu* [A study of "political funding"], p. 81.

tion for this purpose.[27] Somewhat paradoxically, then, the increased individual incentives for financial autonomy under the new regulations had the unforeseen consequence of facilitating both the expansion of factional membership and the modernization of factional structure.

To explain the structural modernization more fully, however, one must focus on one final factor: a major change in the incentives of a particular subset of LDP politicians—factional leaders. The Lockheed incident, which led to the reform of regulations concerning political funding, also had more indirect, psychological effects, especially because it resulted in the indictment and arrest on bribery charges of former prime minister Tanaka. Factional leaders had long monopolized the channels through which political funds were collected, but after Lockheed they became aware of the need to diversify these channels for the purpose of "risk allocation."[28]

Here lies the rational foundation for the restructuring of LDP factions: a de facto collective leadership in which some members shared responsibility for collecting political contributions within each faction was a rational response on the part of a leader to the increased, perceived threat of forfeiting his entire political future in a similar scandal. Because leaders began depersonalizing their funding channels, the decision-making authority within each faction became more decentralized to various functional branches and individual factional members.[29]

In sum, increased individual incentives for seeking financial autonomy

[27] *Asahi Shimbun*, December 12, 1987.

[28] Iwai, *"Seiji Shikin" no Kenkyu*, p. 106.

[29] Further discussion on the consequence of the "decentralization" of factional fund-raising practices can be found in Cox and Rosenbluth, "Electoral Fortunes."

originated in the new regulations governing political contributions, and these explain, at least in part, both the expansion of factional membership and the modernization of factional structure. The latter, however, was also a product of incentives for factional leaders to allocate the "risk" in collecting political contributions. And the former was also a more direct consequence of the dynamic selection process that reduced the number of viable factions, an issue addressed in the next subsection.

"Natural Selection" of LDP Factions

LDP factions seemed to have not only an optimal size but also an optimal number. During the last two decades of the LDP's rule, smaller factions had either disappeared or merged with the five factions, four relatively large ones and the fifth smaller faction, as summarized in Table 6.3. What generated this evolution of LDP factions?

Maurice Duverger, in his classic work on the relationship between the number of political parties and the electoral system, argues that the single-ballot plurality system brings about a two-party system. According to Duverger, this lawlike relationship exists because (1) rational politicians will leave losing parties that are underrepresented ("mechanical effect"), and/or (2) rational voters will not waste their votes on losers ("psychological factor").[30] Steven Reed has extended Duverger's law to the Japanese context and demonstrated empirically that "where *n* is the number of seats in the district . . . elections in simple plurality elections with multimember districts tend to produce competition among $n + 1$ candidates."[31] Duverger's notions of rational politicians and rational voters are consistent with the assumptions adopted in this chapter, and the basic logic of Duverger's law can be extended further to explain the selection process of factions within the LDP.

Obviously the size of each electoral district determines the number of candidates that the LDP (or any party) should nominate in that district: the number of candidates must not exceed *N*. One may aggregate this prediction and claim that the *maximum* number of LDP factions that could have existed under the 1947 electoral arrangement was five, given that there was only 1 district (out of 130) that elected more than five members to the House of Representatives. Such an aggregation might be problematic in a country where the autonomy of local government and political activities is relatively high owing to cultural, linguistic, and regional cleavages.[32] In the case of Japan, however,

[30] Maurice Duverger, *Political Parties.*

[31] Reed, "Structure and Behaviour," p. 336. Gary Cox has since provided a formal proof for Reed's argument (see Cox, "Strategic Voting Equilibria").

[32] See Douglas Rae's treatment of Canada as an exception to the simplest version of Duverger's proposition that plurality formulas cause a two-party system; Rae, *The Political Consequences of Electoral Laws*, p. 94.

TABLE 6.3
The Five Major Factions and Their Leaders

Four Large Factions:

Kakuei Tanaka → Noburu Takeshita[a]
Masayoshi Ohira → Zenko Suzuki → Kiichi Miyazawa
Takeo Fukuda → Shintaro Abe → Hiroshi Mitsuzuka
Yasuhiro Nakasone → Sosuke Uno[b] → Michio Watanabe

One Smaller Faction:

Takeo Miki → Toshio Komoto → Toshiki Kaifu[b]

[a]Takeshita faction broke into two groups in 1993.
[b]Uno and Kaifu became prime ministers, although they did not inherit factional leadership.

the LDP was indisputably a nationwide party that controlled the overwhelming majority of prefectural and municipal offices throughout the country. Given the absence of social cleavages, small localized factions were unlikely to develop. And even if they were to develop, they would have been likely to merge with one another in the long run in order to reduce various kinds of information and transaction costs. Thus it is reasonable to claim that the "rational abandonment" of losing factions in each electoral district led to the gradual elimination of smaller LDP factions at the aggregate party level.

The maximum number, of course, does not mean the optimal number. If rational abandonment is the key mechanism of the selection process, one would predict that the optimal number of LDP factions would be somewhere below five, given that only about a third of the total electoral districts were five-member districts, with the others electing fewer than five representatives. This prediction appears to be consistent with the observed reality that one of the five factions, the Miki/Komoto faction, was small relative to the other four.

To substantiate this claim, I have investigated the distribution of candidates from each faction across different types of electoral districts. If LDP politicians/supporters had disincentives to remain/support candidates of underrepresented factions, one would expect that the members of the fifth faction (the Miki/Komoto faction) and independents, as compared with members of the four larger factions, would be less likely to be candidates in the three-member districts and more likely in the five-member districts. Evidence from the 1990 general election, the last election before the LDP's rule came to an end, supports this hypothesis (see Table 6.4).

There is a considerable difference between the distribution of candidates across three types of electoral districts in the four large factions, on the one hand, and in the Komoto faction and among independents, on the other. Clearly Liberal Democrats who did not belong to one of the four major fac-

TABLE 6.4
Distribution of Factional Candidates in the 1990 Election[a]

	District Size				
Faction	*3*	*4*	*5*	*Other*	*Total*
			Candidates (%)		
Takeshita	24 (29)	24 (29)	34 (41)	1 (1)	83
Nakasone	22 (31)	21 (30)	23 (33)	4 (6)	70
Abe	23 (29)	28 (35)	26 (33)	2 (3)	79
Miyazawa	24 (31)	24 (31)	27 (35)	2 (3)	77
Komoto	6 (19)	10 (31)	14 (44)	2 (6)	32
Independents	5 (19)	3 (12)	14 (54)	4 (15)	26

Source: *Asahi Shimbun*, February 4, 1990.

[a]Includes candidates affiliated with a faction but without official party nomination at the time of election.

tions were more likely to become candidates in the five-member districts and less likely in the three-member districts. I have replicated the same analysis for a few other elections during the 1980s and found that the patterns of distribution were almost identical to the one reported above. The replicated results suggest that the composition of LDP factions, four large factions plus one small faction, was an equilibrium.[33]

In sum, natural selection of LDP factions occurred because, as Duverger would argue, it was rational for LDP politicians and supporters to abandon smaller factions that were underrepresented. The evidence from the few elections in the 1980s seems to indicate that under the 1947 electoral system the optimal number of LDP factions was just below five (four large and one small).

Promotional Incentives and the Rise of LDP Norms

LDP politicians, once (re)elected, pursued promotion within the party, seeking to occupy more lucrative, prestigious, and powerful positions. More specifically, for the leaders of factions, promotion meant becoming the next president of the LDP (and thus the prime minister of Japan). For rank-and-file LDP politicians, promotion meant, at least in the short run, occupying cabinet portfolios and important party positions, such as PARC committee chairs. How do

[33] The static cross-sectional analysis (and the replication of such analyses) that I have conducted may not constitute sufficient proof of an actual selection process which is dynamic in nature. Ideally one would need a large-scale panel survey in order to verify more directly that LDP politicians and LDP supporters acted rationally and that they really abandoned the losing factions over the long run. Given that no such survey was ever conducted, however, I believe that the data and analysis presented here remain the best available evidence.

these secondary incentives of individual Liberal Democrats explain the pattern of promotion and the appointment of influential positions?

Suppose a factional leader was running for the presidency. Because the optimality in the size of factional membership allowed no single faction to comprise a majority within the party, the leader would not only have to consolidate support within his own faction but would also have to form a coalition with at least one other faction. Given the promotion incentives of rank-and-file Diet members, the best, if not the only way to ensure endorsement from the coalition would be to promise that once elected he would deliver a "share" of cabinet portfolios and other important positions to the allied faction. In fact, during the process of presidential selection, the party tended to be divided into two camps, "mainstream" factions that formed the winning coalition and the other, "nonmainstream" factions. And because the absolute number of distributable positions was limited, this tendency translated itself into overrepresentation of the mainstream factions in cabinet and party appointments.

If the elected president were playing a "one-shot game" of coalition building, he might have been tempted to renege *ex post* and not to deliver the promised positions. In such a situation, he would have overrepresented only his own faction because the other factions would not have any means to retaliate against him. However, the nature of the interfactional political process within the LDP was a "repeated game." Because the number of distributable positions, especially cabinet portfolios, was so limited, the president was expected to shuffle his cabinet frequently in order to meet the promotion demands of the rank and file.[34] This meant that if a president had reneged in making his previous appointments, the other faction would have had an opportunity to retaliate, for example, by refusing to participate in the new cabinet, withdrawing from the coalition, and eventually shortening his presidency. It is reasonable to assume that the president himself would have wanted to stay in that position as long as possible, given that it was the most lucrative, prestigious, and powerful position in Japanese political life. Therefore, in order to maintain the coalition and to prolong his incumbency, the elected president had good reason not to renege.

Thus a systematic overrepresentation of the mainstream factions was a direct product of the promotional incentives of individual LDP politicians, especially of factional leaders. It is not surprising that such a pattern was reflected in the actual distribution of public positions up until the late 1960s. This is not the end of the story, however.

Once elected, the president operated under a high degree of political uncertainty because the leaders of other factions, also pursuing party leadership, would soon start fashioning a new coalition in preparation for competing in

[34] In reality, cabinet shuffles occurred about once a year, and a new set of party officials was usually selected at about the same time.

the next presidential selection. Factional leaders in the nonmainstream, especially, had strong incentives to alter the status quo: if their underrepresentation in the cabinet and party were to continue, they might eventually lose the support of their own rank and file. The president therefore had to anticipate new developments and act strategically. More specifically, two kinds of preventative measures were available for the president to prolong his incumbency. First, the president could try to prevent the partner from departing from the existing mainstream coalition by promising the allied partner his future endorsement. In a second, more aggressive strategy, the president could change his coalition partner by making some attractive offers to nonmainstream factions that were then underrepresented.

The first strategy is logically flawed in the sense that the partner had no way, *ex ante*, of preventing the president from reneging once the president finished his own terms of office. Because it could not be credible, the president's promise for future endorsement would not prevent the existing coalition from falling apart. In 1959, for example, President Nobusuke Kishi tried to consolidate his coalition by promising his coalition partner, Banboku Ohno, that upon his resignation he would endorse Ohno as the next president. Even though this promise was given in writing and witnessed by influential business elites and politicians, Ohno later doubted its credibility and strengthened his ties with Kishi's archrival Ichiro Kohno.[35] There was nothing to prevent Kishi from reneging after he decided to resign in 1960, and indeed he supported Hayato Ikeda, not Ohno, as the next president.

The second coalition manipulation strategy, by contrast, seemed to work, at least for a while. This strategy was pursued by President Ikeda during his incumbency. Ikeda was initially supported by the so-called three exbureaucrat factions led by Eisaku Sato, Kishi, and himself. Ikeda later brought the Kohno and Ohno factions into the coalition by delivering cabinet portfolios and important party positions, whereas Sato became his chief enemy when Ikeda sought his third term. This second strategy, however, was not without problems. Ikeda could not continue to manipulate the coalition indefinitely. Because the composition of mainstream and nonmainstream factions had already been completely reversed, Ikeda had run out of options for forming a new winning coalition. Thus, although the coalition manipulation bought some time, it was destined to fail in the long run. In fact, Ikeda's victory over Sato was so marginal that Ikeda, when he finally resigned in 1964, had no choice but to endorse Sato as his successor.

It was in this context that the seniority and interfactional balancing rules evolved as the mechanism for determining promotion and appointment. Having observed the failure of the myopic strategies of his two predecessors,

[35] Goto, Uchida, and Ishikawa, *Sengo Hoshu Seiji no Kiseki* [The Course of Postwar Conservative Politics], p. 139.

President Sato adopted these rules and thus shifted the emphasis of his strategy from the consolidation of the existing coalition to the avoidance of making future enemies. Unconfrontational in that it represented both mainstream and nonmainstream factions with a lawlike regularity, Sato's new strategy allowed little room to maneuver in the distribution of public positions. Nevertheless, this regularity minimized opportunism on the part of other factional leaders because it allowed them to protect, *ex ante*, a "fair share" in cabinet and party positions.

Sato's strategy became institutionalized as party norms that regulated promotion and appointment. Undeniably, Sato was successful in prolonging his incumbency by adopting the seniority and interfactional balancing principles: his ninety-two month reign (from November 1964 to July 1972) was the longest continuous administration in Japanese parliamentary history. A possible explanation for the subsequent institutionalization of these rules is that LDP presidents during the 1970s and 1980s simply copied Sato's strategy. In fact, one president, Takeshita, was frequently quoted as saying that Sato was his mentor and had taught him all the basic skills necessary to run internal party affairs.

This explanation, based on the notion of "learning," would be persuasive only if the copied strategy had continued to produce the same desired outcome. In reality, however, most of the post-Sato LDP presidents (except for Nakasone) were unsuccessful in coping with political uncertainty and in prolonging their terms, even though, for the most part, they adopted the seniority rule and interfactional balancing principles. The fundamental question thus remains: Why did these presidents continue Sato's strategy, despite its apparent failure?

There are two keys to solving this puzzle. First is the expected time limit of any one presidency: as no faction had a majority within the party, no LDP president was expected to remain in that position indefinitely. This further complicated the president's strategic calculations: he had to prepare not only for when he would be out of office but also for the possibility that he would become nonmainstream. The president knew that if he were to deviate from the seniority and balancing rules by overrepresenting his own faction and underrepresenting those of his rivals, he would be likely to suffer retaliation in the future, when a rival took over the presidency. In turn, each factional leader knew that when he became president, he would face the same basic problem. As a result, an optimal outcome for promotion and appointment issues was a system in which both mainstream and nonmainstream were fairly represented with a certain predictability. There existed no Pareto-superior solution, as long as the composition of mainstream and nonmainstream factions was malleable over time and as long as the president (and each other leader) anticipated future retaliation from any potential rivals.

The second key to solving the puzzle lies in the complex nature of the coalition-building game. If the game were being played simply at the interfactional level, the president might not worry about future retaliation; by the time his term was over, all his personal political ambitions would probably have been accomplished and he would have little promotion incentive left. But the game was actually more complicated. Whereas the president might personally be at the end of his own political career, the rank and file of his faction would still have plenty of promotion incentives and they would therefore be concerned about future retaliation from the rival faction. In particular, those seeking to take over the leadership of the faction could be expected to oppose the overrepresented appointments during the current period, in order to avoid underrepresentation resulting from retaliation in future periods, during which they would become the leader. Thus the president was in fact playing a "nested game": his decision to make overrepresented appointments at the interfactional level would have serious political repercussions for his own faction.

In sum, the seniority and balancing rules began as President Sato's strategy for coping with the uncertainty involved in the dynamics of interfactional politics and for prolonging his incumbency. The subsequent institutionalization of these rules had a twofold rational foundation. At the interfactional level, it was a preventative measure with which to constrain the president's abuse of power within the party and thus to protect, *ex ante*, each faction's share of important public positions. At the intrafactional level, it was a preventative measure with which to constrain the factional leader's abuse of power, which would be detrimental to the interests of those who might seek the factional leadership at a future time.

The evolution of factional politics within the LDP from 1955 to 1993 cannot be explained by the unique attributes of Japanese culture and tradition. This chapter has presented an alternative explanation based on a set of standard microanalytic assumptions about the utility functions of relevant actors and their strategic behavior under the given institutional constraints. I have shown that this alternative framework provides a coherent and comprehensive explanation for the evolution of the LDP's internal politics over time. The changes in the pattern of factionalization were determined by the electoral incentives of LDP politicians and LDP supporters. The party norms that regulated appointments and promotions evolved because of the promotion incentives of LDP politicians. Since neither of these two organizational changes can be adequately explained by the conventional political-culture approach, I conclude that the microanalytic perspective provides a more powerful explanation for the evolution of the LDP's intraparty politics.

Before concluding this chapter, let me point to the post-1993 political situation and speculate on the future development of LDP factional politics. It is hard to deny that the nature of the LDP's factional politics started to change in 1993. The initial symptom was the breakup of the ex-Takeshita faction into two groups of roughly the same size. After joining the opposition parties to pass the nonconfidence bill against the LDP government in June, one of these groups, led by Tsutomu Hata, left the LDP and established a new party, the *Shinsei-to*. When the LDP failed to win a majority in the July election, Hata's party played a critical role in forging a non-LDP coalition government with all other opposition parties except the Communists. Thus, for the first time since 1955, internal factional politics led to the breakup of the LDP, and indeed the demise of its long lasting one-party dominance.[36] The newly established government gave priority to the reform of the 1947 electoral arrangement and other laws regulating political contributions and activities of political parties. Although, initially, there was substantial disagreement among the allied parties, the coalition government managed to reach a compromise and the reform bill was passed in February 1994. Instead of the medium-sized electoral districts with a single nontransferable vote, the newly adopted system is a blend of the single-ballot plurality system and proportional representation.

Given that the interfactional dynamics within the LDP were shaped by the institutional context of the electoral system, the nature of factional politics within the LDP is likely to undergo its most significant transformation in the next few years. Even though the LDP politicians' electoral incentives remain intact, the pattern of factionalization will not stay the same since the very basis for the optimal number (and the optimal size) of LDP factions has been replaced by a completely new system. In addition, with regard to the party norms regulating promotion and appointments, it would be difficult to retain all the existing rules. Even though individual LDP politicians will still seek to be promoted within the party, many of these norms were premised on the LDP's assured victory and therefore on the availability of distributable cabinet portfolios and other influential positions.

The above speculation also leads one to reconsider the assumptions adopted in the above analysis, especially those concerning the utility of LDP supporters. I have modified the original Downsian notion and assumed that these supporters vote according to their "expected candidate differential," rather than their "expected party differential." This was justifiable under the 1947 electoral system in which voters had to distinguish individual candidates even from the same party and when the LDP's electoral victory was taken for granted. Under the new system, however, the LDP supporters are likely to take into account the impact of interparty electoral competition rather than the difference between candidates. Within the framework developed in the pre-

[36] See chapter 8.

vious section, the electoral incentives of LDP supporters play only a marginal role in explaining the changes in the factionalization pattern (and these voters are simply irrelevant in explaining the emergence of party norms). Nevertheless, the fundamental change in the electoral behavior of Japanese voters under the new electoral system will certainly add to the forces already operating to change the nature of the LDP's factional politics.

7

POST-1955 CHANGES IN THE JAPANESE PARTY SYSTEM

DURING THE long period of the LDP's one-party dominance from 1955 to 1993, the Japanese party system underwent a significant transformation. As the ruling party's internal factional politics changed over these years, as discussed in the previous chapter, so did the external framework in which the LDP competed with other political parties. The Japan Socialist Party (JSP), established in the same year as the LDP, never became a viable electoral alternative and, contrary to the initially popular projection, a true two-party system never developed in Japan. Instead, by the end of the 1960s, two middle-of-the-road parties, the Democratic Socialist Party (DSP) and the Clean Government Party (CGP), entered the electoral competition.[1] The revival of the multiparty system was accompanied by changes in the degree of the system's polarization. Before the rise of the centrists forces, the Japanese party system was highly polarized and the legislative interactions in the Diet were filled with ideological and even physical confrontations. During the 1970s, however, all-out conflict declined in Parliament, and the LDP and opposition parties started exploring policy compromises through various institutionalized channels of communication.

This chapter examines the determinants of the transformation in the Japanese party system during the post-1955 period. The prevailing view that the "1955 system" reflected a fundamental shift in the underlying socio-ideological cleavage does not fully account for the emergence of the small parties during the 1960s and their suvivial thereafter. While such a macroscopic view may suggest that the extremely polarized nature of the party system induced the rise of centrist forces, it does not provide fine-tuned explanations as to why, under the given circumstances, the DSP and the CGP were able to enter into the electoral race for the House of Representatives. This chapter seeks to establish an alternative interpretation and argues that the change in the number of competing parties was driven by the electoral incentives of individual politicians and voters operating under the constraints of the 1947 electoral law. I thus demonstrate that the institutional framework mediated the structural effect of the socio-ideological factors in determining the optimal number of political parties.

The chapter opens by summarizing the changes in the Japanese party sys-

[1] Some might object to my characterization of the CGP as a centrist party and argue that the emergence of this party represented a shift from a unidimensional to a multidimensional ideological/policy competition. See below on this point.

tem during the post-1955 period. I then critically review the conventional explanations based solely on the socio-ideological perspective and advance an alternative microanalytic interpretation. The chapter ends with a discussion of the implications of the analysis presented here.

Changes in the Japanese Party System, 1955–1993

As documented in chapter 5, both the LDP and the JSP were created in 1955, following the consolidation of the conservative forces on the one hand and of the progressive camp on the other. About a year later, another small party, the Labor-Farmer Party, joined the JSP to complete the earlier wave of partisan realignment. In the subsequent election in 1958, virtually all the lower house seats were distributed between the LDP and the JSP (see Table 7.1). Thus the popular expectation at the time was that the Japanese party system was moving into an Anglo-American type of two-party system.

Contrary to this expectation, the system dominated by the LDP and the JSP did not last long. In 1960 some members of the JSP split off from the party and created the Democratic Socialist Party. In 1967 another centrist party, the Clean Government Party, entered the lower house electoral race.[2] With these new parties, as well as the Japan Communist Party (JCP) whose electoral support grew gradually, the Japanese party system shifted back to a multiparty system by the end of the 1960s (see Table 7.2).

The configuration of the Japanese party system seems to have stabilized since then, at least until the 1990s. Although two other parties, the New Liberal Club (NLC) and the Socialist Democratic Federation (SDF), were established during the 1970s, the former was eventually absorbed by the LDP and the latter was too small to have political significance.[3] The LDP did suffer a long-term decline in its popular support during the 1960s but, benefiting from the fragmentation of the opposition, the LDP managed to form a single-party majority government throughout these years.[4] It was not until 1993 that the Japanese party system went through another fundamental change, when the LDP broke up, new parties were established, and power was finally transferred to a non-LDP coalition government.[5]

[2] The CGP had started its political activities as early as the mid-1950s, but its entry to the lower house electoral race did not take place until 1967.

[3] The NLC was established in 1976 by a handful of politicians who had broken away from the LDP. The SDF was created in 1978 by a small group of politicians who left the JSP. In addition, in the upper house, after the partial adoption of a proportional representation system in 1983, there have been many so-called mini parties, including Rengo no Kai. Because of their limited political influence, I ignore them in the following discussion.

[4] The only exception was the period between 1983 and 1986 during which the LDP made a coalition with the NLC.

[5] See chapter 8 for the analysis of the political change in 1993.

TABLE 7.1
Lower House Seat Distribution after the 1958 Election[a]

Party	*Seat*
LDP	298
JSP	167
Communists	1
Other	1
Total	467

Source: Ishikawa, *Deeta Sengo Seiji-shi* [A data history of postwar politics], p. 121.

[a]These numbers take into consideration some party switching that occurred after the election.

The change in the number of competing political parties was accompanied by the change in the degree of polarization of the post-1955 Japanese party system. Immediately after the LDP and the JSP were established, the system was highly polarized and the legislative interactions in the Diet were filled with confrontations over the issues of national defense, foreign policy, and public order. Moreover, the pushing through of controversial bills by the ruling LDP often led the JSP to mobilize its supporters to protest outside the Parliament building, resulting in general strikes and mass demonstrations.

The rise of the centrist forces during the 1960s, however, foreshadowed the end of the confrontational era in Japanese parliamentary history. Although the JSP retained its Marxist ideological positions (at least until January 1986 when the party declared a new platform), the LDP's legislative behavior changed significantly; that is, despite its continuing parliamentary dominance, the LDP started to engage in frequent consultations with the opposition before the introduction of important bills and/or voting on them. These consultations resulted in the strengthening of various institutionalized channels, such as the House Management Committee and the Diet Countermeasure Committee, through which the LDP and opposition parties communicated and reached policy compromises.[6] Figure 7.1 clearly points to what is often described as a transition from the "politics of confrontation to the politics of compromise" in the Japanese Parliament.[7]

[6] The House Management Committee [Giin Unei Iinkai] is a formally institutionalized committee within each chamber of Parliament, consisting of party representatives. The Diet Countermeasure Committee [Kokkai Taisaku Iinkai], on the other hand, is an informally established forum made up of officials from major political parties. For the latter's increasingly prominent role relative to the former, see Sato and Matsuzaki, *Jiminto Seiken* [The LDP's rule], pp. 130–35.

[7] Watanabe, *Shin Seiji no Joshiki* [New common sense of politics]; Krauss, "Conflict in the Diet."

TABLE 7.2
Lower House Seat Distribution after the 1969 Election[a]

Party	*Seat*
LDP	300
JSP	90
DSP	32
CGP	47
JCP	14
Other	3
Total	486

Source: Ishikawa, *Deeta Sengo Seiji-shi* [A data history of postwar politics], p. 125.

[a]These numbers take into consideration some party switching that occurred immediately after the election. It should also be noted that three members in the "other" category eventually joined the LDP.

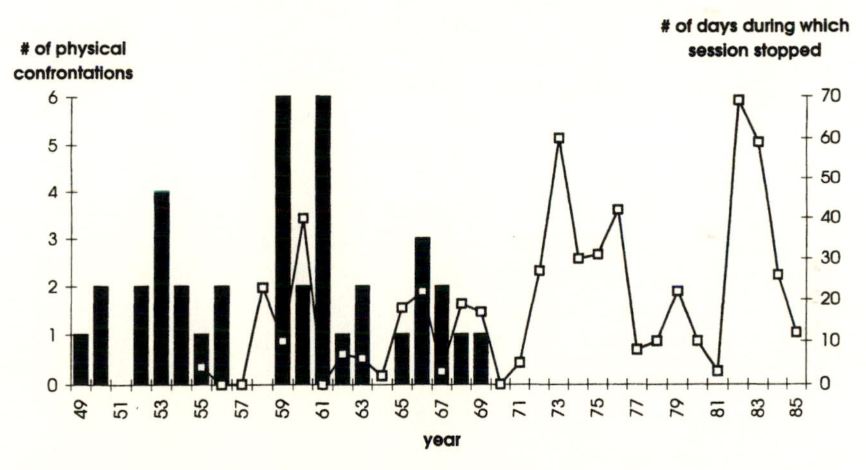

Figure 7.1: Changes in Legislative Interactions. *Source*: Approximated from Sato and Matsuzaki, *Jiminto Seiken* [The LDP's rule], p. 129, Figure 16.

In sum, the Japanese party system underwent a major change during the post-1955 period. The entry of the two viable centrist parties in the 1960s revived the multiparty electoral competition. Further, the Japanese party system's degree of polarization decreased, and the legislative interactions came to reflect more compromise and less confrontation.

Conventional Interpretations

The conventional approaches to Japanese party politics cannot fully account for the changes in the post-1955 Japanese party system described above. Most of the analyses take for granted that the emergence of the two new parties had something to do with the LDP's conciliatory legislative behavior, but the rise itself of these two parties has not yet been adequately explained.

As discussed in chapter 2, the prevailing notion of the 1955 system and the socio-ideological perspective highlight the establishment of the LDP and the JSP as a product of the fundamental shift in the underlying cleavage. Such a view explains the polarization of the Japanese party system for the period immediately after 1955. The central problem with this interpretation, however, is that the polarized party system lasted only a short period or, at most, a decade, which leaves a puzzle: If the socio-ideological shift was truly significant, why was the party system that reflected the shift so unstable?

The fragmentation of the opposition has often been identified as the cause of the LDP's persistent strength throughout the 1970s and 1980s. For example, Seizaburo Sato and Tetsuhisa Matsuzaki argue that the creation of the Democratic Socialist Party, following the departure of the right-wing elements from the JSP, resulted in leftist domination within the JSP and the party's long-term electoral stagnation in subsequent years.[8] However persuasive this may be, it is only in retrospect that one can draw such an interpretation. The question remains as to why the DSP left the JSP in the first place.

Because of the limitations of the socio-ideological explanation, as originally formulated around the concept of the 1955 system, scholars have advanced additional explanatory hypotheses regarding the rise of the centrist parties during the 1960s. For example, with regard to the emergence of the DSP, it is typically argued that the party was created as a result of the Socialists' ideological battle among themselves, which had been carried over from the pre-1955 period. Gerald Curtis presents such an interpretation:

> [Reunification of the JSP in 1955] saddled the JSP with sharp internal differences over whether it should be a class or a mass party, and over national security policy. . . . Although the party's left wing looked as though it were more aggressive and powerful than the right in the late 1950s, economic, social, and political developments had in fact thrown it very much on the defensive. . . . The left's response to these changing realities was to try to drive out of the party those who openly argued that the party should move to the right to meet them and beat down those who advocated "structural reform" as a way to modernize the program of the party's left wing.[9]

[8] Sato and Matsuzaki, *Jiminto Seiken*, p. 18.

[9] Curtis, *Japanese Way of Politics*, pp. 21–22.

For one thing, this account of the formation of the DSP contradicts the claim about the initial polarization of the Japanese party system after 1955. Thus it redirects us to the original key question: If the internal ideological rift within the progressive camp was significant enough to cause the 1960 split, what force brought about the 1955 reintegration of the Socialists in the first place? Moreover, the above interpretation fails to account for the fact that some former Right-Wing Socialists chose not to join the newly created DSP. As Curtis himself admits, the partial nature of the 1960 separation was a source of future ideological struggle within the JSP. This suggests that the creation of the DSP was not entirely a product of ideology/policy differences.[10]

Given that the DSP was created as a result of the split from the JSP, it seems also strange to argue, as do some proponents of the socio-ideological approach, that the exceptionally rigid nature of the Japanese cleavage prevented the JSP from adopting moderate social-democratic policy positions.[11] Since at least some Socialists were prepared to and in fact did adopt such positions in 1960, the question is not why the JSP failed to converge to the ideological center but why some Socialists did converge while others failed to do so. The socio-ideological perspective, preoccupied with a macrolevel analysis of the underlying cleavage structure, cannot provide such a fine-tuned prediction.

Another prevailing perception regarding the division between the JSP and the DSP focuses on the difference between these two parties in terms of the ideologies of their support base, namely, different labor unions. True, the JSP, at least until the realignment of the Japanese labor movements in 1987, was closely aligned with Sohyo (General Council of Japanese Trade Unions), and the DSP with Domei (All Japan Labor Federation). The former, representing public sector workers deprived of a right to strike, sustained far more militant Marxist rhetoric than the latter. The difference in the two parties' underlying support from the labor movement, however, does not explain the initial split because the creation of the DSP preceded the formation of Domei by four years.[12] Only after the DSP proved unsuccessful in the elections of 1960 and 1963 did the party turn to Domei for votes, candidates, and organizational assistance. At least originally the leaders designed the DSP as a centrist party, and they were seeking far broader electoral support than particular labor groups.

[10] With respect to the fact that not all former Right-Wing Socialists left the JSP in 1960, Curtis points to the personal and factional rivalry among the former Right-Wingers, namely, between Suehiro Nishio who led the defecting group and Jotaro Kawakami who decided to remain in the JSP (see ibid., pp. 22–23). Contrary to what is implied by Curtis, some members of the Kawakami faction actually joined Nishio in leaving the JSP. Thus, the personal/factional rivalry also fails to account for the DSP's creation.

[11] See, in particular, the work of Hideo Otake, cited in chapter 2.

[12] The development of the Japanese labor movement in the late 1950s and the early 1960s was actually extremely complicated. True some moderate labor organizations were formed even before the establishment of the DSP in 1960 but, at least until 1962, the labor union that wanted an alternative to Sohyo were not fully united.

If the conventional view that stresses the 1955 socio-ideological shift has difficulty explaining the creation of the DSP, it is almost impossible for such an account to explain the rise of the second centrist party, the Clean Government Party. This is because of the anomalous origins of the CGP compared with other Japanese political parties. The CGP initially began as a political arm of the Soka Gakkai, a lay organization of the Nichiren Soshu sect of Japanese Buddhism.[13] The party therefore had no ideological roots in labor or leftist movements.

Faced with the difficulty in accounting for the CGP (and the DSP), some scholars in the socio-ideological tradition have argued that the societal and ideological foundations of the 1955 system had actually eroded over the years and that this erosion explained the fragmentation of the opposition. It is typically claimed that Japan's rapid industrialization during the 1960s marginalized and politically left behind those voters who had recently moved from rural to urban areas. With regard to the CGP, in particular, scholars seem to agree that the CGP's electoral support (and Soka Gakkai's popularity) flowed from those urban voters who had no place in the existing political system. These voters included nonunionized workers in small factories, small business owners, and clerical workers.[14]

This line of argument is generalized and best articulated by Scott Flanagan. He rejects the interpretation that "the appearance of Center parties simply represents a movement to fill the unoccupied middle ground on the traditional Left-Right ideological continuum."[15] Using "affect thermometer" survey results, Flanagan conducts a factor analysis and concludes that, although "we see clearly that the primary defining dimension in Japan's political space is still the bipolar confrontation between the establishment Right . . . and the establishment Left,"

> [the factor analysis] suggests that a second dimension of political competition is beginning to emerge, but one that is as yet ill defined. . . . We can characterize this dimension as a cleavage between rural constituencies, the establishment, and the Old Politics, represented by the farmers, courts and police . . . and urban constituencies, the antiestablishment, and the New Politics, represented by the emerging Center parties, the Communists, the student movement, and radicals.[16]

This analysis, however, has a major methodological flaw. Contrary to what is claimed above, nothing in Flanagan's evidence suggests that the rise of centrist forces reflected the emergence of a new socio-ideological cleavage.

[13] The CGP officially broke its ties with the Soka Gakkai in 1970, after it was publicized that the latter tried to stop publication of a book critical of the organization.

[14] See Takabatake, "Taishu Undo no Tayoka to Henshitsu" [The diversification and transformation of mass movements]; and White, *The Sokagakkai and Mass Society*.

[15] Flanagan, "Electoral Change in Japan," p. 180.

[16] Ibid., pp. 181–82.

Because his evidence comes from a one-time cross-sectional survey, it is impossible to draw conclusions about *intertemporal* changes in the Japanese cleavage structure. In order to demonstrate that "a second dimension of political competition is beginning to emerge," Flanagan would have needed pooled survey data for at least two different points in time, before and after the rise of the centrist parties.[17] Unfortunately, such data are not available for the Japanese case. The lack of data is critical in the socio-ideological approach, since there is no practical way, other than survey data, to identify the effect of the socio-ideological cleavage independent of observing the party system.[18]

With regard to the second, less tangible change in the party system, namely, the decrease in the degree of the system's polarization, many observers point to the changes in the pattern of party interactions in Parliament, especially the LDP's increasing conciliatory legislative behavior. At least two different explanations apply, although each has its shortcomings.

First, consistent with the thrust of the socio-ideological perspective, some analysts have focused on the shift in the underlying societal demands for legislative activities. Kenzo Uchida, for example, stresses that the consensus-building style of parliamentary interactions started as early as 1965, and he attributes much of this change to the LDP's successful economic policies under the administrations of Hayato Ikeda and Eisaku Sato. He claims that economic growth during the 1960s had the consequence of "weakening the opposition's criticism and power" and that "domestic, distributional, and therefore budgetary issues (and budget-related bills) replaced ideological issues concerning the national destiny."[19]

Aside from the methodological problem of failing to measure *ex ante* the society's legislative needs (independent of the actual legislative activities), this line of reasoning is problematic because it is ambiguous about why domestic and distributional issues are necessarily easier to compromise on. Some of the budgetary issues related to agriculture, education, and labor policies could have been as confrontational as diplomatic issues, and indeed, in the mid- and late 1960s, the LDP often had to railroad bills through Parliament in these areas.

[17] The same methodological flaw can be found in Ronald Inglehart's article, which undoubtedly influenced Flanagan and which discusses more generally the changing values in Western industrial democracies (see "The Changing Structure of Political Cleavages"; see also Inglehart, *The Silent Revolution*).

[18] It should also be noted that one cannot draw conclusions regarding the relationship between the changing socio-ideological structure and the rising centrist forces based on electoral data for the lower house. As I demonstrate in the next section, these small centrist parties did not nominate candidates in all districts. Thus the center parties' votes did not reflect the underlying party support for their ideological/policy positions.

[19] Uchida, "Seito nai, kan no Tetsuzuki" [Intra- and interparty procedure]," pp. 36, 42 (translation by Kohno). See also Kosaka, "Kyoko Saiketsu no Seijigaku" [Politics of snap-voting], pp. 50–69.

The second explanation focuses not so much on the changes in the society's legislative demands per se as on the gradual decrease in the margin of the LDP's majority, which, as discussed above, is often regarded as a consequence of such changes. Thus, in apparent contrast to the first explanation, this alternative explanation points to the decline of the LDP's bargaining power vis-à-vis the opposition as the cause of its conciliatory legislative behavior.[20] Often raised along with such a claim is the institutional structure of the Japanese Parliament, especially its committee systems. As Ellis Krauss elaborates:

> In allocating seats on committees the lower house follows a complex procedure, but its basic thrust is distribution according to a party's proportion of seats in the full house. The major factor complicating seat allocation, however, is the custom that the committee chairman does not vote in committee decisions except in the case of a tie. On the two odd-numbered (25-member) standing committees this presents no problem. . . . But on the remaining fourteen standing committees which are even numbered . . . this custom complicates the definition of what constitutes a majority of the committee. . . . To control both the chairman and a voting majority, the LDP must have at least a majority of 21–19 on the forty-member committee . . . Thus to have an "effective majority" (also called in Japan a "stable majority") control of both the committee chairmanship and a voting majority on all standing committees, a party must have almost 53 percent (271) of the seats in the 511-seat lower house. To control all special as well as standing committees would require an even larger majority.[21]

As Krauss himself recognizes, however, the LDP retained its majority in the full house throughout these years. Given that the number of committee seats, their distribution, the selection of committee chairs, and the custom that the chair does not vote are all governed by either legislation or convention, and not by the Constitution, the LDP could have changed these rules. Furthermore, there is no reason to believe that the loss of its majority *surplus* would necessarily lead the LDP to adopt a more conciliatory style of parliamentary strategy. It is at least plausible that a decline in bargaining power could lead to even more confrontational tactics.

Hence the conventional literature cannot adequately explain the two aspects of the changes in the post-1955 Japanese party system, namely, the change in the number of competing viable parties or the decrease in the degree of the system's polarization. In what follows I offer an alternative explanation which, consistent with the rest of this study, is based on a microanalytic framework.

[20] See Krauss, "Conflict in the Diet"; see also Tani, "Kokkai ni okeru Seito no Rippo Kodo ni kansuru Doutai Bunseki" [Dynamic analysis of parties' legislative behavior in the national Diet], pp. 168–90.

[21] See Krauss, "Conflict in the Diet," p. 259.

Incentives, Institutions and Party Competition in Japan

Let us begin the analysis by considering the second aspect of the change in the post-1955 party system, namely, the decreased level of the system's polarization. Figure 7.2 summarizes the legislative behavior of all parties (after the DSP and the CGP both won some seats in the lower house), as measured by the degree of support for the LDP-sponsored bills in the lower house.

Assuming the unidimensionality of the ideological/policy space, Figure 7.2 enables one to identify the CGP and the DSP clearly as centrist forces or as parties left of the LDP but right of the JSP (and the JCP); that is, for most of the period under consideration here (1967–85), the CGP and the DSP, as well as the NLC, recorded a higher rate of support for the LDP-sponsored bills than the JSP. This aggregate evidence yields a simple explanation for the change in the mode of legislative interactions: it was brought about by the new parties whose ideological positions were close enough to those of the LDP so that the latter could explore policy compromises.[22]

What made it possible, then, for these small parties to enter the electoral race? As adherents of the conventional socio-ideological perspective would argue, the entry of these newcomers would not have occured if the party system created in 1955 had not been so polarized. To the extent that the two existing parties, the LDP and the JSP, were so far apart ideologically, there was enough space for the smaller parties to enter in the middle. However, although the nature of the socio-ideological configuration was certainly a necessary condition, that alone was not sufficient to fragment the opposition. The rise of centrist forces cannot be adequately explained without considering more microanalytic factors, namely, the incentives of individual political actors and the institutional constraints under which they interacted.

In order to see this, let us go back and once again consider Maurice Duverger's classic formulation of the relationship between electoral law and the party system. The basic intuition behind "Duverger's law" is the notion that (1) rational politicians will leave losing parties that are underrepresented ("mechanical effect"), and/or (2) rational voters will not waste their votes on losers ("psychological factor"). Thus, under the single-ballot plurality system, parties will be selected out, at least in the long run, to produce a two-party

[22] Another development should be noted here, well documented by many observers of legislative interactions, namely, the exclusion of the JCP from Diet Countermeasure Committee meetings since the early 1980s. The LDP may have needed to exclude the radical Communists in order to facilitate effective dialogue and policy compromises with other opposition parties. Some veteran politicians have suggested that the exclusion of the JCP took place precisely for this reason (see Ito, "Kensho 'Kokutai-Seiji' no Kozai" [Examining the merits and demerits of the "politics of the Diet Countermeasure Committee"].

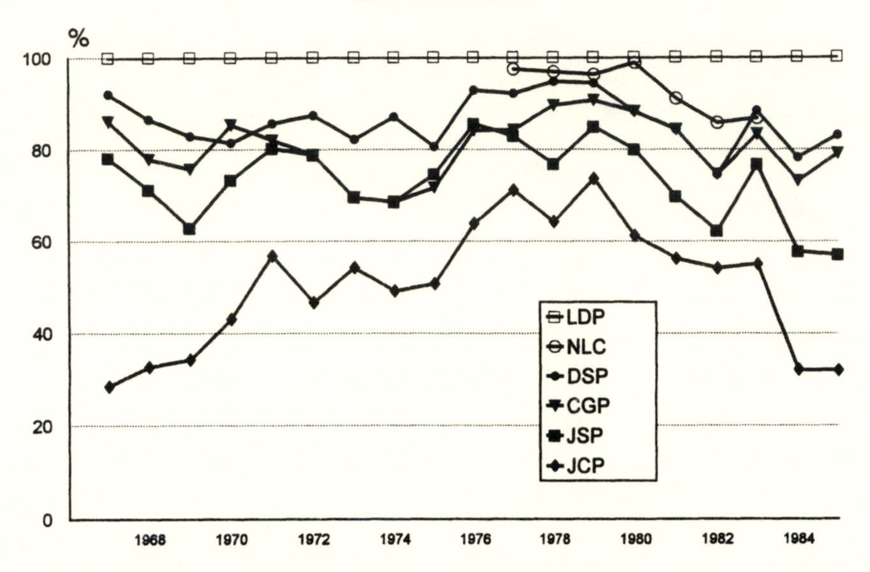

Figure 7.2: Pattern of Partisan Policy Sponsorship. This figure reflects each party's legislative support and opposition for and against the bills passed by the House of Representatives in each year. Bills that were passed by the lower house but not by the upper house are excluded. *Source*: Sato and Matsuzaki, *Jiminto Seiken* [The LDP's rule], p. 139, Figure 17.

system.[23] As discussed in the previous chapter, recent studies have extended Duverger's original insights and supported a more general proposition that a system with a single nontransferable vote and with district size M will produce a competition among $M + 1$ actors.[24]

Was this logic at work for the evolution of the Japanese party system?[25] Since the Japanese electoral system for the lower house remained the three- to five-member district system throughout the period from 1947 to 1993, the first question to consider is the emergence of the quasi-two-party system in 1955. The available evidence suggests that the mechanism of "rational abandonment" was clearly in operation in inducing this earlier shift in the Japanese party system. Figure 7.3 traces the ratio of the number of elected candidates in relation to the total number of candidates who ran in general elections.

These aggregate data show that Japan's postwar parliamentary democracy started with too many candidates. In the aftermath of the war, major as well as minor political parties nominated their own candidates without much coordination, and, as a result, these candidates entered the electoral race with, on

[23] Duverger, *Political Parties*.

[24] Reed, "Structure and Behaviour"; Cox, "Strategic Voting Equilibria."

[25] In the following analysis I ignore the "aggregation problem" with Duverger's law for the same reasons discussed in the previous chapter.

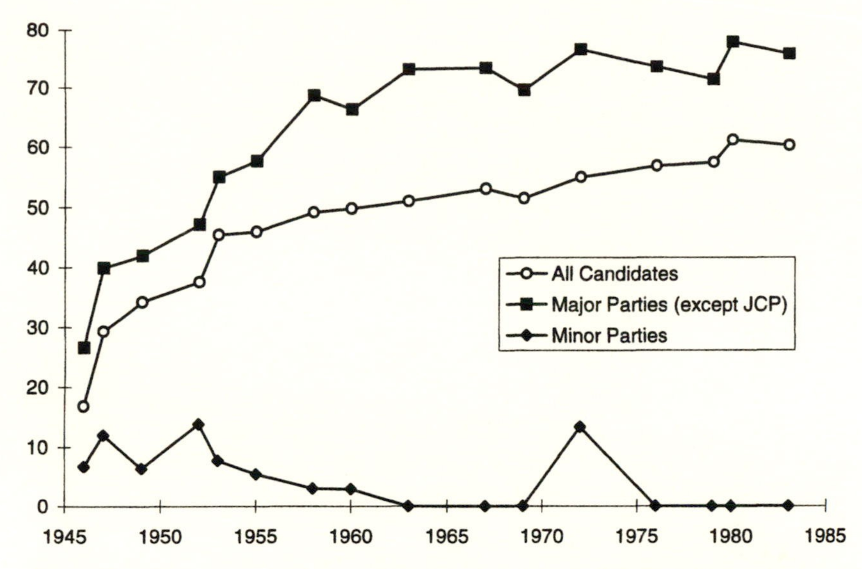

Figure 7.3: Average Success Rate of Candidates in Postwar General Elections. *Source*: Ishikawa, *Deeta Sengo Seiji-shi* [A data history of postwar politics].

average, far less than a 50 percent chance of winning a seat. The selection mechanism, however, started to weed out those candidates who had little chance of electoral success. This is evident in the trend of an increasing success rate for those running from major political parties in contrast to the decreasing success rate for those from minor parties.[26]

One would expect, however, that the quasi-two-party system established in 1955 was not an equilibrium, given that most electoral districts in Japan elected three or more candidates.[27] Evidence to support this expectation is provided by the trends of candidates' success rates presented above. According to Figure 7.3, the average success rate for all candidates, even after it leveled off around 50 percent, has increased throughout the 1960s and 1970s, despite the emergence of the small parties during those decades. That the ratio did not go down suggests that the entry of the DSP and the CGP (and the NLC and the

[26] It was in this context that the mergers of the conservative and progressive parties occurred in 1955. To the extent that they were competing for the same pool of voters, the conservative parties, as did the progressive parties, had an incentive to coordinate their nominations, thus avoiding excessive competition among themselves. As I have demonstrated in chapter 5, however, the conservative merger and the Socialist reunification cannot be fully explained without considering the parties' electoral strength at the time and their relative bargaining power in forming a coalition government.

[27] Throughout most of the period under consideration here, there was only one single-member district and only a few two-member districts.

SDF) to the electoral race was part of the structure-induced process of reaching the optimal number of political parties.

In accordance with the recent extension of Duverger's insights, one can claim more specifically that the *maximum* number of parties that can exist under the 1947 Japanese electoral arrangement was six, given that only one district elected more than five members to the house. The maximum number, of course, is not necessarily an optimal number. If the magnitude of electoral districts is the key institutional constraint, one would predict that the optimal number of political parties in Japan would have been somewhere below six because only about a third of the electoral districts were five-member districts (with the others electing fewer than five members). This prediction appears to be consistent with the observed reality that there were five long-standing parties since the 1960s (the LDP, JSP, DSP, CGP, and JCP) and two minor parties, one of which disappeared (the NLC), the other having always been politically inconsequential (the SDF).

To substantiate these claims I have investigated the distribution, across different types of electoral districts, of candidates who ran from the three small centrist parties in their first few elections. If, as Duverger would argue, the electoral system provides disincentives for rational politicians and rational voters to remain members or support members of underrepresented political parties, one would expect that the small parties would be less likely to run their candidates in three-member districts and more likely to run them in five-member districts. Evidence from the cases of the DSP, CGP, and NLC all yield results supporting this hypothesis.

The case of the DSP, the first small party to emerge in 1960, is in fact extremely useful in illuminating the strategy of candidate nominations. The DSP, in its first general election in 1960, endorsed 105 candidates, 1 in almost every electoral district (see Table 7.3), as its leaders initially designed the party as a broadly based centrist party "seeking to form a government within five years."[28]

The results of the election, however, were disastrous as the DSP elected only seventeen members (see Table 7.4). Based on this experience, the DSP in the next election reduced its number of candidates by approximately half, this time clearly concentrating on larger districts (see Table 7.5).

In contrast to the DSP, the CGP in its first election in 1967 took a conservative strategy, nominating only thirty-two candidates. Note, however, that the CGP's pattern of candidate nominations was similar to the DSP's 1965 election (see Table 7.6).

Because the CGP was successful in its first election (electing twenty-five members), it more than doubled the number of candidates in the next election

[28] This remark was made by Suehiro Nishio, the first chairman of the DSP, quoted in Sato and Matsuzaki, *Jiminto Seiken*, p. 18.

TABLE 7.3
Distribution of 105 Candidates from the Democratic Socialist Party across Different-Sized Districts in the 1960 Election[a]

		District Size		
		3	*4*	*5*
Candidates (%)	Yes[b]	33 (82.5)	34 (87.2)	36 (94.7)
	No	7 (17.5)	5 (12.8)	2 (5.3)
	Total	40	39	38
	X^2 = 2.8			

Source: Asahi Shimbun, November 22, 1960.
[a]Excludes one single-member district.
[b]Includes one five-member district and one four-member district in which two candidates from the DSP ran.

TABLE 7.4
Success and Failure of 105 Candidates from the Democratic Socialist Party across Different-Sized Districts in the 1960 Election

	District Size		
	3	*4*	*5*
Success (%)	3 (9.1)	5 (14.3)	9 (24.3)
Failure (%)	30 (90.9)	30 (85.7)	28 (75.7)
Total	33	35	37
X^2 = 3.1			

Source: Asahi Shimbun, November 22, 1960.

TABLE 7.5
Distribution of 59 Candidates from the Democratic Socialist Party across Different-Sized Districts in the 1963 Election[a]

		District Size		
		3	*4*	*5*
Candidates (%)	Yes	12 (30.0)	22 (56.4)	25 (65.8)
	No	28 (70.0)	17 (43.6)	13 (34.2)
	Total	40	39	38
	X^2 = 10.8 (significant at .01 level)			

Source: Asahi Shimbun, November 23, 1963.
[a]Excludes one single-member district.

TABLE 7.6

Distribution of 32 Candidates from the Clean Government Party across Different-Sized Districts in the 1967 Election[a]

		District Size		
		3	4	5
Candidates (%)	Yes	5 (11.6)	10 (25.6)	17 (42.5)
	No	38 (88.4)	29 (74.4)	23 (57.5)
	Total	43	39	40
	X^2 = 10.2 (significant at .01 level)			

Source: Asahi Shimbun, January 31, 1967.
[a]Excludes one single-member district.

in 1969. The shift to such an offensive strategy notwithstanding, the CGP did not depart from the established pattern of candidate nominations, again concentrating on larger districts (Table 7.7).

Evidence from the NLC in its first election in 1976 also reveals the same nomination pattern (Table 7.8). Although, unlike the cases of the DSP and CGP described above, the results here are not statistically significant, it is worth noting that there was redistricting before this election and that three of the seven three-member districts in which the NLC candidates ran had previously been five-member districts; this might account for the statistical insignificance.

Taken together, the cases of the DSP, CGP, and NLC yield remarkably consistent results in support of the hypothesis that candidates from smaller parties were less likely to run in three-member districts and more likely to run in five-member districts.

To illustrate the significance of my findings, let me emphasize two points. First, if the electoral districting were such that larger districts were concentrated in urban areas, the evidence presented here might not be particularly revealing. If this had been the case, the above set of results could be interpreted as support for the socio-ideological argument that the rise of centrist forces reflected the new political agenda of urban voters. The grouping of the three different sizes of electoral districts, however, did not coincide with the urban/rural distinction or with industrial demographics. Densely populated prefectures, such as Tokyo, were subdivided into several electoral districts, some of which were three- and four-member districts, whereas certain rural prefectures, such as Shimane and Yamanashi, constituted single five-member districts precisely because of their small populations. Given this, the above results point to the independence, as well as validity, of the microanalytic interpretation that the revival of the Japanese multiparty system was driven by the electoral system under which rational voters and politicians had to operate.

TABLE 7.7
Distribution of 76 Candidates from the Clean Government Party across Different-Sized Districts in the 1969 Election[a]

		District Size		
		3	*4*	*5*
Candidates	Yes	15 (34.9)	27 (69.2)	34 (85.0)
(%)	No	28 (65.1)	12 (30.8)	6 (15.0)
	Total	43	39	40
	X^2 = 23.4 (significant at .01 level)			

Source: Asahi Shimbun, December 29, 1969.
[a]Excludes one single-member district.

TABLE 7.8
Distribution of 25 Candidates from the New Liberal Club across Different-Sized Districts in the 1976 Election[a]

		District Size		
		3	*4*	*5*
Candidates	Yes	7 (14.9)	5 (12.2)	13 (31.7)
(%)	No	40 (85.1)	36 (87.8)	28 (68.3)
	Total	47	41	41
	X^2 = 5.9			

Source: Asahi Shimbun, December 7, 1976.
[a]Excludes one single-member district.

TABLE 7.9
Number of Districts Where Cooperation and Competition Took Place between the CGP and the DSP in the 1979 Election

	District Size			
	3	*4*	*5*	*Total*
Cooperation (%)	11 (39.3)	9 (32.1)	8 (28.6)	28
Competition (%)	3 (8.8)	10 (29.4)	21 (61.8)	34

Source: Asahi Shimbun, October 9, 1979.

Second, the historical context in which each of those three small parties, the DSP, CGP, and NLC, was created differed considerably and, consequently, the social backgounds of the supporters of each party varied from labor union members to Buddhists to neo-Conservatives. That the results were statistically significant and remarkably consistent across the three cases, *despite such variations*, illustrates the generalizability of the theoretical claim expressed in the form of the hypothesis. In other words, individual politicians and voters are independent decision makers, and they act rationally and strategically beyond specific historical and social contexts.

Related evidence that sheds light on the electoral strategy of the small parties can be drawn from the data on the electoral cooperation that such parties often engaged in during the campaign. If the district size operates as an institutional constraint, as argued above, one would expect that it would be easier for candidates from the CGP and DSP to *coexist* in large districts, such as those electing five (or more) seats. Smaller districts, on the other hand, would present a "prisoners' dilemma" because these parties knew that it would be extremely difficult for both their candidates to succeed in such districts, whereas their votes, if combined, might be sufficient to elect one of the two candidates. An obvious solution would be to coordinate the candidate nomination process between these parties. Thus it was not surprising that the DSP and CGP actually began coordinating their candidate nominations as early as 1972.

It was not until the 1979 general election, however, that these two parties officially engaged in large-scale electoral cooperation. In fourteen districts the CGP refrained from nominating candidates and supported DSP candidates, while the DSP returned the favor to the CGP in fourteen other districts.[29] A closer analysis of the pattern of electoral cooperation clearly reveals the electoral incentives and strategies of these small parties (see Table 7.9).

As expected, the DSP-CGP cooperative arrangements were concentrated in smaller districts in which it would have been difficult for both these parties to run viable candidates. In larger districts, on the other hand, the two parties were more likely both to nominate their candidates and to engage in direct competition with each other. This suggests that the behavior of these two small parties was driven by their own electoral incentives and their strategy under the given institutional constraints.

Finally, one caveat must be made here. The above analysis does not apply to the Japan Communist Party. When the quasi-two-party system was established in 1955, the JCP did not merge with the Socialists even though the JCP and the leftist element of the JSP were going after the same pool of voters. One could argue that if the Japanese electoral law had been a pure Anglo-

[29] This number includes one independent candidate affiliated with the DSP at the time of the election, who later joined the party.

American plurality system, the JCP would have had no choice but to merge with the JSP in 1955 and that the JCP's independence itself reflected the institutional bias toward a multiparty competition. Yet the pattern of the JCP's candidate nominations after 1955 reveals that the JCP was an exception: it has consistently nominated more than a hundred candidates, one in almost every electoral district, despite the repeated low success rate of its candidates.

Even though the size of the electoral districts did not constrain the JCP's nomination pattern, however, it did influence its candidates' electoral fate. For example, in the 1979 election, in which the JCP won more seats than in any other previous election, nineteen out of the total thirty-nine successful candidates came from five-member districts, eleven from four-member districts, and only nine from three-member districts. Thus, even in the JCP's case, the district size was clearly a relevant factor constraining individual political actors.

In sum, the revival of the multiparty system during the 1960s was a product of the competitive and strategic behavior of rational voters and politicians operating under institutional constraints. Given the nature of the 1947 electoral system, it was not surprising that the party system dominated by the LDP and JSP lasted less than five years (during which time only one general election was held). The subsequent "stabilization" of the number of parties reflected Duverger's logic for determining the optimal number of competing parties.

This chapter has explored the determinants of the evolution of the Japanese party system during the period between 1955 and 1993. The conventional socio-ideological perspective may offer some insights into why the small centrist parties were able to enter the electoral competition, but it is not a sufficient explanation for the overall post-1955 changes. I have developed instead a microanalytic explanation, which is consistent with the rest of this study. I argue that the change in the level of the system's polarization was brought about by the change in the number of competing parties, which in turn was driven by the electoral incentives of rational politicians and rational voters operating under the constraints of the 1947 electoral law.

The multiparty system which thus reemerged during the 1960s remained stable for the next two decades. In 1993, however, the equilibrium was finally broken after the failed attempt to revise the 1947 electoral system, which led the LDP to split and forced the party to end its long one-party rule. That a major political change was triggered by an initiative to reform the existing electoral law itself indirectly supports the claims made in this chapter that the Japanese party system is shaped by the institutional context that constrains individual political actors. Given that the electoral law was subsequently revised by the non-LDP coalition government, it is likely that the nature of the

Japanese party system will undergo a major transformation in the next few years, as will the nature of LDP's factional politics analyzed in the previous chapter.

This, of course, begs the question: What led the LDP in 1993 to initiate the electoral reform? It is precisely the analysis of the process of the 1993 political change to which the next chapter is devoted.

8

THE POLITICAL CHANGE IN 1993

JAPANESE party politics underwent a major change in 1993. After a series of political scandals paralyzed the government of the Liberal Democratic Party, a group of self-claimed "reformers" joined the opposition in passing a nonconfidence bill and eventually left the party. In the general election subsequently held in July, the LDP failed to obtain a majority. Although the LDP remained the largest party in Parliament, in both the upper and lower houses, it failed to prevent other parties from forming a non-LDP coalition. Shinsei-to and Sakigake, the two new parties created by the LDP renegades, joined forces with the Socialist Party (JSP), the Democratic Socialist Party (DSP), the Clean Government Party (CGP), the Socialist Democratic Federation (SDF), and the Japan New Party (JNP), another newly created party, to nominate as Prime Minister Morihiro Hosokawa, leader of the JNP. Thus, after thirty-eight years in power, the LDP was forced to retreat to the opposition camp.[1]

The 1993 political change was significant, not only because it ended the LDP's one-party rule but also because it resulted in a transformation of the Japanese electoral system. Prime Minister Hosokawa realized that his mandate largely lay in political reform and placed the utmost priority in revising the 1947 electoral law.[2] After much bargaining with the LDP, the Hosokawa government managed to pass the package of reform bills in March 1994 and replaced the old electoral system with a hybrid of a single-member plurality and a proportional representation system.[3] Thus the 1993 political change is destined to have sweeping, long-term effects on Japanese politics, altering the landscape of the party system and the fundamental "rules of the game" for party competition in Japan.

This chapter examines the series of events that led to the transition of power from the LDP to the non-LDP coalition government and explores the determinants of these events. Given the magnitude of this political change, arguments are likely to continue for many years about its causes and consequences. Some preliminary analyses and explanations have already been presented, but they

[1] The opposition thus consisted of the LDP and the Japan Communist Party (JCP) which also did not join the coalition government.

[2] See chapter 3 for a discussion of the creation of this electoral system.

[3] The coalition had to seek a compromise with the LDP largely because there were elements within the JSP that were expected to oppose such a hybrid system, preferring a pure proportional representation system.

are far from complete. In this chapter I offer an explanation which, consistent with the rest of this study, highlights politicians' individual incentives and the strategic interactions of political parties under a given set of constraints. More specifically, I argue that the pattern of the LDP's breakup, which eventually caused the party to lose its majority, can be explained by the reaction of electorally vulnerable politicians to mounting public pressure for political reform. I also demonstrate that the establishment of the non-LDP coalition government, headed by Hosokawa, reflected both the preelection strategic maneuvering of political parties under the electoral uncertainty and their relative bargaining power in the postelection negotiation.

The chapter begins with a description of the events that led to the demise of the LDP's rule and the establishment of the non-LDP coalition government. Next, I critically assess the scholarly analyses offered thus far to explain this political change and then present an alternative microanalytic interpretation.

Facts

For the sake of clarity, I divide the process of the 1993 political change into two parts: (1) the period up to the passage of the nonconfidence bill against the LDP government, and (2) the period of postelection interparty bargaining that led to the creation of the non-LDP coalition government.[4]

The Collapse of the LDP Government

The beginning of the end of the LDP's one-party dominance came with the emergence of a new large-scale political scandal, involving a trucking company, Sagawa Kyubin, in February 1992.[5] In light of the mounting public pressure, the LDP government, headed by Prime Minister Kiichi Miyazawa, had no choice but to stress its commitment to political reform and to reopen the discussions for revising the existing electoral system, which had been put

[4] In reconstructing the following course of events, I have used numerous newspaper reports and articles. Some of the editorial articles from *Asahi Shimbun* were later compiled into a book: Asahi Shimbun Seiji-bu, *Seikai Saihen* [The realignment of a political landscape]. Another important source of information is Uchida, Hayano, and Sone, *Dai-Seihen* [The big political change]. In the interests of simplicity I will only specify sources for quotations and for instances where the article was based on editorial speculation.

[5] It should be emphasized that even before the Sagawa Kyubin case the Japanese political scene had, since the late 1980s, been plagued by two other major scandals, one involving Rikuruuto (originally the publishing company of an employment information magazine that issued millions of dollars worth of its own stock at below-market prices to politicians) and the other involving Kyowa (a company that bribed a former cabinet minister in charge of regional development in Hokkaido prefecture). Indeed, it was the surfacing of the Rikuruuto scandal in particular that had led the LDP government (then headed by Noboru Takeshita) to establish an advisory board (Dai Hachi-ji Senkyo Seido Shingikai) in 1989 to advise on political reform, including a proposal for revising the existing electoral system.

off since late 1991.[6] Ultimately, what prompted the passage of the nonconfidence bill against the LDP government in June 1993 was Miyazawa's failure to deliver on his commitment to revise the electoral system.[7] The process leading up to that point, however, was long and complex.

As an immediate result of the scandal, Shin Kanemaru, the LDP's vice-president, was convicted in September 1992 of accepting five hundred million yen from Sagawa in violation of the political contribution regulations. In the course of the investigation it became clear that Kanemaru was hiding a large amount of money from the tax office. As a result he was arrested in early 1993 for allegedly violating the income tax law. Kanemaru was the head of the LDP's largest faction, the Takeshita faction, and had long been depicted as the most powerful politician in Japan. His conviction and subsequent arrest therefore had an enormous impact on the following course of events.

Most important, the decline of Kanemaru's influence triggered the growth of an internal power struggle within the Takeshita faction. On October 28, 1992, two weeks after Kanemaru resigned, Keizo Obuchi was selected as the new leader of the faction. Dissatisfied with this result, Obuchi's rival, Ichiro Ozawa, formed an informal study group, and, on December 18, he and forty-three followers established a new faction and chose Tsutomu Hata as their leader. The Ozawa/Hata faction tried to portray itself as a group of reformers within the party.[8] At a press conference Hata emphasized that, with regard to the fate of electoral reform, his faction would be willing to compromise with opposition parties, thus implying the possibility of exploring party realignment beyond existing party lines.

While the Takeshita faction was experiencing turmoil, Prime Minister Miyazawa was putting together a new reform package. On December 22 the LDP's Executive Council decided to endorse the introduction of a single-member plurality electoral system. On January 22, 1993, the day that the ordinary session was convened, Miyazawa reiterated in Parliament his pledge

[6] After the Rikuruuto scandal, a consensus seemed to emerge among the public that the main cause of the excessive "money politics" was the existing electoral system which fostered intense factional competition within the LDP (cf. chapter 6). An earlier attempt to revise this system had been made during the summer of 1991 by Prime Minister Toshiki Kaifu who, among other things, tried to introduce a hybrid of a plurality and a proportional representation system, as proposed by the advisory board. Kaifu was forced to abandon his reform package (and ultimately to resign), not only because of the resistance from the opposition parties that preferred a system closer to pure proportional representation but also because he failed to forge a consensus for the proposed reform within the LDP. Since this earlier round of debates resulted in bitter internal fighting, newly chosen Prime Minister Miyazawa did not initially engage in discussions on substantive electoral reform.

[7] In this chapter I will not address aspects of political reform other than electoral reform. The reform of the electoral system was, as discussed below, by far the most contentious and important issue. For the content of the reform, see Christensen, "Electoral Reform in Japan."

[8] Ozawa was unquestionably the most powerful within the group, although Hata was chosen as the leader because he had a better public image. I therefore refer to this group throughout the chapter as the Ozawa/Hata faction.

for political reform. After the annual budget was passed, on April 2, the LDP put forward its package of reform bills for Diet deliberation.

Anticipating future difficulties in dealing with opposition parties, Miyazawa was also concerned with the unity of his party, especially given that the (former) Takeshita faction had gone through such a bitter split. Miyazawa therefore sought to appease the self-claimed reformers within the LDP. On April 6 he offered Hata the position of minister of foreign affairs, one of the most important cabinet positions. Hata, however, declined the offer, stating that political reform was his highest priority at that time.

In response to the LDP's proposal, the Socialists and the CGP, on April 8, presented their joint package of reform bills, including a proposal for introducing a German-style proportional representation electoral system. Because the LDP's and JSP-CGP's proposals were opposed to each other on the critical issue of a new electoral system, the upcoming legislative debate was expected to result in a stalemate. What prevented a stalemate from developing was another proposal made public on April 17 by a private group called Seiji Kaikaku Suishin Kyogi-kai (headed by a respected business leader, Masao Kamei), consisting of scholars, business elites, and labor representatives (the "Kamei group"). The electoral system this group envisioned was similar to the hybrid system proposed by the LDP in 1991, but the group was also receptive to the opposition's concern that a single-member district competition (even under such a hybrid system) would be biased in favor of larger parties. It therefore adopted a mechanism that would automatically correct the bias in deciding the distribution of seats assigned to the proportional representation portion.

Since the Kamei group's proposal was seen as a possible basis for compromise, the momentum for political reform was maintained. On May 25 the group representing junior members within the LDP gave Miyazawa signatures collected from 219 (out of a total of 381) LDP Diet members, urging that political reform be realized during the current Diet session even at the cost of compromising with opposition parties. On May 28 leaders from all the opposition parties except the Communists gathered and agreed that, based on the plan presented by the Kamei group, they would work together to put forward a proposal that could forge an agreement with the LDP. As pressure was mounting both in and outside his own party, on May 31, Miyazawa appeared on television and made explicit his determination to carry out political reform during the current Diet session.[9]

[9] There had been speculation that Miyazawa himself was initially reluctant about instituting political reform and was of the view that, if the political ethics of individual politicians were strengthened, institutional reform would not be necessary. It was later reported that he changed his view during early May when the JSP leaders approached Miyazawa and told him that their party would accept the Kamei group's plan. Because this plan was similar to the LDP's 1991 proposal, Miyazawa became more convinced that he could consolidate support within the LDP and that political reform was possible. It has been said that this conviction led him to make the statements he did on television (see Asahi Shimbun Seiji-bu, *Seikai Saihen*, pp. 25–27).

Despite Miyazawa's pledge, however, the senior hard-liners within the LDP refused to cooperate and lobbied hard against any compromise with the opposition. The younger group and the self-claimed reformers urged Miyazawa to show stronger leadership, but Miyazawa continued to rely on Party Secretary Seiroku Kajiyama for the task of unifying party opinions. After weeks of unsuccessful attempts to persuade the hard-liners, Kajiyama apparently gave up his efforts and, on June 14, told reporters that the LDP would not compromise and that the reform would be carried out not in the current session but after the upper house election scheduled two years hence.

As it became clear that the consensus building within the LDP was not succeeding, the opposition parties were preparing to present a nonconfidence bill against the Miyazawa government. Afraid that the Ozawa/Hata faction (and other rank-and-file members) would join the opposition, Miyazawa tried to extend the Diet session another two months in order to deliberate the reform bills further and asked the Speaker of the House, Yoshio Sakurauchi, to intervene on the matter. The JSP, CGP, and DSP, however, refused to accept Sakurauchi's arbitration. Therefore, on June 17, the three opposition parties presented the nonconfidence bill.

As the LDP-opposition dialogue was failing, the focus inevitably turned to the Ozawa/Hata faction. Anticipating the presentation of the nonconfidence bill, the leaders of this faction had gathered on June 16 and decided that if such a bill were presented they would uniformly support it. Hata himself had earlier thought that his faction should abstain in such a vote, whereas Ozawa consistently had insisted that abstention would send an ambiguous message to the constituencies. Hata apparently had changed his view by June 16, as he became convinced, through numerous telephone conversations with Miyazawa and Kajiyama, that even if the Diet session were extended, such an extension would not guarantee successful reform.

Hence the nonconfidence bill was passed in the early evening of June 18 by a vote of 255 to 220. Forty LDP members, including most of the members of the Ozawa/Hata faction, voted yes, while eighteen other LDP members were absent for the vote. On the same day Miyazawa dissolved the lower house and called a general election.

The Birth of a Non-LDP Coalition Government

During the two-month period between the passage of the nonconfidence bill and the establishment of the non-LDP coalition government, Japanese political parties were engaged in intense preelection maneuvering and postelection bargaining for coalition formation. During that process it was the three newly created parties that were crucial in deciding the final coalition outcome.

Two of these three parties were created immediately after the general election was called. First, on June 18, eleven members of the LDP left the party, and ten of them, led by Masayoshi Takemura, went on to establish a new party called "Sakigake" on June 21. Then, on June 22, forty-four members of the Ozawa/Hata faction left the LDP, and the next day they created a new party called "Shinsei-to."

Subsequently, these two parties explored means of cooperating with other parties. The leaders of Shinsei-to met with the leaders of the other four traditional opposition parties (the JSP, CGP, DSP, and SDF). Some of the latter group were seeking to ally with the LDP, but Shinsei-to convinced them that such an alliance would be political suicide for their parties given the salience of the reform issue. The five parties therefore agreed that they would seek to establish a non-LDP coalition government (excluding the JCP).[10] Sakigake, on the other hand, strengthened its ties with another new party, the JNP, led by Morihiro Hosokawa.[11] The latter two parties agreed not only that they would cooperate in the upcoming election, mutually endorsing candidates, but also that they would establish a uniform parliamentary force after the election.

The election was held on July 18. No party obtained a majority (see Table 8.1), and thus began the intense interparty bargaining for coalition formation. Although Shinsei-to and the other four parties had already committed to the establishment of a non-LDP (and non-JCP) coalition government, they alone did not have enough seats to form a parliamentary majority. Since the LDP also fell short of a majority, the focus turned to the two new parties, Sakigake and the JNP. These two parties, clearly recognizing that they held the key to a majority coalition, took a series of initiatives in the interparty negotiations.

On July 19, in accordance with the preelection agreement, the JNP and Sakigake joined forces to register as a single party (*kaiha*) in the lower house. On the same day Takemura and Hosokawa agreed that they would soon propose a policy outline that would form the basis for coalition negotiations. Furthermore, on July 20, on a live television program in which leaders of various parties appeared, Takemura suggested that each party's acceptance of the hybrid electoral system (of plurality and proportional representation) be the critical precondition for participation in a coalition. Finally, on July 23, the two parties formally announced their policy outlines (including the introduction of the hybrid system) and told reporters that they would seek to establish a government committed to political reform.

The Sakigake-JNP initiative forced other parties to take the defensive. In particular, it posed difficulties for the JSP, which was internally divided after its unprecedented defeat in the election. Whereas some members of the JSP stressed the importance of participating in a coalition (and thus ending the LDP's rule), others were more concerned with rebuilding the party itself. The

[10] In light of this development several labor unions, which had traditionally supported only the JSP or DSP candidates, decided that they would also endorse some new conservative candidates while terminating their support for the leftist elements in the JSP which were expected to oppose a coalition with the center/conservative parties.

[11] The JNP was formed in May 1992 and therefore had no seats in the lower house.

TABLE 8.1
Lower House Seat Distribution after the 1993 Election[a]

Party	*Seats*	*(Seats Held Previously)*
LDP	223	(222)
Independents (Pro-LDP)	10	(8)
JSP	70	(134)
CGP	51	(45)
Shinsei-to	55	(36)
DSP	15	(13)
Sakigake	13	(10)
JNP	35	(0)
SDF	4	(4)
Independents (Anti-LDP)	20	(7)
JCP	15	(16)
Others	0	(2)
Total	511	

Source: Asahi Shimbun, July 19, 1993.

[a]These numbers represent party affiliations immediately after the election. There was some party switching thereafter, but it was largely inconsequential to the following course of events and is thus ignored.

latter group, although outnumbered by the former, expressed vocal opposition to the proposed hybrid electoral system, arguing that the introduction of such a system would even further erode the party's support. Concerned with the JSP's impasse, other parties, especially Shinsei-to, applied strong pressure on the leaders of the JSP to make their decision quickly. On July 26 the JSP finally decided to accept the Sakigake-JNP proposal.[12]

The Sakigake-JNP initiative also put the LDP on the defensive. When Takemura specified his precondition for a coalition on the July 10 television program, Hiroshi Mitsuzuka, chair of the LDP's Policy Affairs Research Council, promptly responded that the LDP would be prepared to accept the hybrid electoral system. A consensus within the party then suddenly seemed to appear, as even those LDP members who were regarded as reluctant about political reform also started to endorse the hybrid system. On July 26, just as the

[12] Originally the JSP had scheduled a meeting of local representatives to take place on July 27 before the party's Central Executive Committee would make an official party decision. Shinsei-to, however, urged the JSP leaders to speed up the decision-making process, informing them that the LDP had been trying hard to lure members of the JNP and Sakigake into the LDP's camp. The JSP held a Central Executive Committee meeting and made its decision on the evening of July 26.

JSP and other parties responded favorably to the proposal, the LDP leaders also made it clear that they were prepared to accept the hybrid electoral system specified as the precondition by the JNP and Sakigake.

As the JNP and Sakigake joined forces, they exercised clear leverage vis-à-vis both the LDP and the non-LDP camps. There was nevertheless a difference in attitudes between the two parties. Hosokawa of the JNP was much more eager to go along with the non-LDP coalition option. For example, on July 22, even before the two parties formally set out the preconditions for coalition, he told reporters that he would prefer a non-LDP government. It was later reported that on the day Hosokawa made his remark, Shinsei-to's Ozawa offered his support to Hosokawa as prime minister. Takemura, on the other hand, was much more reserved and his party, Sakigake, tried to maintain official neutrality, at least until other parties made their counteroffers. It was also reported that Takemura, after having been informed about Ozawa's secret meeting with Hosokawa, complained to Ozawa himself that such an offer was premature.[13]

Sakigake's apparent neutrality was the only source of the LDP's hope. Since Prime Minister Miyazawa had already indicated his intention to resign, the discussion focused on the selection of a new party leader whose commitment to reform would be appealing, especially to Sakigake. The most obvious candidate was Masaharu Gotoda, a deputy prime minister/minister of justice, and he was approached and pressured to run by a number of LDP members. Gotoda, however, firmly declined to stand for the party leadership, citing his age and poor health as his reasons. He was seventy-eight years old and was in the hospital being treated for diabetes from July 18 to July 25, the most critical week of the coalition-building process.[14]

Having received counteroffers from both the LDP and non-LDP camp, it was finally time for the JNP and Sakigake to announce their coalition partner officially. By this point Sakigake's reservation had apparently disappeared, and, on July 27, Takemura agreed with Hosokawa to participate in the non-LDP group. On July 28, when these two informed the LDP of their coalition with the rival camp, the LDP's PARC chair, Mitsuzuka, tried to lure them back by saying that he would do his best to persuade Gotoda to become the new party leader. The two leaders, however, responded coolly and told Mitsuzuka that the terms of the LDP's counterproposal still needed to be more concrete.

On the same day the seven parties announced their formal agreement to

[13] Asahi Shimbun Seiji-bu, *Seikai Saihen*, pp. 137, 168.

[14] The LDP eventually selected Yohei Kohno, chief cabinet secretary, as the new leader. Kohno had an image of being a reformer with a fresh view not only because he was not a leader of an existing faction but also because he had once rebelled against the LDP and had become the founder of the New Liberal Club in 1976. At the meeting of party delegates on July 30 to select the new leader, Kohno, supported by a majority of rank-and-file members, defeated Michio Watanabe, a veteran factional leader, by a vote of 208 to 159.

establish a coalition government. On July 29 the leaders of these seven parties (and one other party in the upper house) agreed (1) to nominate Hosokawa as prime minister, and (2) to nominate a member of the JSP as speaker of the house. On July 31 Takemura made it public that he had been asked to become the chief cabinet secretary in the new government. On August 6, after electing Takako Doi, the former JSP leader, as speaker, Hosokawa was elected as the new prime minister. Three days later, on the same day that Hosokawa promised political reform before the end of the calender year, the cabinet ministers were appointed.[15]

Conventional Interpretations

Because of the magnitude of the political change (and its anticipated long-term consequences), scholars have yet to establish a thorough and systematic explanation for the series of events described in the previous section. Some preliminary analyses and explanations have been presented but, as reviewed below, they are either unsubstantiated or limited in their analytical scope.

The first type of explanation focuses on the broader international context in which the 1993 Japanese political change took place. Eiji Tomimori, for example, argues that the "1955 system," characterized by the conservative one-party dominance, was a product of the Cold War and that it was into the maintenance of this procapitalist system that businesses had to pour seemingly endless resources, thus facilitating "money politics," the LDP's factionalism and corrupt relationships among businessmen, politicians, and bureaucrats. According to Tomimori, the demise of this system was inevitable because the ending of the Cold War eliminated its structural foundations.[16] In the same vein, Takashi Inoguchi emphasizes the impact the end of the Cold War had on the foreign policy of the United States toward its allies. He draws parallels between Japan and Italy, both of which saw the long-standing dominant party collapse. According to Inoguchi, these changes took place because U.S. policy makers had become less concerned with preserving conservative regimes in these countries and began to make tougher demands in return for the provision of collective security.[17]

This type of explanation is merely impressionistic and not well supported by evidence. Even if it were true that the changing international environment

[15] The JSP occupied six ministerial positions, Shinsei-to occupied five, and the CGP occupied four, while the DSP, the SDF, Sakigake, and the JNP each occupied one position. Three other positions were assigned to nonpartisan ministers.

[16] Tomimori, "55-nen Taisei Hokai no Imi" [The significance of the demise of the 1955 system]. Note that Tomimori's conception of the "1955 system" is an illustration of the socio-ideological perspective reviewed critically in chapter 2.

[17] Inoguchi, "Japanese Politics in Transition"; Inoguchi, *Gendai Nihon Gaiko* [Contemporary Japanese diplomacy], esp. pp. 273–87.

was an important part of the background, the more precise pattern with which the change in Japanese domestic politics actually occurred cannot be explained by such a macroscopic view. For example, as far as the 1993 electoral outcome was concerned, it was not the conservative camp but rather the progressive forces, namely, the JSP, that suffered the most dramatic defeat. The LDP, in fact, remained the largest parliamentary group, obtaining more seats than it had had after the defection of the Ozawa/Hata group but before the election. Furthermore, the Cold War hypothesis does not answer the question regarding the timing of the political change; that is, why did the ending of the Cold War in 1989 not affect the fate of the LDP much earlier? The LDP had tried to pursue political reform in 1991 (after having won the general election), and this earlier reform attempt, although also unsuccessful, did not lead to the breakup of the party nor the demise of its dominance.

The second set of analyses focus more closely on the pattern of Japanese voting behavior in the 1993 election. Some analysts, such as Ikuo Kabashima and Michitoshi Takabatake, highlight the realignment within the conservative camp and emphasize the significance of the fact that the voters now had conservative options other than the LDP.[18] Others, including Masumi Ishikawa, emphasize that the election had the lowest turnout rate in postwar history (67.2 percent) and speculate as to how the pervasive "political distrust" not only provided an incentive for the conservative camp to realign but also caused the overall decline of old establishment parties, such as the JSP, CGP, JCP, and DSP.[19]

These analyses of the electoral outcome, however, are not helpful in illuminating the cause of the demise of the LDP government. Since the LDP maintained its number of seats, much of the collapse of the LDP's regime must be attributed to the preelection breakup of the party itself. None of the above voting analyses explain why the LDP broke up in the first place or the pattern of its breakup. Ishikawa is probably correct in suggesting that the unprecedented level of public political distrust (born out of the series of scandals) provided the incentive for conservative politicians to portray themselves as "reformers," but such a view begs the question as to why the political distrust did not entail an even greater realignment of the conservative camp, rather than the partial breakup of the LDP eventuated by the departure of the Ozawa/Hata group.

[18] Kabashima, "'Shin-Hoshujidai' no Makuake" [The opening of a "new conservative era"]; Kabashima, "Shinto no Tojyo to Jiminto Itto Yui Taisei no Houkai" [The rise of new parties and the collapse of the LDP's one-party dominance system]; and Takabatake, "'Shinto Gensho' de Nani ga Okitanoka?" [What happened with a "new party boom"].

[19] See, for example, Ishikawa, "5-to e no Aki, Kiken de Hyomei" [Expressing frustration toward the five parties through abstention]. Ishikawa is clearly under the influence of the Michigan school of voting studies, which suggests that the decline of party identification leads to party realignment (see Angus Campbell et al., *Elections and the Political Order*).

The criticisms developed here are not to deny that the end of the Cold War and the pervasiveness of the public political distrust had something to do with the collapse of the LDP's one-party dominance. However, although these structural factors might have been significant, they alone cannot account for the way the political events unfolded in 1993. In what follows I develop an alternative, more microanalytic explanation that illustrates how the competitive and strategic behavior of self-interested actors led to the demise of the LDP and to the establishment of the non-LDP coalition government.

Electoral Vulnerability, Bargaining Power, and the 1993 Political Change

In order to understand the causal chain of events that led to the 1993 political change, one must focus on the incentives of competing actors and the range of options open to them in the changing strategic environment.

The Breakup of the Former Takeshita Faction

The collapse of the LDP's one-party regime was triggered by the two-way split of the then Takeshita faction in December 1992. As demonstrated in chapter 6, the pattern of the LDP's factionalization was shaped by the existing electoral system, as it constrained the behavior of individual LDP politicians and LDP supporters. In this regard, the breakup of one of the existing major factions represented an anomalous development and, as such, it should have been "corrected" at least in the long run through an institutional selection mechanism.

Ultimately what prevented such a corrective mechanism from functioning was the increasing prospect of political reform and thus the increasing expectation that the institutional framework for party competition itself might be altered in the near future. When the Miyazawa government reopened discussions for electoral reform, after the Sagawa Kyubin scandal surfaced in February 1992, the public's political distrust had already reached a point where individual politicians had to make their commitment to political reform explicit. Precisely because the existing electoral system was viewed as the cause of LDP's factionalism, which in turn was viewed as the source of excessive "money politics," the revision of the 1947 electoral law was to become the central issue in the reform debate.

The mounting public distrust, however, did not affect the LDP politicians evenly, and the need to demonstrate their commitment to reform varied among individuals. Because of the subsequent arrest of their leader, Shin Kanemaru, members of the former Takeshita faction were particularly sensitive to the public demand for reform. It was especially important, therefore, for Ichiro

TABLE 8.2
Profile of the Obuchi and Ozawa/Hata Group in Terms of Their Parliamentary Affiliation

	Lower House	*Upper House*	*Total*
Obuchi	28	34	62
Ozawa/Hata	35	9	44

Source: Nihon Keizai Shimbun (evening edition), December 18, 1992.

Ozawa, who had been regarded as Kanemaru's best student, to portray himself as "reformer" in the party. Immediately following the arrest of Kanemaru for tax evasion in March 1993, Ozawa began to criticize his former mentor openly. Furthermore, it is reasonable to suggest that young/junior members within the party were particularly vulnerable, as they had not yet firmly established their networks of support in their own constituencies. Veteran politicians, on the other hand, were probably less sincere about their commitment to reform because it was under the existing system that they had been reelected.

The creation of the Ozawa/Hata faction as a group of (self-claimed) reformers must be understood in this context. True, the reason this faction emerged was the struggle for leadership between Obuchi and Ozawa, but the promotion motives of these two leaders cannot alone explain the pattern with which they formed separate groups. To highlight how the varying degree of electoral vulnerability of rank-and-file members led to the split, I have analyzed the profile of those politicians who followed Ozawa and those who supported Keizo Obuchi. When the Ozawa/Hata faction was established, forty-four members (of the former Takeshita faction) supported it, whereas sixty-two remained faithful to Obuchi.[20] As summarized in Tables 8.2 and 8.3, the support base for each group was quite different.

First, the Ozawa/Hata group received more support from lower house members, whereas an overwhelming majority of upper house members supported Obuchi (see Table 8.2). Because the ongoing discussion on political reform focused primarily on the revision of the electoral system for the House of Representatives, one would expect that members of the upper house felt less public pressure.

Second, clear differences existed between the lower house supporters for each group, in terms of their number of reelections. As Table 8.3 shows, most of the members who had been elected only once or twice chose to join the Ozawa/Hata camp. These members, as they had been recruited only recently, were indeed electorally vulnerable and had reason to be vocal about their

[20] *Nihon Keizai Shimbun* (evening edition), December 18, 1992. Four members remained neutral.

TABLE 8.3
Profile of the Lower House Members of the Obuchi and Ozawa/Hata Group in Terms of the Number of Their Re-elections

Number of Reelections	*Obuchi*	*Ozawa/Hata*
1	2	7
2	3	12
3	4	3
4	3	0
5	4	4
6	4	1
7	1	2
8	1	6
9	1	0
10 or more	5	0
Total	28	35

Source: Nihon Keizai Shimbun (evening edition), December 18, 1992.

commitment to political reform.[21] Much of Obuchi's support, on the other hand, came from less vulnerable senior members of the faction.

In sum, individual LDP politicians reacted differently to growing public pressure for political reform. The above evidence suggests that the incentives of the electorally vulnerable members, in particular, were the important determinant of the breakup of the former Takeshita faction.

As indicated in the previous section, this breakup in December 1992 led to the creation of a new party, Shinsei-to, and therefore lay the foundation for the establishment of the future non-LDP government several months ahead. This is not to suggest, however, that the Ozawa/Hata faction had intended all along to leave the LDP. Creating a new faction within an existing party is one thing, but creating a new party is quite another, since the latter involves much higher organizational costs and can be risky electorally. Thus, as argued below, the following course of events, including Ozawa's and Hata's revolt against the LDP, may not have been what they had originally anticipated.

The Dissolution of the House and Creation of Sakigake

It is difficult to know at what point Ozawa and Hata concluded that their group had to leave the LDP altogether. With the benefit of hindsight, they appear to

[21] Of those twenty-four politicians of the (former) Takeshita faction elected for the first or second time in the previous election, only one finished top in the constituency. Among the nine rookies, four won the last seat in a multimember district competition; among the fifteen elected for the second time, four were winners of the last seat and three were winners of the second last seat (*Asahi Shimbun*, February 20, 1990.)

have chosen the correct strategy because they were eventually able to form a non-LDP coalition government. *Ex ante*, however, leaving could have been costly and risky. Furthermore, as evidenced by Hata's and Ozawa's initial disagreement as to how to deal with the nonconfidence bill against the Miyazawa government, individual members probably had different visions as to the group's future.[22]

In so far as the group was driven by the desire to send a clear reform message, it may have been inevitable that eventually it would join the opposition in supporting the nonconfidence bill. The strategy after that, however, was far from definite. The members of the Ozawa/Hata faction knew that their collective yes vote would guarantee the bill's passage, but there was uncertainty as to whether in fact that would lead to a general election. Constitutionally, the government could either dissolve the house (and thus call an election) or resign en masse.[23]

It has been suggested that the group's strategist, Ozawa, made a miscalculation on this matter. He thought that the LDP would not choose to call an election but rather would replace Miyazawa with a new leader, under whom discussions of political reform with the opposition parties could be resumed. The person Ozawa had in mind was Deputy Prime Minister Masaharu Gotoda who by then had already attracted wide support from the reform-minded junior members of the LDP. Miyazawa's decision to dissolve the house was therefore a surprise. Ozawa was later quoted as saying: "Why did Mr. Gotoda agree to Prime Minister Miyazawa's dissolution of the house? I was positive he would oppose it. If it had been the resignation of the cabinet en masse [instead of the dissolution], he surely could have become prime minister. I still don't understand."[24]

Had Gotoda been chosen as the new LDP president at this point, the Ozawa/Hata faction would have had the option of remaining in the LDP. In light of Gotoda's leadership and his commitment to reform, the Ozawa/Hata group could have reinstated itself as the mainstream force within the party.[25]

[22] It is reported that another influential member of the group, Kozo Watanabe, had earlier told Ozawa that he would oppose the group's departure from the LDP (Asahi Shimbun Seiji-bu, *Seikai Saihen*, p. 40).

[23] Article 69 of the Constitution stipulates: "If the House of Representatives passes a nonconfidence resolution, or rejects a confidence resolution, the Cabinet shall resign en masse, unless the House of Representatives is dissolved within ten (10) days."

[24] Quoted in Asahi Shimbun Seiji-bu, *Seikai Saihen*, p. 43 (translation by Kohno).

[25] The selection of Gotoda as the new LDP leader would not have been the only pretext the Ozawa/Hata group could have used to remain in the LDP. It is reported that in the last telephone conversation between Hata and Miyazawa (on June 18) before the dissolution of the house, Hata offered to agree to extend the Diet session if Miyazawa would release Party Secretary Kajiyama and two other top party officials from their duties. Miyazawa is said to have angrily declined the offer (Ibid., p. 35). Such a change in party leadership would have been taken as a sufficient expression of reform commitment, which could at least have delayed the departure of the Ozawa/Hata faction.

Gotoda's endorsement of (or his lack of opposition to) a general election, however, left Ozawa and Hata no option but to dissociate themselves from the LDP. In other words, they were finally forced to pay the price of portraying themselves as reformers, build a new party, and start an electoral campaign from scratch.[26]

In addition to the "Gotoda" factor, what confused the strategy of the Ozawa/Hata group even more was the creation of Sakigake only hours after the house was dissolved. Unlike the Ozawa/Hata faction, this group, led by Masayoshi Takemura, had maintained its low-key posture within the LDP until the very last moment, even voting against the nonconfidence bill.[27] While Sakigake was far smaller, the sudden creation of another new political party was a blow to the Ozawa/Hata group, as the latter could no longer monopolize the banner of rebellious reformers. Furthermore, as Sakigake began strengthening its ties with Morihiro Hosokawa's JNP, the range of options open to the Ozawa/Hata group narrowed considerably. If there had not been a Sakigake-JNP alliance, Ozawa/Hata's Shinsei-to would still have held the key bargaining leverage in the postelection negotiations, given that neither the LDP nor the non-LDP camp was likely to obtain a majority. With the rise of the Sakigake-JNP bloc, however, Shinsei-to's leverage over the LDP disappeared because the LDP now had an alternative, more appealing coalition partner. Hence Ozawa and Hata were left with no choice but to engineer an alliance with the "left," that is, the traditional opposition parties such as the CGP, DSP, and JSP. In fact, because the LDP was likely to remain the largest party, Shinsei-to had to unite the opposition parties into a coherent anti-LDP force *before* the election so that the LDP would not be able to exploit division within the non-LDP camp during the postelection coalition-building negotiations.

Thus, because of Sakigake's preelection maneuvering, Shinsei-to was losing its control on the course of events. Meanwhile, the preelection collaboration between Sakigake and the JNP was extremely beneficial not only for Takemura but also for the JNP leader, Hosokawa. Hosokawa knew, of course, that Sakigake would be too small by itself to have significant clout in the postelection coalition negotiations. But he was unsure of his own party's electoral prospects because, unlike Shinsei-to and Sakigake which consisted largely of LDP renegades, virtually all the JNP's candidates were running for the first time for the lower house. Thus the endorsement from Sakigake was a good strategy for Hosokawa, both for electoral and future coalition purposes.[28]

[26] This raises the question as to why Gotoda forfeited his rare opportunity for promotion. That he subsequently chose to be hospitalized during the critical week of the coalition-building process suggests, as reported elsewhere (Ibid., p. 146), that he did not want to become prime minister and that he perhaps wanted to retire from politics, leaving behind his image as a hard-core reformer not interested in power and prestige.

[27] Ibid, pp. 51–54.

[28] The uncertainty may have been mitigated by the JNP's stunning success in the Tokyo metropolitan election, which had been held before the general election.

To the extent that the JNP's electoral performance was uncertain, Hosokawa's interest in holding the key balance of power in the postelection negotiations converged with Takemura's. When the election was over, however, and the uncertainty gone, the interests of the two leaders began to diverge. As discussed below, this tension between the JNP and Sakigake became the basis for the formation of the non-LDP coalition government. But before moving on to an analysis of the postelection bargaining, let us examine more closely the results of the 1993 general election.

The Electoral Success of the New Parties

In so far as the outcome of the 1993 general election is concerned, unquestionably the winners were the three newly created parties—the JNP, Shinsei-to, and Sakigake. As indicated in Table 8.4, these parties performed well relative to other parties in terms of their overall success rates.[29]

As argued in chapters 6 and 7 in this study, the existing electoral system imposes significant constraints for individual politicians and competing political parties, and one has no reason to believe that the 1993 election was an exception. In order to assess the institutional impact on the three parties' electoral strategy, I have investigated the distribution of electoral districts in which none of these three parties had candidates. There were thirty-three such districts, and they were distributed as shown in Table 8.5.

These results, although not statistically significant, point to the tendency of the three newly created parties to nominate more candidates in larger-sized districts, suggesting that the multimember district electoral system facilitated the rise of these parties.[30] Thus, although the pervasive political distrust might have been the ultimate cause of these new parties' appearance, the impact of this structural factor was mediated through the institutional framework of party competition. Had there been a single-member plurality system, the establishment and electoral success of these parties would have been more difficult.

Having identified the institutional effect of the electoral system generally, let us now focus more closely on the three parties' electoral strategy and show how this effect contributed to their electoral success. As indicated earlier, Shinsei-to and Sakigake were made up of LDP renegades and therefore most of their candidates had already developed bases in their own constituencies. The JNP, on the other hand, was a party of new candidates.[31] One would

[29] The CGP's rate is high, but this should be treated as an exception.

[30] Note that these results were consistent with the findings of the electoral strategy of smaller LDP factions (see chapter 6) and of the middle-of-the-road parties that appeared in the 1960s (see chapter 7).

[31] This also explains the lower success rate of the JNP compared with the other two parties reported in Table 8.4.

TABLE 8.4
Success Rates of Seven Major Parties in the 1993 Election

Party	*Number of Candidates*	*Number of Seats*[a]	*Success Rates (%)*
LDP	285	223	78.2
JSP	142	70	49.3
CGP	54	51	94.4
Shinsei-to	69	55	79.7
DSP	28	15	53.6
Sakigake	15	13	86.7
JNP	55	35	63.6

Source: Asahi Shimbun, July 5, 1993; July 19, 1993.
[a]These entries represent party affiliations immediately after the election.

TABLE 8.5
Distribution of Eighteen Districts with No New Party Candidates across Different-Sized Districts in the 1993 Election

		District Size				
		2	*3*	*4*	*5*	*6*
Candidates	No	4 (50)	12 (30.8)	10 (29.4)	7 (15.2)	0 (0)
(%)	Yes	4 (50)	27 (69.2)	24 (70.6)	39 (84.8)	2 (100)
	Total	8	39	34	46	2
	$X^2 = 6.6$					

Source: Asahi Shimbun, July 6, 1993.

TABLE 8.6
Distribution of 55 Candidates from the Japan New Party across Different-Sized Districts in the 1993 Election

		District Size				
		2	*3*	*4*	*5*	*6*
Candidates	Yes	1 (12.5)	10 (25.6)	19 (55.9)	23 (50)	2 (100)
(%)	No	7 (87.5)	29 (74.6)	15 (44.1)	23 (50)	0 (0)
	Total	8	39	34	46	2
	$X^2 = 13.7$ (significant at .01 level)					

Source: Asahi Shimbun, July 5, 1993.

TABLE 8.7
Success and Failure of 55 Candidates from the Japan New Party in the 1993 Election[a]

	District Size				
	2	*3*	*4*	*5*	*6*
Success (%)	0 (0)	5 (50)	10 (52.6)	17 (73.9)	2 (100)
Failure (%)	1 (100)	5 (50)	9 (47.4)	6 (26.1)	0 (0)
Total	1	10	19	23	2
$X^2 = 6.1$					

Source: Asahi Shimbun, July 20, 1993.
[a]Excludes one candidate who was not an official JNP candidate at the beginning of the campaign period.

expect, then, that the JNP's candidate nomination would reveal an especially distinctive pattern.

As Table 8.6 shows, the candidates from the JNP were clearly concentrated in larger districts.[32] Furthermore, the results of Table 8.7 suggest that the electoral success or failure of the JNP candidates was also influenced by the size of their districts in which they were competing.

The JNP was a party of entirely new candidates and, as such, it is fair to say that it faced the toughest campaign. The JNP was nevertheless electorally successful, benefiting from the multimember district arrangement of the existing electoral system.

The Formation of the Hosokawa Government

During the postelection negotiations that led to the formation of the Hosokawa government, the bargaining power of political parties did not directly reflect their relative size in terms of their parliamentary seats. As already argued, the JNP and Sakigake ultimately held the balance of power because, while joining forces, they did not make a preelection commitment to either the LDP or the non-LDP camp. The LDP and the JSP, on the other hand, were not able to exercise much leverage, even though they remained the two largest parties.

The explanation for the lack of the LDP's bargaining leverage is straightfor-

[32] A similar pattern of candidate nomination cannot be found for Shinsei-to and Sakigake, presumably because these two parties were created by former LDP members. Both these parties, however, did nominate new candidates for the election, in addition to those who had originally defected from the LDP. This leads one to expect a contrast across different-sized districts between the distribution of incumbent (and previously affiliated) candidates and that of new candidates. The results of the analysis are mixed. With regard to Sakigake, one can detect that new candidates, relative to the incumbents, were concentrated in the larger districts, although the sample here is too small to be conclusive. With regard to Shinsei-to, this trend was not apparent.

ward: most other parties, after having voted for the nonconfidence bill, ran electoral campaigns seeking to establish a non-LDP government. Otherwise the LDP could have explored a liaison with the traditional centrist parties, namely, the DSP and CGP, for a majority coalition. But because these two parties increased their "audience costs" vis-à-vis their own supporters in terms of their anti-LDP commitment, the credibility of the CGP and DSP as potential coalition partners for the LDP was lost.[33] For this reason the LDP had to turn to the JNP-Sakigake alliance and had no choice but to accept their preconditions immediately after the election.

The lack of bargaining power of the second largest party, the JSP, was far more puzzling. Even though the JSP suffered an unprecedented defeat in the election, it was still the largest among the seven non-LDP parties. Because there was no immediate sign of a further breakup within the LDP, a non-LDP coalition government could not have been formed without the JSP's participation.[34] Nevertheless, the JSP not only failed to select its own leader for prime minister, but it exercised little leverage in influencing the platform of the Hosokawa government, as evidenced by its concession to accept the hybrid electoral system proposed by the JNP and Sakigake.

The critical development that determined the fate of the JSP was the LDP's decision, expressed as early as July 21, to accept the hybrid system as a compromise. This meant that electoral reform would probably pass in the forthcoming Diet session and that the next general election would be held under the new system. Although many of the details would still have to be worked out, approximately half the total seats under the new system would likely be determined by a single-seat plurality competition. The prospect of the adoption of the new system made it difficult for the JSP to remain outside the non-LDP coalition. An element within the JSP strongly opposed the introduction of even a partial plurality electoral system, but its opposition was irrelevant now that the LDP appeared willing to accept the JNP-Sakigake proposal. Since the LDP was still a force to be reckoned with, the JSP now had an incentive to participate in the coalition in order both to have input into the details of the electoral reform and to compete in the forthcoming election with the LDP candidates from within the coalition. In short, given the expectation of institutional reform, its own future electoral concerns prevented the JSP from exercising its bargaining power in the coalition-building negotiations.

The JSP's decision to participate in the non-LDP camp set the stage for the JNP and Sakigake to choose their coalition partners. One important question remains: Why did these two parties choose to side with the non-LDP group

[33] For an explanation of the concept of "audience costs," see footnote 22 in chapter 5.

[34] The LDP was not likely to go through another major split as long as it still had a chance of forming a majority coalition with the JNP and Sakigake. Three members led by Mutsuki Kato left the LDP (eventually to join Shinsei-to), but their departure was only after the seven non-LDP parties agreed formally to establish a coalition government on July 28.

rather than the LDP? The answer with regard to the JNP is straightforward; the former outbid the latter. The non-LDP group had offered Hosokawa the position of prime minister. The LDP, on the other hand, was struggling to persuade Gotoda to become the new party leader. This explains why Hosokawa leaned toward the non-LDP camp, even before the JNP and Sakigake jointly announced their policy outline. For Hosokawa, the collaboration with Sakigake was only important *before* the election when he was unsure of his party's electoral performance. Now that the JNP had won far more seats than had Sakigake, the JNP was clearly the stronger partner of the two. Thus, when Ozawa offered support for his premiership, nothing prevented Hosokawa from accepting.

The decision for Sakigake's Takemura, on the other hand, was more complicated. Takemura knew that, given the size of his party, his bargaining leverage in the interparty negotiations was contingent on the unity of the JNP-Sakigake partnership. Thus, provided Sakigake and the JNP could act uniformly, Takemura's preferred strategy would have been to wait as long as possible to see whether the LDP or the non-LDP camp would come up with a better a coalition offer.[35] Takemura, however, could not pursue this strategy because he knew that Hosokawa's incentive to maintain the two-party collaboration had declined. When Ozawa, well aware of the potential tension between Takemura and Hosokawa, made a secret deal with Hosokawa, Takemura knew that his "wait-and-see" strategy would not work.

Thus Takemura had to reformulate his strategy, as he was gradually leaning toward the non-LDP camp. He might have welcomed the selection of Hosokawa as prime minister, if the JNP had not won as many seats and the two parties could have remained equal partners. Now that there was such disparity in the size of the two parties, the selection of Hosokawa would not directly benefit Takemura and his party. For Hosokawa, on the other hand, the fate of Sakigake was no longer a major concern. Knowing this, Takemura took the offensive and announced that Hosokawa had asked him to become chief cabinet secretary even before Hosokawa was formally designated prime minister in the Diet.[36] This intentional leak had the effect of highlighting "the JNP-Sakigake partnership" and thus forcing Hosokawa to take Sakigake seriously. This strategy worked: despite the pressure from Shinsei-to to appoint someone

[35] If there had been no tension between the JNP and Sakigake, these two parties probably would have exercised even more bargaining power collectively, vis-à-vis both the LDP and non-LDP camps, in terms of cabinet positions and policy influence. This interpretation points to the party's dilemma with the ultimate bargaining power in a coalition-building process, which I have discussed in my analysis of the Katayama government formation in chapter 4. As I pointed out, such a party would be vulnerable to an internal split precisely because of the increased expectation that it would be part of the majority coalition. Its concern would therefore shift from how to participate in to how to lead the coalition.

[36] It is impossible to verify whether Hosokawa actually asked Takemura to take the position. Hosokawa was reportedly unhappy with Takemura's leak (Asahi Shimbun Seiji-bu, *Seikai Saihen*, p. 200).

else, Takemura was indeed chosen as the new secretary when the Hosokawa government was established on August 9.[37]

In sum, the formation of the non-LDP government headed by Hosokawa was a product of complex interactions among political actors involved in the coalition-building process. The bargaining power of political parties was determined not only by the relative size of their parliamentary share but also by their preelection commitment, future electoral concerns, as well as the strategy of other parties involved in the negotiation. Although the JNP and Sakigake held the key to the balance of power, the tension between the two parties prevented them from exercising even greater leverage.

The series of events in 1993 resulted in the collapse of the LDP's one-party regime that had ruled Japan for nearly four decades. As is the case with any political change of such magnitude, it would be impossible to explain the transition of power from the LDP to the non-LDP coalition government without taking into account some basic exogenous forces, such as the pervasion of public distrust that was born out of a series of financial scandals. The explanations that rely exclusively on these structural causes, however, fail to explain the more precise pattern with which the 1993 political change took place. To understand more fully the causal chain of events, one needs to focus, microanalytically, on the basic incentives of individual political actors and their strategic behavior under the given institutional constraints.

In this chapter I have shown that such a microanalytic perspective provides a coherent and comprehensive explanation for the 1993 political change. The breakup of the Takeshita faction was a product of the electoral vulnerability of those politicians who needed to show their commitment to political reform. The establishment of the Hosokawa government was a reflection of the relative bargaining power of political parties and their strategic maneuvering in the coalition-building negotiations. The analyses and evidence presented here are thus consistent with those in the rest of the study: they reveal that the underlying logic of competition and strategic interaction among political actors drives political outcomes in Japan.

As pointed out earlier, the 1993 political change resulted in a transformation of the electoral system, and it will therefore have long-term consequences for Japanese party politics. The details of the bargaining over the electoral reform, as well as the pattern of the partisan realignment, deserve systematic scholarly investigation of their own. But however Japanese party politics unfolds in the future, the fundamental nature of political parties competing for power and public influence under Japan's parliamentary democracy will most likely remain unchanged.

[37] This obviously was not a final solution to the tension between these two parties. Despite the earlier agreement to merge into a new single party, the two parties repeatedly put off their meeting to discuss the merger and eventually decided not to join forces.

9

CONCLUSION

THE PRECEDING chapters of this study have analyzed the fundamental nature of competitive democracy in Japan. The analysis has shown that the Japanese political actors are as self-seeking as those elsewhere and that the existing institutional arrangements, especially the electoral laws, operate as constraints on these actors' behavior. Ever since these institutional arrangements were being established in the aftermath of World War II, Japanese political parties have been engaged in incessant and fierce competition for votes, parliamentary seats, and legislative influence. Likewise, individual politicians have constantly been seeking opportunities to maximize their chance of reelection and promotion within their own parties. As Joseph Schumpeter argued more than half a century ago, competition is the defining characteristic that distinguishes democracy from other types of political regimes.[1] In this sense one can expect that the future pattern of interactions between Japanese political parties and individual politicians will not deviate, at the most fundamental level, from those documented in this study.

From a more theoretical standpoint, this study can be seen as an attempt to demonstrate the usefulness of the microanalytic approach that focuses on individual actors and the given set of constraints. As I have demonstrated throughout the book, this approach can establish consistent explanations for various important changes in postwar Japanese party politics. At the same time I have pointed out the inadequacies of interpretations based on the three conventional theoretical approaches summarized in chapter 2. I do not claim that political-culture, historical, or socio-ideological factors are irrelevant in determining the evolution of Japanese parliamentary democracy. In some of the cases discussed, in fact, these macrostructural factors were critical, such as in providing a "focal point" in the interparty bargaining during the electoral reform process in 1947 (chapter 3) and in setting the basic boundaries within which party competition had to take place during the post-1955 period (chapter 7). What I claim, however, is that, even in these cases, an analysis preoccupied with the macrostructural determinants can only provide partial insight and limited predictions. Generally the impact of political-culture, historical, and socio-ideological factors is likely to be mediated through more specific institutional arrangements that in turn constrain the behavior of individual actors. Thus, in order to explain the details and more precise patterns with which political events develop, one needs to go beyond the macrolevel analysis and

[1] Schumpeter, *Capitalism, Socialism and Democracy.*

examine the incentives, bargaining power, and strategies of the individual political actors who are making actual choices.

As noted in chapter 1, the analytical exercise of this study may have implications beyond the Japanese context and, more generally, for the field of comparative politics. Given the "uniqueness" or "distinctiveness" often associated with Japan in the family of advanced industrial democracies, if the microanalytic approach can produce consistent explanations for a country like Japan, it must be applicable to other countries whose cultural, historical, and societal backgrounds are not believed to be so unique or distinctive. Because comparative politics is such a diverse field, broad generalizations cannot be justified, but at least for the analysis of party politics in a democratic setting, one can conclude that the microanalytic framework provides effective tools and valuable insights.

The microanalytic approach, of course, has its own shortcomings, one of which may be that it does not account for the events and phenomena in question in a perfectly falsifiable manner. As some of the previous chapters indicate, there are often sudden "exogenous shocks" that are influential on the final political outcomes, as was the case with the effect of MacArthur's announcement on the 1947 coalition building (chapter 4), that of Ogata's death on the 1955 conservative merger (chapter 5), and the pervasive political distrust on the 1993 political change (chapter 8). It is impossible to incorporate, *ex ante*, the impact these shocks have on individual preference-formation processes, and, given the unexpected nature of these shocks, it would probably be inappropriate to do so.

The advantage of the microanalytic focus, however, is that it can reconstruct individual preferences and options available at each point in time *as history unfolds*. Put another way, it can re-create the strategic environment in which the relevant actors interacted just as those actors perceived it. It is only in this manner of reconstruction that one can understand the impact of the exogenous shocks (and the actors' responses to them) in sorting out the causal chain of events. In essence, then, the microanalytic approach helps one to avoid relying on hindsight and instead to establish more forward-looking interpretations.

Explorations of the microfoundations of Japanese politics, similar to the one conducted in this book, have already been presented in other subfields within Japanese political studies, especially in public policy analyses.[2] These early applications have triggered a heated controversy in and outside the scholarly literature, leading some traditional Japanologists to reject the utility of the microanalytic models outright.[3] In these criticisms, the studies based on

[2] Ramseyer and Rosenbluth, *Japan's Political Marketplace*. See also Cowhey and McCubbins, eds., *Structure and Policy in Japan and the United States*.

[3] See, for example, Johnson and Keehn, "A Disaster in the Making."

such models are said to be "completely ahistorical" and "tell us little about why and how these systems change."[4] Such criticism, however, is misguided. There is nothing unique about the microanalytic models that make their mode of analysis "ahistorical" or "insensitive to change." As I hope is evident from the previous chapters, a microanalytic exploration can indeed take historical facts seriously and account for important political changes.

The primary purpose of this study has been positive in the sense of describing and interpreting the postwar evolution of Japan's party politics. The arguments and analyses advanced here, however, have normative implications as well; that is, despite suggestions some Japanologists made to the contrary, Japan's parliamentary democracy is no more "uncommon" and no less democratic than any other advanced industrial democracy in the world.[5] Japan is a nation based on a system of parliamentary democracy in which elections take place, politicians and societal forces organize political parties, and political parties compete for power and influence. As in any other Western nation, it is the fundamental logic of competition and strategic interactions that drives the dynamics of party politics in Japan.

As noted at the outset of this study, party competition has been a neglected area in contemporary Japanese political studies. It should also be re-emphasized that most observers of Japanese politics have thus far failed to recognize the importance of the microanalytic approach. Hence this study has attempted to fill the vacuum in the literature and to stress two points that must be addressed in future research. First, political parties are clearly an important set of actors and their competitive interactions must be taken seriously in understanding the dynamics of postwar Japanese politics. Political parties matter, not only because of their increasing policy-making capacity but also because of their role in shaping basic political institutions and determining the pattern of government formation in Japan's parliamentary democracy. Second, individual incentives, bargaining power, and strategic interactions are important analytical concepts that are useful in studying contemporary Japan. A search for the microfoundations of the observed behavioral outcomes, without relying so heavily on macrostructural factors distinctive to the Japanese context, will further enhance the opportunities to compare the politics of Japan with that of other advanced industrial democracies.

[4] Ibid., p. 16.

[5] See, for example, Pempel, *Uncommon Democracies*; and Curtis and Ishikawa, *Doken Kokka Nippon* [Construction state Japan].

BIBLIOGRAPHY

NEWSPAPERS AND DATA SOURCES

Asahi Shimbun.

Nihon Keizai Shimbun.

Shugiin and Sangiin, eds. *Gikai Seido Shichiju-nen-shi: Shiryo-hen* [Seventy year history of parliamentary institutions: documents-volume]. Tokyo: Okurasho Insatsu-kyoku, 1962.

Shugiin Jimukyoku. *Dai Nijuni-kai Shuugiin Giin Sosenkyo no Kekka* [The results of the twenty-second House of Representative election]. Tokyo: Okurasho Insatsu-kyoku, 1950.

BOOKS AND ARTICLES

Akiyama, Youichiro. *Senkyo* [Elections]. Tokyo: Daiichi Houki, 1973.

Asahi Shimbun Seiji-bu. *Seikai Saihen* [The realignment of a political landscape]. Tokyo: Asahi Shimbun-sha, 1993.

Austen-Smith, David, and Jeffrey Banks. "Elections, Coalitions, and Legislative Outcomes." *American Political Science Review* 82 (1988): 405–22.

Axelrod, Robert. *Conflict of Interest.* Chicago: Markham, 1970.

Babb, James. "The Statics and Dynamics of Japan Socialist Party Ideology." Paper presented at the annual meeting of the American Political Science Association, Chicago, 1992.

Baerwald, Hans H. *Party Politics in Japan.* Boston: Allen and Unwin, 1986.

Baron, David P. "A Spatial Bargaining Theory of Government Formation in Parliamentary Systems." *American Political Science Review* 85 (1991): 137–64.

Bawn, Kathleen. "The Logic of Institutional Preferences: German Electoral Law as a Social Choice Outcome." *American Journal of Political Science* 37 (1993): 965–89.

Befu, Harumi. *Japan: An Anthropological Introduction.* San Francisco: Chandler, 1971.

Calder, Kent E. *Crisis and Compensation: Public Policy and Political Stability in Japan, 1949–1986.* Princeton, N.J.: Princeton University Press, 1988.

Campbell, Angus, Phillip E. Converse, Warren E. Miller, and Donald E. Stokes. *Elections and the Political Order.* New York: Wiley, 1966.

Christensen, Raymond V. "Electoral Reform in Japan: How It Was Enacted and Changes It May Bring." *Asian Survey* (July 1994): 589–605.

Christensen, Raymond V., and Paul Johnson. "Toward a Context-Rich Analysis of Electoral Systems: The Japanese Example." *American Journal of Political Science* 39 (1995): 575–98.

Cowhey, Peter F., and Mathew D. McCubbins, eds. *Structure and Policy in Japan and the United States.* New York: Cambridge University Press, 1995.

Cox, Gary W. "Strategic Voting Equilibria under the Single Nontransferable Vote." *American Political Science Review* 88 (1994): 608–21.

———. "Is the Single Nontransferable Vote Superproportional? Evidence from Japan and Taiwan." *American Journal of Political Science*, forthcoming.

Cox, Gary W., and Frances Rosenbluth. "The Electoral Fortunes of Legislative Factions in Japan." *American Political Science Review* 87 (1993): 577–89.

Cox, Gary W., and Emerson Niou. "Seat Bonuses under the Single Nontransferable Vote System: Evidence from Japan and Taiwan." *Comparative Politics* 26 (1994): 221–36.

Crombez, Christophe. "Minority Governments, Minimum Winning Coalitions, and Surplus Majorities in Parliamentary Systems." *European Journal of Political Research* 29 (1996): 1–29.

Curtis, Gerald L. *Election Compaigning Japanese Style*. New York: Columbia University Press, 1971.

———. *The Japanese Way of Politics*. New York: Columbia University Press, 1988.

Curtis, Gerald L., and Masumi Ishikawa. *Doken Kokka Nippon* [Construction state Japan]. Tokyo: Kobun-sha, 1984.

David, Paul. "Clio and the Economics of QWERTY." *American Economic Review* 75 (1985): 332–37.

Doi, Takeo. *Amae no Kozo* [The structure of dependence]. Tokyo: Kokubun-do, 1971.

Downs, Anthony. *An Economic Theory of Democracy*. New York: Harper and Row, 1957.

Duverger, Maurice. *Political Parties: Their Organization and Activity in the Modern State*. New York: Wiley, 1963.

Fearon, James D. "Deterrence and the Spiral Model: The Role of Costly Signals in Crisis Bargaining." Paper presented at the annual meeting of the American Political Science Association, San Francisco, 1990.

———. "Counterfactuals and Hypothesis Testing in Political Science." *World Politics* 43 (1991): 169–95.

Ferejohn, John. "Rationality and Interpretation: Parliamentary Elections in Early Stuart England." In *The Economic Approach to Politics: A Critical Reassessment of the Theory and Rational Action*, ed. Kristen Monroe. New York: Harper Collins, 1991.

———. "The Spatial Model and Elections." In *Information, Participation, and Choice: An Economic Theory of Democracy in Perspective*, ed. Bernard Grofman. Ann Arbor: University of Michigan Press, 1993.

Flanagan, Scott C. "Electoral Change in Japan: A Study of Secular Realignment." In *Electoral Change in Advanced Industrial Democracies: Realignment or Dealignment?* ed. Russell J. Dalton, Scott C. Flanagan, and Paul Allen Beck. Princeton, N.J.: Princeton University Press, 1984.

Fukui, Haruhiro. *Party in Power: The Japanese Liberal Democrats and Policy Making*. Berkeley: University of California Press, 1970.

———. "Electoral Laws and the Japanese Party System." In *Japan and the World: Essays on Japanese History and Politics in Honour of Ishida Takeshi*, ed. Gail Lee Bernstein and Haruhiro Fukui. London: MacMillan, 1988.

Fukunaga, Fumio. "Sengo ni okeru Chu-Senkyoku-sei no Keisei Katei" [The formation process of the medium-sized district system in the postwar era], *Kobe Hogaku Zasshi* 36 (1986): 403–58.

Fundenberg, Drew, and Eric Maskin. "The Folk Theorem in Repeated Games with Discounting or with Incomplete Information." *Econometrica* 54 (1986): 533–54.

Goto, Motoo, Kenzo Uchida, and Masumi Ishikawa. *Sengo Hoshu Seiji no Kiseki* [The course of postwar conservative politics]. Tokyo: Iwanami-shoten, 1982.

Hrebenar, Ronald J. "The Changing Postwar Party System." In *The Japanese Party System: From One-Party Rule to Coalition Government*, ed. Ronald J. Hrebenar. Boulder: Westview, 1986.

Ide, Yoshinori. "Hoshu Choki Seiken-ka no Tochi" [The administration under the conservative long ruling]. In *55-nen Taisei no Keisei to Houkai* [The formation and decline of the 1955 system], ed. Nihon Seiji Gakkai. Tokyo: Iwanami-shoten, 1979.

Inglehart, Ronald. *The Silent Revolution: Changing Values and Political Styles among Western Publics*. Princeton, N.J.: Princeton University Press, 1977.

———. "The Changing Structure of Political Cleavages in Western Society." In *Electoral Change in Advanced Industrial Democracies*, ed. Dalton, Flanagan, and Beck.

Inoguchi, Takashi. *Gendai Nihon Gaiko* [Contemporary Japanese diplomacy]. Tokyo: Chikuma-shobo, 1993.

———. "Japanese Politics in Transition: A Theoretical Review." *Government and Opposition* 28 (1993): 445–55.

Inoguchi, Takashi, and Tomoaki Iwai. "Zoku Giin" no Kenkyu [A study of "policy tribes"]. Tokyo: Nihon Keizai Shimbun-sha, 1987.

Iseri, Hirofumi. *Habatsu Saihensei* [Factional realignment]. Tokyo: Chuo Koron-sha, 1988.

Ishida, Takeshi. *Kindai Nihon Seiji Kozo no Kenkyu* [A study on modern Japanese political structure]. Tokyo: Mirai-sha, 1956.

———. *Sengo Nihon no Seiji Taisei* [Postwar Japan's political system]. Tokyo: Mirai-sha, 1961.

Ishikawa, Masumi. *Deeta Sengo Seijishi* [A data history of postwar politics]. Tokyo: Iwanami-shoten, 1984.

———. "5-to e no Aki, Kiken de Hyomei" [Expressing frustration toward the five parties through abstention]. *Asahi Shimbun*, July 23, 1993.

Ito, Tatsumi. "Kensho 'Kokutai-Seiji' no Kozai" [Examining the merits and demerits of the "politics of the Diet Countermeasure Committee"]. *Chuo Koron* (December 1990): 130–46.

Iwai, Tomoaki. *"Seiji Shikin" no Kenkyu* [A study of political funding]. Tokyo: Nihon Keijai Shimbun-sha, 1990.

Johnson, Chalmers. "Japan: Who Governs? An Essay on Official Bureaucracy." *Journal of Japanese Studies* 2 (1975): pp. 1–28.

———. *MITI and the Japanese Miracle: The Growth of Industrial Policy, 1925–1975*. Stanford: Stanford University Press, 1982.

Johnson, Chalmers, and E. B. Keehn. "A Disaster in the Making: Rational Choice and Asian Studies." *The National Interest* (Summer 1994): 14–22.

Kabashima, Ikuo. "Yukensha no Ideorogi" [Ideologies of the electorate]. In *Nihonjin no Senkyo Kodo* [The Japanese electoral behavior], ed. Joji Watanuki et al. Tokyo: Tokyo Daigaku Shuppan-kai, 1986.

———. "'Shin-Hoshujidai' no Makuake" [Opening of a "new conservative era"]. *Mainichi Shimbun*, July 20, 1993.

———. "Shinto no Tojyo to Jiminto Itto Yui Taisei no Houkai" [The rise of new parties and the collapse of the LDP's one-party dominance system]. *Leviathan* 15 (1994): 7–31.

Kinoshita, Takeshi. *Katayama Naikakushi-ron* [On the history of the Katayama cabinet]. Kyoto: Houritsu Bunka-sha, 1982.

Kohno, Masaru, and Yoshitaka Nishizawa. "A Study of the Electoral Business Cycle in Japan: Elections and Government Spending on Public Construction." *Comparative Politics* 22 (1990): 151–66.

Kosaka, Masataka. "Kyoko Saiketsu no Seijigaku" [Politics of snap-voting]. *Chuo Koron* (November 1969): 50–69.

Krasner, Stephen D. "Sovereignty: An Institutional Perspective." *Comparative Political Studies* 21 (1988): 66–94.

Krauss, Ellis S. "Conflict in the Diet: Toward Conflict Management in Parliamentary Politics." In *Conflict in Japan*. ed. Ellis S. Krauss, Thomas P. Rohlen, and Patricia G. Steinhoff. Honolulu: University of Hawaii Press, 1984.

Kyogoku, Jun'ichi. "Seiji Ishiki no Henyou to Bunka" [Transformation and diversification of political consciousness]. In *Gendai Nihon no Seiji Katei* [Political process of contemporary Japan], ed. Yoshitake Oka. Tokyo: Iwanami-shoten, 1958.

Laver, Michael, and Kenneth A. Shepsle. "Coalitions and Cabinet Government." *American Political Science Review* 84 (1990): 873–90.

———. "Government Coalitions and Intraparty Politics." *British Journal of Political Science* 20 (1990): 489–507.

Lebra, Takie. *Japanese Patterns of Behavior*. Honolulu: University of Hawaii Press, 1976.

Lee, Kap Yun. "Shuugiin Senkyo de no Seito no Tokuhyo-su to Giseki-su" [Political parties' votes and seats in the House of Representative elections]. *Leviathan* 10 (1992): 109–31.

Leiserson, Michael. "Factions and Coalitions in One-Party Japan: Interpretation Based on the Theory of Games." *American Political Science Review* 62 (1968): 770–87.

Lijphart, Arend, Rafael Lopez Pintor, and Yasunori Sone, "The Limited Vote and the Single Nontransferable Vote: Lessons from the Japanese and Spanish Examples." In *Electoral Laws and Their Political Consequences*, ed. Bernard Grofman and Arend Lijphart. New York: Agathon, 1986.

Lipset, Seymour M., and Stein Rokkan. "Cleavage Structures, Party Systems, and Voter Alignments: An Introduction." In *Party Systems and Voter Alignments: Cross-National Perspectives*, ed. Seymour M. Lipset and Stein Rokkan. New York: Free Press, 1967.

Martin, Lisa L. "Credibility, Costs, and Institutions: Cooperation on Economic Sanctions." *World Politics* 45 (1993): 406–32.

Maruyama, Masao. *Gendai Seiji no Shiso to Kodo* [The ideologies and movements of contemporary politics]. Tokyo: Mirai-sha, 1964.

Masumi, Jun'nosuke. "1955-nen no Seiji Taisei" [The political system of the year 1955]. *Shiso* (June 1964): 55–72.

———. *Gendai Seiji* [Contemporary politics]. Tokyo: Tokyo Daigaku Shuppan-kai, 1985.

Mill, John Stuart. *System of Logic*. As excerpted in *Comparative Perspectives: Theories and Methods*, ed. Amitai Etzioni et al. Boston: Little Brown, 1970.

Miyake, Ichiro. "Seito Shiji no Ryudosei to Anteisei" [Fluidity and stability in party support]. In *Nempo Seijigaku 1970* [Annual political science report], ed. Nihon Seiji Gakkai. Tokyo: Iwanami-shoten, 1970.

———. *Seito Shiji no Bunseki* [An analysis of party support]. Tokyo: Sobun-sha, 1985.

Miyake, Ichiro, Tomio Kinoshita, and Jun'ichi Aiba. *Kotonaru Reberu no Senkyo ni okeru Tohyo Kodo no Bunseki* [The analysis of voting behavior at various levels]. Tokyo: Sobun-sha, 1967.

Miyake, Ichiro, Yasushi Yamaguchi, Michio Muramatsu, and Eiichi Shindo. *Nihon Seiji no Zahyo: Sengo Yonju-nen no Ayumi* [The coordinates of Japanese politics: The trace of postwar forty years]. Tokyo: Yuuhikaku, 1985.

Miyazaki, Ryuji. "Nihon ni okeru 'Sengo Demokurashii' no Koteika" [Consolidation of "postwar democracy" in Japan]. In *Sengo Demokurashii no Seiritsu* [Formation of postwar democracies], ed. Kazuo Inudo et al. Tokyo: Iwanami-shoten, 1988.

Mochizuki, Mike M. "Managing and Influencing the Japanese Legislative Process: The Role of Parties and the National Diet." Ph.D. diss., Harvard University, 1982.

Murakami, Yasusuke. "Shin Chukan Taishu Seiji no Jidai" [The age of New Middle Mass politics]. *Chuo Koron* (December 1980): 202–29.

———. "The Age of New Middle Mass Politics." *Journal of Japanese Studies* 8 (1982): 29–72.

———. *Shin Chukan Taishu no Jidai* [The age of New Middle Mass]. Tokyo: Chuo Koron-sha, 1984.

Murakami, Yasusuke, Seizaburo Sato, and Shumpei Kumon. "Datsu 'Hokaku' Jidai no Torai" [The arrival of the post-"conservative-progressive" Era]. *Chuo Koron* (February 1977): 64–95.

———. *Bunmei to Shite no Ie Shakai* [Family society as civilization]. Tokyo: Chuo Koron-sha, 1979.

Muramatsu, Michio. "Seisaku Katei" [Political process]. In *Nihon Seiji no Zahyo: Sengo Yonju-nen no Ayumi* [The coordinates of Japanese politics: The trace of postwar forty years], ed. Ichiro Miyake et al. Tokyo: Yuuhikaku, 1985.

Muramatsu, Michio, and Ellis Krauss. "Bureaucrats and Politicians in Policymaking: The Case of Japan." *American Political Science Review* 78 (1984): 126–46.

Nakamura, Kikuo, ed. *Gendai Nihon no Seiji Bunka* [The political culture of contemporary Japan]. Kyoto: Mineruva-shobo, 1975.

Nakane, Chie. *Tate-Shakai no Ningen Kankei* [Human relations of vertical society]. Tokyo: Kodan-sha, 1967.

Noguchi, Yukio. *1940-nen Taisei: Saraba "Senji Keizai"* [The 1940 system: Good-bye wartime economy]. Tokyo: Toyo Keizai Shimpo-sha, 1995.

North, Douglass C. *Institutions, Institutional Change, and Economic Performance.* New York: Cambridge University Press, 1990.

Nihon Seiji Gakkai, ed. *55-nen Taisei no Keisei to Houkai* [The formation and decline of the 1955 system]. Tokyo: Iwanami-shoten, 1979.

Ohishi, Kaichiro. "Sengo Kaikaku to Nihon Shihonshugi no Kozo Henka: Sono Renzoku-Setsu to Danzetsu-Setsu" [Postwar reforms and the structural changes of Japan's capitalism: Continuity hypothesis and discontinuity hypothesis]. In *Sengo Kaikaku* [Postwar reforms], vol. 1, ed. Tokyo Daigaku Shakai Kagaku Kenkyu-jo. Tokyo: Tokyo Daigaku Shuppan-kai, 1974.

Oka, Yoshitake, ed. *Gendai Nihon no Seiji Katei* [Political process of contemporary Japan]. Tokyo: Iwanami-shoten, 1958.

Oka, Yoshitake. "Gendai Nihon Seiji ni okeru Gaiatsu, Hannou" [Foreign pressure, reactions in Contemporary Japanese politics]. In *Gendai Nihon no Seiji Katei* [Political process of contemporary Japan], ed. Yoshitake Oka. Tokyo: Iwanami-shoten, 1958.

Okazaki, Tetsuji, and Masahiro Okuno, eds. *Gendai Nihon Keizai Sisutemu no Genryu* [The origins of the contemporary Japanese economic system]. Tokyo: Nihon Keizai Shimbun-sha, 1993.

Otake, Hideo. *Gendai Nihon no Seiji Kenryoku, Keizai Kenryoku* [Political power and economic power in contemporary Japan]. Tokyo: San-Ichi-shobo, 1979.

———. *Adenaua to Yoshida Shigeru* [Adenauer and Shigeru Yoshida]. Tokyo: Chuo Koron-sha, 1986.

———. "Nihon Shakai-to Higeki no Kigen: Gunkoku-Shugi Fukkatsu no Kenen to Sengo Shakai-Shugi Seito" [The origins of the Japan Socialist Party's tragedy: Concerns for revival of militarism and postwar socialist political parties]." *Chuo Koron* (October 1986): 146–61.

———. *Sai-Gunbi to Nashonarizumu* [Rearmament and Nationalism]. Tokyo: Chuo Koron-sha, 1988.

———. "Defense Controversies and One-Party Dominance: The Opposition in Japan and West Germany." In *Uncommon Democracies: The One-Party Dominant Regimes*, ed. T. J. Pempel. Ithaca, N.Y.: Cornell University Press, 1991.

———. "Rearmament Controversies and Cultural Conflicts in Japan: The Case of the Conservatives and the Socialists." In *Creating Single-Party Democracy: Japan's Postwar Political System*, ed. Tetsuya Kataoka. Stanford: Hoover Institution Press, 1992.

Pempel, T. J. *Policy and Politics in Japan*. Philadelphia: Temple University Press, 1982.

———. "Introduction. Uncommon Democracies: The One-Party Dominant Regimes." In *Uncommon Democracies: The One-Party Dominant Regimes*, ed. T. J. Pempel. Ithaca, N.Y.: Cornell University Press, 1991.

———. "Conclusion. One-Party Dominance and the Creation of Regimes." In *Uncommon Democracies: The One-Party Dominant Regimes*, ed. T. J. Pempel. Ithaca, N.Y.: Cornell University Press, 1991.

Pempel, T. J., ed. *Uncommon Democracies: The One-Party Dominant Regimes*. Ithaca: Cornell University Press, 1990.

Rae, Douglas W. *The Political Consequences of Electoral Laws*. New Haven, Conn.: Yale University Press, 1967.

Ramseyer, J. Mark, and Frances McCall Rosenbluth. *Japan's Political Marketplace*. Cambridge, Mass.: Harvard University Press, 1993.

Reed, Steven R. "The People Spoke: The Influence of Elections in Japanese Politics, 1949–1955." *Journal of Japanese Studies* 14 (1988): 309–39.

———. "Structure and Behaviour: Extending Duverger's Law to the Japanese Case." *British Journal of Political Science* 20 (1990): 335–56.

———. *Making Common Sense of Japan*. Pittsburgh: University of Pittsburgh Press, 1993.

Richardson, Bradley M. *The Political Culture of Japan*. Berkeley: University of California Press, 1974.

———. "Party Loyalties and Party Saliency in Japan." *Comparative Political Studies* 8 (1975): 32–57.

———. "Constituency Candidates versus Parties in Japanese Voting Behavior." *American Political Science Review* 82 (1988): 695–718.

Richardson, Bradley M., and Scott C. Flanagan. *Politics in Japan*. Boston: Little, Brown, 1984.

Riker, William H. *The Theory of Political Coalition*. New Haven, Conn.: Yale University Press, 1962.

Sato, Seizaburo, and Tetsuhisa Matsuzaki. *Jiminto Seiken* [The LDP's rule]. Tokyo: Chuo Koron-sha, 1986.

Scalapino, Robert, and Jun'nosuke Masumi. *Parties and Politics in Contemporary Japan*. Berkeley: University of California Press, 1962.

Schumpeter, Joseph A. *Capitalism, Socialism, and the Democracy*. New York: Harper, 1942. Rev. ed. 1950.

Shinobu, Seizaburo. "Dokusen Shihon to Seiji" [Politics of monopolistic capitalism]. In *Gendai Nihon no Seiji Katei* [Political process of contemporary Japan], ed. Yoshitake Oka. Tokyo: Iwanami-shoten, 1956.

———. *Sengo Nihon Seijishi, 1945–1952* [Political history of postwar Japan, 1945–1952], Vols. 1–3. Tokyo: Keisou-shobo, 1965.

Shupe, Anson D., Jr. "Social Participation and Voting Turnout: The Case of Japan." *Comparative Political Studies* 12 (1979): 229–58.

Simon, Herbert A. "Human Nature in Politics: The Dialogue of Psychology with Political Science." *American Political Science Review* 79 (1985): 293–305.

Soma, Masao. *Nihon Senkyo Seido-shi* [The history of Japan's electoral systems]. Fukuoka: Kyushu Daigaku Shuppan-kai, 1986.

Strom, Kaare. *Minority Government and Majority Rule*. Cambridge: Cambridge University Press, 1990.

Sugiyama, Mitsunobu. "Hoshuka Shakai-ron no Sai-Kento" [Rethinking the conservative society thesis]. *Chuo Koron* (August 1981): 173–91.

Takabatake, Michitoshi. "Taishu Undo no Tayoka to Henshitsu" [The diversification and transformation of mass movements]. In *55-nen Taisei no Keisei to Houkai* [The formation and decline of the 1955 system], ed. Nihon Seiji Gakkai. Tokyo: Iwanami-shoten, 1979.

———. " 'Shinto Gensho' de Nani ga Okitanoka?" [What happened with a "new party boom"?]. *Ekonomisuto* (August 3, 1993): 52–57.

Tani, Katsuhiro. "Kokkai ni okeru Seito no Rippo Kodo ni kansuru Doutai-Bunseki" [Dynamic analysis of parties' legislative behavior in the national Diet]. *Leviathan* 4 (1989): 168–190.

Tani, Satomi. "The Japan Socialist Party before the Mid-1960s: An Analysis of Its Stagnation." In *Creating Single-Party Democracy: Japan's Postwar Political System*, ed. Tetsuya Kataoka. Stanford: Hoover Institution Press, 1992.

Thayer, Nathaniel B. *How the Conservatives Rule Japan*. Princeton, N.J.: Princeton University Press, 1969.

Tomimori, Eiji. *Sengo Hoshu-to Shi* [History of postwar conservative parties]. Tokyo: Nihon Hyoron-sha, 1977.

———. "55-nen Taisei Hokai no Imi" [The significance of the demise of the 1955 system]. *Sekai* (August 1993): 58–61.

Tomita, Nobuo, Akira Nakamura, and Ronald J. Hrebenar, "The Liberal Democratic Party." In Hrebenar, *The Japanese Party System*.

Tsebelis, George. *Nested Games: Rational Choice in Comparative Politics*. Berkeley: University of California Press, 1990.

Tsuji, Kiyoaki. "Kanryo Kiko no Onzon to Kyoka" [The preservation and strengthening of bureaucratic institutions]. In *Gendai Nihon no Seiji Katei* [The political process of contemporary Japan], ed. Yoshitake Oka. Tokyo: Iwanami-shoten, 1958.

———. *Shinban: Nihon Kanryo-sei no Kenkyu* [New edition: A study of Japanese bureaucracy]. Tokyo: Tokyo Daigaku Shuppan-kai, 1969.

Uchida, Kenzo. *Sengo Nihon no Hoshu Seiji* [Conservative politics of postwar Japan]. Tokyo: Iwanami-shoten, 1969.

———. "Seito nai, kan no Tetsuzuki" [Intra- and Interparty procedure]. In *Nempo Seijigaku 1985* [Annual political science report], ed. Nihon Seiji Gakkai. Tokyo: Iwanami-shoten, 1986.

Uchida, Kenzo, Toru Hayano, and Yasunori Sone. *Dai-Seihen* [The big political change]. Tokyo: Toyo Keizai Shimpo-sha, 1994.

Verba, Sidney, Norman H. Nie, and Jae-on Kim. *Participation and Political Equality: A Seven Nation Comparison*. Cambridge: Cambridge University Press, 1978.

Ward, Robert, E., and Akira Kubota. "Family Influence and Political Socialization in Japan: Some Preliminary Findings in Comparative Perspective." *Comparative Political Studies* 3 (1970): 140–75.

Watanabe, Tsuneo. *Habatsu: Nihon Hoshuto no Bunseki* [Factions: An analysis of the Japanese conservative party]. Tokyo: Kobun-do, 1964.

———. *Shin Seiji no Joshiki* [New common sense of politics]. Tokyo: Kodan-sha, 1977.

Watanuki, Joji. *Politics in Postwar Japanese Society*. Tokyo: University of Tokyo Press, 1977.

Watanuki, Joji, Ichiro Miyake, Takashi Inoguchi, and Ikuo Kabashima. *Nihonjin no Senkyo Kodo* [The Japanese electoral behavior]. Tokyo: Tokyo Daigaku Shuppan-kai, 1986.

White, James W. *The Sokagakkai and Mass Society*. Stanford: Stanford University Press, 1970.

———. *Migration in Metropolitan Japan: Social Change and Political Behavior*. Berkeley: Institution of East Asian Studies, University of California, 1984.

Yakushiji, Taizo. *Seijika vs Kanryo* [Politicians vs bureaucrats]. Tokyo: Toyo Keizai Shimpo-sha, 1987.

Yamaguchi, Yasushi. "Seiji Tenkan to 'Chukan-so Mondai'" [Political change and the "Middle Class Problem"]. *Sekai* (November 1977): 154–71.

———. "Sengo Nihon no Seiji Taisei to Seiji Katei: Sono Tokushitsu to Henyo" [The political system and process of postwar Japan: Characteristics and transformation]. In *Nihon Seiji no Zahyo: Sengo Yonju-nen no Ayumi* [The coordinates of Japanese politics: The trace of postwar forty years], ed. Ichiro Miyake et al. Tokyo: Yuhikaku, 1985.

SUBJECT INDEX

AUTHOR INDEX